HUMAN NATURE

Love the Lord your God w/ all your mind, strength, soul.
the link between the brain, body & Spirit

cognitive therapy(?)   (co. (u, Th)
— mind over matter
— change the way we think to change the way we act.

CBT

cog.
change thoughts to produce a change in beh.
(ccogn.)

Beck, Ellis
— talk about it.

BT
skinner
conditioning.

HUMAN NATURE

Reflections
on the Integration of
Psychology and Christianity

Malcolm Jeeves

TEMPLETON FOUNDATION PRESS

PHILADELPHIA AND LONDON

Templeton Foundation Press
300 Conshohocken State Road, Suite 670
West Conshohocken, PA 19428
www.templetonpress.org

Originally published in 1997 by Baker Books and APOLLOS
2006 Templeton Foundation Press Edition
© 1997 by Malcolm A. Jeeves

Templeton Foundation Press helps intellectual leaders and others learn about science research on aspects of realities, invisible and intangible. Spiritual realities include unlimited love, accelerating creativity, worship, and the benefits of purpose in persons and in the cosmos.

Library of Congress Cataloging-in-Publication Data

Jeeves, Malcolm A., 1926–
  [Human nature at the millennium]
  Human nature : reflections on the integration of psychology
and Christianity / Malcolm A. Jeeves.
      p. cm.
  Originally published: Human nature at the millennium.
Grand Rapids, Mich. : Baker Books ; Leicester, UK : APOLLOS, c1997.
With new pref.
  Includes bibliographical references and index.
  ISBN-13: 978-1-932031-96-6 (pbk. : alk. paper)
  ISBN-10: 1-932031-96-0 (pbk. : alk. paper) 1.
Christianity—Psychology. 2. Psychology, Religious. 3. Man
(Christian theology) 4. Psychology. I. Title.
  BR110.J38 2006
  261.5'15—dc22
                                2005031390

Typeset and designed by Gopa & Ted2, Inc.
Printed in the United States of America

06 07 08 09 10   10 9 8 7 6 5 4 3 2 1

To Ruth,
For unfailing support

Contents

PREFACE TO THE 2006 EDITION

THE NATURE OF HUMAN-NESS is central to many disciplines: psychology, anthropology, sociology, theology, soteriology, and eschatology to name a few. The questions raised are daunting and the aim of this book remains to offer guidelines to help develop critically constructive, open-minded, biblically based thinking, which faces squarely the relevant current scientific evidence. In addressing any questions about the implications of science for our understanding of human-ness it is crucial to remember that the outcome of any study of human nature will necessarily be limited by the focus of the investigations and the techniques used. In this book the focus is on psychology, particularly at its interfaces with neuroscience and evolutionary biology. The investigators' techniques include natural observation, case histories, cognitive modeling (including artificial intelligence insights), and experimental investigation using single-cell recording and brain scanning of humans and animals.

Scarcely a day passes without the media telling us about the latest exciting developments in research at the interface of psychology and neuroscience. But these are not purely academic matters. The implications of some of them will ultimately, we trust, give hope to those for whom the consequences of brain damage come very close to home. As I write, the national press in Britain is giving detailed coverage of the untimely death of Mo Mowlam, one of its leading politicians. The *London Times* traces out the changes in Mo Mowlam's personality and behavior as she suffered from a brain tumor and the subsequent consequences of the necessary surgery to give her temporary relief.

The week following the *Times* report on Mo Mowlam, one of Britain's main TV channels presented a one-hour program on the once-renowned conductor Clive Wearing. Twenty years ago he was hit by a virus that led to encephalitis that targeted a crucial part of the brain-processing memory. Since then he has lived in the eternal present. He has no memory of his wedding to his wife Deborah eighteen months before his illness. He knows nothing about what she does or of their past life. Despite all of this he remains charming, cheerful, and witty. The damage to his brain has changed his mental life and, to a degree, his personality forever.

Fifty years ago B. F. Skinner and his behaviorism were in their heyday and few self-respecting scientific psychologists in North America would have dared to talk about the mind or mental life. Today everything has changed. The 1990s, declared by the U.S. Senate as "The Decade of the Brain" has now been succeeded by "The Decade of the Mind."

Neuropsychology and neuroscience journals regularly cover exciting advances in our understanding of how our minds and our behavior depend upon the efficient working of the physical substrate of our brains. The progress of the cognitive revolution highlighted in the Preface to the 1997 edition continues unabated. The readiness of psychologists and neuroscientists to write about the mind and mental life is indicative of this welcome development.

Trends identified in 1995 when I wrote this book have accelerated and expanded in a way we could not then have imagined. But the basic issues, of how properly to relate the developing scientific portraits of human nature to traditional religious and humanist portraits, remain. These issues are so important that concerned non-Christians are publicizing them by assembling essays under titles such as *The New Brain Sciences: Perils and Prospects* by Dai Rees and Steven Rose.[1] They, and we, recognize that in many respects some emerging issues have become even more pressing as the actual, and potential, practical, moral, and ethical implications of advances in cognitive neuroscience become clearer.

The study of mind and the readiness to research it and to talk about it has not only come to the forefront of psychology's interface with neuroscience. Something analogous has occured at psychology's interface with evolutionary biology. For some psychologists it has become *the* major topic in contemporary psychology. For them developments in evolutionary psychology, displayed in the new *Handbook of Evolutionary Psychology*,[2] have been so impressive and so rapid that they have seen them as grounds for mounting a takeover bid of the whole of psychology.

During this past decade a new awareness has also developed of a potential natural bridge between neuroscience and evolutionary psychology through the earlier discovery by Giacomo Rizzolatti of so-called "mirror neurons," which fire either when performing certain actions or when observing another doing so. One high-profile research neurologist in North America believes that Rizzolatti's discoveries in this field will be as far reaching for psychology as the deciphering of the structure of DNA was for biology. Thus V. S. Ramachandran has written "I predict that mirror neurons will do for psychology what DNA did for biology."

As you read this book you cannot remind yourself too often of the account given by Paul Vitz (see chapter 9) of the ways in which some psychologists, and no doubt also some neuroscientists, readily and perhaps unthinkingly shift their categories from the scientific to the philosophical and to the normative and then move without justification to theories of moral obligation. In so doing they blur the conceptual boundaries between science and the broader views of humankind already richly available in literature, philosophy, and religion that come to us from centuries past. That some psychologists and neuroscientists are either unaware of or unwilling to expose their own metaphysical and moral presuppositions will continue to be a problem and particularly so if they seek to invoke what they believe is the authority of science to authenticate their opinions.

For the thoughtful Christian, developments in neuropsychology and evolutionary psychology inevitably raise challenging questions about basic doctrinal and pastoral matters. How free are we to make responsible judgments? Are we embodied souls or mere DNA-reproducing machines controlled by invariant physico-chemical reactions? Are we apes on the way up? Angels on the way down? Sinners for whom Christ died or helpless pawns in a post-modern jungle? Pilgrims on a journey or flotsam in a flood?

One topic about our Christian understanding of ourselves that has received more attention than others has been the essential nature of the human person. The accelerating and accumulating scientific evidence of the intimate interdependence of mind and brain, what used to be called soul and body, has sent us back, with the help of biblical scholars, to reexamine what the ancient texts say about the soul. As a result, the past decade has witnessed a series of books focusing on ways in which developments in psychology, neuroscience, and evolutionary psychology prompt a reexamination of some of our traditional Christian ways of thinking about the human person. I have added a new reading list at the end of this preface listing some of the more readily available books and journal articles that represent the variety of responses from those who, whilst sharing the same basic Christian beliefs, interpret the impact that this new science has had on our understanding of human nature in different ways. Study the evidence, both biblical and scientific, and make up your own mind.

In closing this new preface, I wish to reiterate my special thanks to my very good friends and colleagues, professors Warren Brown and David Myers, and to Dr. Kenneth Boa who gave me permission to draw upon his Oxford doctoral thesis in writing chapter nine.

The following books and journal articles illustrate in detail how many of the issues raised in the 1997 edition of *Human Nature* have been amplified and widely discussed in the past ten years. Each in turn gives many further references to original source materials.

BOOKS

Brown, Warren S., H. Newton Maloney, and Nancey Murphy. *Whatever Happened to the Soul? Scientific and Theological Portraits of Human Nature*. Minneapolis: Augsburg Fortress, 1998.

Green, Joel B. and Stuart L. Palmer, eds. *In Search of the Soul: Four Views of the Mind-Body Problem*. Downers Grove: InterVarsity Press, 2005.

Green, Joel B. *What about the Soul?: Neuroscience and Christian Anthropology*. Nashville: Abingdon Press, 2004.

Hasker, William. *The Emergent Self*. Ithaca: Cornell University Press, 1999.

Jeeves, Malcolm, ed. *From Cells to Souls and Beyond: Changing Portraits of Human Nature*. Grand Rapids: William B. Eerdmans Publishing Company, 2004.

Jeeves, Malcolm A., and David G. Myers, eds. *Psychology Through the Eyes of Faith*. 2nd. ed. San Francisco: HarperSanFrancisco, 2003.

Myers, David G. *Intuition: Its Powers and Perils*. New Haven: Yale University Press, 2002.

Rees, Dai, and Stephen Rose, eds. *The New Brain Sciences: Perils and Prospects*. Cambridge: Cambridge University Press, 2004.

JOURNAL ARTICLES

Jeeves, Malcolm. "Changing portraits of human nature." *Science and Christian Belief* 14, no. 1 (2002): 3–32.

Jeeves, Malcolm. "How free is free?" *Science and Christian Belief* 16, no. 2 (2004): 101–22.

Jeeves, Malcolm. "Human nature without a soul?" *European Review* 12, no.1 (2003): 45–64.

Jeeves, Malcolm. "Neuroscience, evolutionary psychology and the image of God." *Perspectives on Science and Christian Faith* 57, no. 3 (2005): 170–86.

Torrance, Alan. 2004. "Developments in neuroscience and human freedom: Some theological and philosophical questions." *Science and Christian Belief* 16, no. 2 (2004): 123–139.

Preface to Original Edition

It has been twenty years since I wrote *Psychology and Christianity: The View Both Ways*. It is instructive to reflect on the changes that have taken place in psychology over the past two decades. They vividly illustrate the intensity of the scientific research effort and the pace of discovery in psychology and related fields during that period. For thirteen of those twenty years I have served as an editor of one of the leading international scientific journals reporting research in behavioral and cognitive neuroscience, for three of them as its editor in chief. One spin-off from such editorial work is the privilege of, almost daily, receiving manuscripts reporting exciting research at the frontiers of cognitive neuroscience. The cumulative effect of such research is that it underlines repeatedly the ever-tightening links among brain, mind, and behavior and has resulted in new issues moving onto center stage within psychology. Consequently, fresh challenges have arisen as we ask what implications, if any, current psychological knowledge has for traditional Christian beliefs.

On both sides of the Atlantic psychologists have been intimately involved in national research initiatives. In the United States, we are halfway through the "Decade of the Brain," declared by the U.S. Senate in 1990. In Britain, an interdisciplinary research center on brain and behavior has been established, funded by the major research councils. Almost every day the media report exciting developments in, for example, our understanding of the neural basis of memory and vision, Alzheimer's disease, schizophrenia, depression, the possible neural bases of sexual orientation and aggression, and a myriad of other issues where research depends crucially on what is happening at the interface between psychology and neuroscience. Discussion of the possible implications of such research for religious beliefs has also, at times, been given wide publicity. One such instance, occurring in the past year, is the appearance of the fascinating book *The Astonishing Hypothesis* by Nobel Laureate Francis Crick. The subtitle of the book, *The Scientific Search for the Soul*, says it all. Crick, and no doubt others, believe that developments in neuroscience and psychology *do* have implications for some traditional Christian beliefs.

One feature of the past two decades in psychology has been the continuing cognitive revolution. After gathering momentum in the early 1970s, it has become a major influence in psychology and neuroscience. "Mind talk" is respectable again after more than a half century when psychologists, primarily in the United States, were able to foist upon generations of students the belief that the only thing worth studying was behavior, and that any reference to mental life was, in some unspecified way, unscientific. During this same period the combined efforts of cognitive scientists and neuroscientists have developed into the discipline of cognitive neuroscience. Such collaboration has produced an impressive increase in research in neuropsychology.

Another issue that has received wide publicity and in which research in psychology is coupled with that in another discipline, in this instance, genetics, is sexual orientation. The general public is most aware of it in the ongoing, and at times ill-tempered, debate about the roots and fruits of sexual orientation. Here, sadly, scientific integrity has been constantly under threat by claims and counterclaims of what this or that preliminary scientific finding means for wider issues of sexual orientation and practice. The evidence has, at times, been hijacked, used selectively, and distorted by the gay rights movement so that it becomes extremely difficult for the nonexpert to disentangle fact from fiction and science from ideology.

While still constituting a relatively small part of the sum total of academic psychology, personality theories and psychotherapy represent a significant part of applied psychology and clinical practice. It has been four decades since psychologists, such as Hans Eysenck in Britain and Paul Meehl in America, called into question some of the claims made for the effectiveness of psychotherapy. With the demand for the services of psychotherapists and counselors seemingly increasing exponentially over the past two decades, this issue has recurred from time to time but has been somewhat overwhelmed by the understandable desire of psychotherapists to satisfy the evident demand for their services. One of the outcomes has been that the commitment of psychotherapists to relieve suffering, wherever possible, has, sadly, outrun the time or the effort they seem to have been able to allocate to examining the scientific basis of the therapy in which they are engaged and assessing its effectiveness.

This issue has been given high prominence by the widely acclaimed book by Robyn Dawes, *House of Cards*, subtitled *Psychology and Psychotherapy Built on Myth*. In it he pin-points issues that perhaps have not received the attention they deserve among Christians. So concerned have we been to satisfy the needs of those suffering, by applying this or that form of psychotherapy, that we have, at times, forgotten the requirement and commitment of the Christian not to depart from the truth, but at all times to "tell the story as it really is."

In addition to specific issues, such as sexual orientation and psychotherapy, there are more general pervasive issues recurring across the board as we detect consensus views emerging about human nature widely shared by scientists working on mind, brain, and behavior. Thus, taken together, much neuropsychological research has pointed almost uniformly to the ever-tightening link among mind, brain, and behavior. One result is that it has raised, generally and with a fresh urgency, issues such as the extent to which we actually do have freedom of choice in our thinking and behaving. In the domain of sexual orientation, this in turn raises important questions for Christians for whom moral choice and responsibility are not optional extras. More specifically, among Christians it raises questions of the status of terms we have become so familiar with in the past such as soul, spirit, body.

Most recently, and across a surprisingly wide spectrum of scientists, a new interest has developed in a topic hitherto, almost exclusively, a concern of philosophers, though occasionally of psychologists. I refer to consciousness. A century ago it held center stage in psychology but since then it has, seemingly, been banished to the wings. Because of its central prominence today I have devoted two chapters to it. Physicists and mathematicians have played a major role in the rediscovery of consciousness. They have also helped us reexamine issues such as determinism by indicating the possible relevance of chaos theory and others like it to enduring concerns about determinism, freedom, and responsibility.

Bearing in mind the variety of issues raised above, I have written with several, at times distinct, readerships in mind—first, for Christian psychology students, both undergraduate and postgraduate, who are faced in many of their courses with a mass of evidence indicating an increasing knowledge of the biological substrates of cognition and behavior. Such courses also emphasize the unity of the organism. Most depend heavily on research on animals, as well as humans, for the discoveries being reported. They naturally raise in the minds of some students questions about human nature as it is compared with animal nature, and about the components of human nature in terms of the soul and the spirit, and the interrelationship between them and the body. For instance, do animals have souls? Are animals living souls? Does our spiritual awareness depend on the intactness of our brains or, in some mysterious way, does spirituality stand apart from our biological substrate? I have devoted one chapter to the relation among neural processes, psychological states, and spiritual awareness and in so doing I have attempted deliberately to deal with issues which, for some, can cause considerable distress and concern.

Mindful of the differing expertise and expectations of those who read this book, I should like to alert you to the way in which some chapters are more demanding, in terms of technical scientific background, than others. The consciousness chapters (10 and 11), for example, will be, I suspect, somewhat challenging. However, in an effort to convey the flavor of those chapters, and any others that you may be inclined to skip, I have included, at the end of every chapter, a *Taking Stock* section, giving you the main points in nontechnical language. By reading these sections you will, I hope, be able, at least, to get the basics of what I have been saying and what I think it may or may not imply for Christian beliefs.

At times I fear that, despite my best efforts, I shall have appeared more confident and dogmatic about some of the things I have written than I really am. My basic hope is that the material of this book will, at least, enable Christian students and others to reaffirm a clear commitment to enthusiastic involvement in the scientific enterprise as it is represented in research and practice in psychology and neuroscience. For the Christian, this world is, as a well-known hymn puts it, "my Father's world." It is, I believe, part of our commitment and responsibility, as Christian stewards and disciples, to be involved, as our talents permit, in studying and exploring our Father's world, of which we are ourselves a part. In so doing we shall, I believe, discover each day more of how "wonderfully and fearfully made" we are.

Without the warm invitation from Fuller Theological Seminary to deliver their 1995 Integration Lectures, it is unlikely that this book would have been written at this particular time. While the lecture material probably makes up less than a fifth of the present book, it was the need to prepare for those lectures that set me to work on a range of contemporary issues at the interface among psychology, neuroscience, and Christian beliefs. I am deeply indebted to the president and academic staff of Fuller, and in particular to Professor Warren Brown, for many stimulating discussions during my visit to Pasadena. I am also indebted to my good friend Professor David Myers, who read parts of the manuscript and offered many helpful suggestions. In particular, through his encyclopedic knowledge as a very successful textbook writer, he drew my attention to references that are not in my special research area in psychology but of which I needed to be aware. I thank him warmly. I acknowledge my special indebtedness to Dr. Kenneth Boa. In chapter 9, where I compare psychological and theological accounts of human needs, I make, with his permission, extensive reference to his Oxford doctoral thesis on this topic. Finally, I am especially grateful to Mrs. Diane Lawrie and Mrs. Lesley Ferrier for their patient and dedicated help at the word processor.

Human Nature

CHAPTER I

APPROACHING MODERN PSYCHOLOGY

Psychology has not added up to an integrated science,
and it is unlikely ever to achieve that status. . . .
For the most part, psychologists (like other academics) go about their
daily research and writing without agonizing about the actual or potential coherence of their field.
—Howard Gardner, William James Lecture, 1988

The considerable advances that have been made in the
scientific study of human nature in this century make
this the right time for a fruitful integration of the
science and theology of human nature.
—Fraser Watts, Inaugural Starbridge Lecture, 1995

PSYCHOLOGY'S CLAIM TO BE A SCIENCE

PSYCHOLOGY CONTINUES to make strong and, at times, strident claims
to being a science. It has been more than a century since William James
wrote to his friend Thomas W. Ward, "It seems to me that perhaps the
time has come for psychology to begin to be a science."[1] In his 1988
William James Lecture entitled "Scientific Psychology: Should We Bury
It or Praise It?"[2] Howard Gardner of Harvard expressed the view that
"psychology has not added up to an integrated science, and it is unlikely
ever to achieve that status." He continued: "What does make sense is to
recognize important insights that have been achieved by psychologists;
to identify the contribution which contemporary psychology can make
to disciplines which may some day achieve a firmer scientific status; and
finally to determine whether at least parts of psychology might survive

as participants in a conversation which obtains across major disciplines." He also pointed out that, "for the most part, psychologists (like other academics) go about their daily research and writing without agonizing about the actual or potential coherence of their field." Equally, it is my impression that the majority of psychologists do not spend much time agonizing over whether their work is scientific or in reading the latest debates among philosophers about what does or does not constitute "*the* scientific method." Perhaps they should; but they don't. They are perhaps content to accept as their primary goal being scientific in the sense, as Ziman[3] has put it, of producing "reliable knowledge."

As Hendrika Vande Kemp[4] has pointed out, scientists rely on the testimony of past witnesses (see any textbook or review paper), on intuition, on reason and observation (the hypothetico-deductive method), and on serendipity (finding one thing in the process of looking for something else). Like Skinner, she points out that it is very difficult to capture in words what scientists actually do, and reiterates with approval Skinner's[5] warning that "it is a mistake to identify scientific practice with the formalized constructions of statistics and scientific method. These disciplines have their place, but it does not coincide with the place of scientific research" (360). This point is well exemplified by what some of those scientists who have made the greatest impact this century have done and said. Nobel Laureate Francis Crick[6] is a good if somewhat provocative example, with his book on science entitled *What Mad Pursuit?* In *The Astonishing Hypothesis*, he stresses his belief that the study of consciousness is a scientific problem:

> If there is any lesson to be learned from this book it is that we can now see ways of approaching the problem experimentally. . . . Philosophers have had such a poor record over the last two thousand years that they would do better to show a certain modesty rather than the lofty superiority that they usually display. . . . I hope that more philosophers will learn about the brain to suggest ideas about how it works, but they must also learn how to abandon their pet theories when the scientific evidence goes against them or they will only expose themselves to ridicule (257).

These are strong words indeed: Clearly there are philosophers and there are philosophers, but by ignoring all philosophers scientists may expose themselves to ridicule. It seems to me that the body of the book (the science) contrasts strangely with the naïveté of its opening and closing few pages (the philosophy); I believe a reader should forget about the "astonishing naïveté" of the *Astonishing Hypothesis* and enjoy the good science.

After reviewing the science in the book, Fraser Watts wrote, "So much for the serious science. Grafted on to this are the polemics and philosophy, especially the 'astonishing hypothesis' of the title." He continues: "It is not difficult to spot that this reductionist position is neither a necessary presumption nor an inevitable conclusion from the science. Neither is it anything new: just a reversion to the extreme physicalist view of mind that was fashionable up to 30 years ago!"[7]

It seems extremely difficult for the scientist working at the cutting edge also to be a philosopher; likewise, the philosopher would have to work overtime to acquire the background knowledge and skills to philosophize from a sound base of contemporary scientific knowledge. (Some readers may well conclude this statement is an advanced apologia for later philosophical howlers in this book. And they may be right!)

What is clear is that insofar as psychology's claim to be a science is justified, it behooves anyone discussing the integration of psychology and Christian belief to seek to profit from the lessons, at times hard learned, from earlier attempts to integrate science and Christian beliefs by more established sciences such as physics, astronomy, geology, and zoology. By so doing we may not only avoid expending unnecessary effort in reinventing the wheel but may, more importantly, learn from earlier mistakes and hence be better equipped to avoid repeating them in the context of our discussions of the psychology-faith relationship.

Another prerequisite to any discussion of the integration of psychology and Christian beliefs is that one make as clear as possible what is being subsumed under the heading of psychology. Despite the fact that there is some variability in how psychologists set the boundaries of their discipline, a broad consensus exists about the main features of the territory of psychology today. We turn first, therefore, to an overview of the psychological landscape at the turn of the millennium.

PSYCHOLOGY AT THE TURN OF THE MILLENNIUM

Norman Munn, author of one of America's most widely used university textbooks of psychology in the 1940s, expressed a view about the status of psychology that is little changed today. He wrote:[8] "The scientific status of psychology depends on its methods—not on what it studies. Its methods are basically the same as those of the other natural sciences, but the nature of its subject matter introduces methodological problems which the other sciences do not have." David Myers,[9] author of today's most widely used textbook of psychology in North America, writes: "Psychology is a science that seeks to answer all sorts of questions about us all: how we think, feel, and act." Myers then goes on to warn student readers of the disappointments they face if they come to the discipline with the wrong expectations and unaware of its limits. He writes: "If you ignore psychology's limits and expect it to answer the ultimate questions posed by the Russian novelist Leo Tolstoy in 1904—Why should I live? Why should I do anything? Is there in life any purpose which the inevitable death that awaits me does not undo and destroy?'—you are destined for disappointment. If instead," he goes on, "you expect that psychology will help you better understand why people, yourself included, feel, think, and act as they do—or if you enjoy exploring such questions—then you should find the study of psychology both fascinating and applicable to life."

It is interesting that both Munn and Myers, at the beginning of their textbooks, emphasize the need to know something about psychology's history properly to understand it in the present; thus Munn wrote, "It is difficult to give the student a meaningful definition of psychology until he is acquainted with certain aspects of its long and interesting history." Myers explains that we can only really understand what psychology is trying to do if we understand how it arose in the first place. Despite these similarities between Munn and Myers, one notable difference has occurred in the past fifty years. While Munn could confidently assert in 1946 that "psychology *no longer implies the study of the mind*," he had clearly changed his views by 1971, which saw the publication of his *The Evolution of the Human Mind*. Myers echoes this change of view when he writes that "psychology is *the science of* behavior and *mental processes*." These changes illustrate the emergence of what has been called the "cognitive revolution" in psychology, beginning in the late 1950s and dominant in the past decade.

As we shall see in a moment, the very diversity of subject matter subsumed under contemporary psychology leads to a corresponding diversity in the methods and techniques employed by different groups of research psychologists. It soon becomes evident, for example, that the relative objectivity and reproducibility of empirical findings vary enormously, depending on the subdiscipline of contemporary psychology under consideration; on whether you are studying the responses of single cells in the cortex of an alert and awake monkey on seeing a familiar face; on whether you are measuring interhemispheric transmission times in normal human beings; on whether you are studying working memory in Alzheimer's patients; on whether you are studying racial attitudes in inner-city populations; or on whether you are interested in cross-cultural differences in attitudes and beliefs. These areas are today all labeled psychology, even though they differ widely in the investigative techniques they use, the reproducibility of their findings, and their links with cognate disciplines.

There are several ways of trying to arrive at a consensus of what constitutes psychology today. One is to examine the contents page of a typical university textbook of psychology; another, to scrutinize the contents of the *Annual Review of Psychology*; another, to look at the titles of papers appearing in psychological journals; another, to look at research funding given to different sub-branches of contemporary psychology. Putting together the results of these approaches produces the beginning of a consistent picture. It contains at least the study of the following:

✦ basic sensory processes whereby we gather information from the world we live in (sight, hearing, taste, touch, smell)

✦ the way in which we process information gathered through the senses

✦ basic processes of conditioning and learning, which in turn is complemented by

✦ an effort to investigate how we store the information so acquired—in other words, the study of memory; the latter also requires us to devote considerable energies to

✦ understanding how we retrieve stored information and gain access to it as and when we need it. And then there is the further area, greatly influenced today by artificial intelligence and computer studies, of

✦ our attempts to understand complex processing, traditionally described as thinking. Even when such information has been gathered there remains

✦ the further large area of psychological inquiry that devotes itself to understanding how we organize and execute the motor responses we make after we have successfully gathered and processed information from the environment.

In all these diverse areas psychologists, like other scientists, have developed models and proposed theories, sometimes expressed mathematically and often formulated in terms of information flow diagrams, in order to understand the mechanisms at work and to enable predictions to be made about what will happen if certain specific kinds of further experiments are carried out. This kind of work seems to occupy at least a third of the total field of modern psychology. If one then adds in the parallel studies, also carried out by psychologists, seeking to understand the biological bases undergirding the psychological processes already listed, that adds up to a further third of the total psychological landscape.

There remains the further one-third, which is made up of the very important issues for psychologists as they study how the development of all the processes listed above take place from birth through death; of how we relate to one another in social situations; and, finally, of how we each come to have our unique personalities, this requiring us to investigate how we can best understand and describe human personality. In this book our focus will be primarily on basic sensory and cognitive processes and their biological substrates; on the part played by psychological, neural, and genetic factors in determining behavior; and on issues arising from such research for Christian beliefs. Others have already written at length about the issues concerning social psychology, notably, David Myers, while Mary Van Leeuwen and Paul Vitz have concentrated on personology.

PSYCHOLOGY AND CHRISTIANITY— HINTS OF WHAT INTEGRATION CANNOT MEAN

It should already be apparent that, as we talk about the relation of Christian belief to psychology, there are certain things that integration *cannot* mean. It cannot presumably mean that, in the study of sensation and perception, we expect Weber's law to differ depending on whether the experimenter is a Christian or a non-Christian and whether we are using as our experimental subjects those who hold Christian beliefs or those who do not. The same applies to studies of the processes of depth perception and stereopsis. Likewise, in the case of cognition and learning, we do not expect the principles of classical conditioning to differ between Christians and non-Christians, nor do we expect the schedules of reinforcement found to apply in operant conditioning to differ between Christians and non-Christians. Or, in the case of memory, it is difficult to think of any reason why the information-processing models currently fashionable in the psychological marketplace to help us understand memory processes will differ between Christians and non-Christians. Presumably the serial position effect in learning word lists will be the same for Christians and non-Christians. Neither do we have any grounds, on the basis of Christian belief, for selectively modifying the distinction usefully made between declarative memory and procedural memory. Any attempt to integrate or incorporate Christian beliefs with psychological theorizing in these areas of contemporary psychology would clearly be misplaced, or, to put it more strongly, would not make sense—in fact, would be "nonsense."

As one moves into another area where the study of sensory and cognitive processes is prominent but focused on different questions, namely, developmental psychology, we can ask whether we have any grounds for believing that, for example, the stages we now identify in the normal motor development of a child are likely to differ between Christians and non-Christians. Presumably we do not believe that a new theory of motor development should be developed that integrates or incorporates Christian beliefs with the empirical evidence. Neither, presumably, do we expect the milestones of cognitive development, in so far as they are an accurate account (and here the developmental milestones proposed by Piaget are debatable), to differ between Christians and non-Christians. Any attempt to mix Christian beliefs with psychological accounts is guaranteed to cause confusion and to make nonsense of both, since it is clear evidence of a failure to recognize the different domains to which the two kinds of knowledge belong and the different categories they use for expressing that knowledge.

FORESHADOWING THE SPECIAL PROBLEMS OF PERSONOLOGY

There does, however, remain a further part of the psychological land-scape where the issues of integration are more problematic. Although these aspects of the contemporary landscape form a relatively small part of the total psychological scene, it is nevertheless here that the greatest amount of debate and discussion about how properly to relate psychology and Christian belief has occurred.

As regards their relatively minor contribution to basic research and academic psychology we note several points. First, considering the *Annual Review of Psychology*, it is interesting to see how a roughly constant proportion of these volumes has been devoted to personality annually over the past forty years. Thus, if one looks at volume 1 of the *Annual Review of Psychology*, produced in 1950, we find that, out of its eighteen chapters, one was on personality, one on clinical methods—psychotherapy, and one on counseling methods—therapy. The following year, 1951, in volume 2 there were again eighteen chapters, again one on personality, one on psychotherapy, and one on counseling. In 1968, volume 19, made up of fifteen chapters, contained only one chapter on psychotherapeutic processes; the following year, 1969, volume 20, which contained twenty-two chapters, had one on personality and one on psychotherapeutic processes. Coming now to the contemporary scene, volume 45 (published in 1994) contained eighteen chapters, with one on personality assessment and one on interpersonal relationships.

This brief scan of the *Annual Review* indicates that of the total psychological scene the proportion of space allotted to personality theory and psychotherapy has varied over the years, from about one-sixth to one-eleventh. However, because it occupied a relatively small amount of the total psychological scene (and, therefore, warns us against making psychology synonymous with personality theory), nevertheless, for those discussing the relation of psychology and Christian belief, it has loomed large. There are good reasons for this. Although personality theory, or personology as it is called these days, occupies a relatively small part of the total landscape of academic psychology, nevertheless it does represent a large proportion of the applications of contemporary psychology, particularly by clinical psychologists and psychotherapists. It is for this reason, as well as others, that it is an important issue that has to be addressed in any comprehensive discussion of the relation of psychology and Christian belief. We shall therefore devote two chapters of this book to considering recent trends in relating personality theory and psychotherapy to Christian beliefs.

The fact that it does not make sense to talk about integrating Christian beliefs with specific areas of psychological knowledge does not preclude the identification of recurring themes or pervasive issues in much psychological writing that imply things about our general understanding of human nature and that may or may not be at variance with some of our traditional Christian beliefs about human nature. After all, the Bible is full of profound insights into human nature and the human situation, both individually and in society at large. There are, I suggest, several pervasive themes or recurring issues that we meet as we look at the claims of contemporary psychology and consider whether, and in what way, they may challenge some of our basic Christian beliefs and possess the seeds of potential conflict.

First, as we saw, psychologists devote much effort to understanding basic cognitive mechanisms and to studying the biological, primarily neural, substrates of those processes. We believe that the accumulating evidence points to an ever-tightening link between mental processes and their biological substrates. This raises the question, What do we mean when in Christian teaching we talk about mind, soul, spirit? Are these separate entities that are linked together in some definable way? Certainly contemporary neuropsychology seems to demand a rethinking of the nature of humankind. In this regard, witness the title of Antonio Damasio's exciting recent book, *Descartes' Error.* Do we believe Descartes made an error? Second, studies using animals help our understanding of human cognition and behavior. Work today by psychologists, ethologists, and sociobiologists on nonhuman primates and other animals maintains and extends a long tradition in psychological research. As this work has developed, mindlike behavior in nonhuman primates has been studied increasingly, and raises questions about the relation of human nature to animal nature. Do animals possess souls? Does the spirit uniquely separate man from animals? Third, there are issues that recur as we consider what personologists have to say about human nature. How should we relate their theories of human nature to traditional Christian views of human nature? Finally, the study of consciousness has, in the past five years, moved onto center stage in many discussions of human nature by physicists, biologists, and neuroscientists as well as psychologists. Does what is being said on this topic have any earth-shaking, or for that matter faith-shaking, implications for Christian belief?

TAKING STOCK

1. Any claim to talk about the integration of psychology and Christian belief must deal with psychology as it actually is today. It will not do to confine our discussion to some small section (for example, focusing exclusively on personology) and fail to take account of the vast majority of the psychological landscape as it is at the end of this century.

2. Today psychology has very strong links with neuroscience and cognitive science, with a marked emphasis on an understanding of the neural basis of behavior, including mind and not excluding personality.

3. While applied topics such as clinical psychology, and the inclusion in that of personality theory, loom large for many psychologists who are practitioners, that set of topics, nonetheless, is a relatively small part of the total psychological landscape. Thus, to talk about integration with only that in mind is tantamount to letting the tail wag the dog.

4. Any close scrutiny of the actual nature of scientific psychology quickly alerts us to what integration *cannot* mean. For example, since many aspects of contemporary psychology express their results in mathematical equations, it makes little sense to talk about the "incorporation" of Christian beliefs into mathematical equations. There is no question of adding another constant into Weber's law or into the Fechner fraction on the grounds of Christian belief!

5. There are a number of pervasive themes in contemporary psychology that may well raise deep issues for our traditional Christian understanding of human nature. In particular, we have identified the way in which research on brain and mind has converged during this century to underline the unity of the human person. That, in turn, demands that we think carefully, and *biblically*, when we talk about the soul.

6. Developments in cognitive neuroscience have underlined that several levels of analysis are required to tackle the research problems we face.

Moreover, the accounts given at one level do nothing to exclude or make irrelevant accounts given at other levels. We also believe that accounts of human nature given in terms of cognitive neuroscience do not make superfluous insights traditionally found enlightening from literature, art, and religion. The accounts at these other levels are certainly not made redundant by the results of research in cognitive neuroscience.

7. The reductionistic trap is not a thing of the past. Eternal vigilance is called for. As Sperry put it, "The meaning of the message will not be found in the chemistry of the ink." We have no need to be defensive about the scientific study of the link between mind and brain. Of itself it does not threaten human dignity; rather, the knowledge derived from such study can, in principle and ultimately in practice, enable us to treat one another with greater respect and understanding. A distinguished Canadian psychiatrist, Dr. Lipowski,[10] has wisely said, "Neither brainless nor mindless psychiatry could do justice to the complexity of mental illness and to the treatment of patients. A comprehensive, biopsychosocial approach to our field is needed." We should echo his words and say neither brainless nor mindless psychology can do justice to the complexity of the tasks we face in seeking to understand mental life and human behavior. A comprehensive biopsychosocial approach to such problems is essential. And, we would add, both the biological and the psychological aspects of mind are real; they are different and are not reducible the one to the other. As Damasio[11] put it, "It is not only the separation of mind and brain that is mythical: the separation between mind and body is probably just as fictional. The mind is embodied, in the full sense of the term, not just embrained" (118).

CHAPTER 2

SCIENCE AND FAITH

Learning from the Past

I am free, I am bound to nobody's word, except those inspired
by God; if I oppose those in the least degree, I beseech God
to forgive me my audacity of judgment, as I have been moved
not so much by longing for some opinion of my own as by
love for the freedom of science.
—Nathaniel Carpenter, *Philosophia Libera*, 1622

Christians had nothing to fear if astronomy discovered new
worlds, geology new ages, or anthropology extinct races
and species. Rather would the Christian welcome joyfully
and appropriate each successive revelation.
—Lewis W. Green, *Lectures on the Evidences of Christianity*, 1854

IN SO FAR AS psychology's claim to be a science is valid, it follows that
the status of psychological knowledge shares that enjoyed by all knowledge coming from the scientific enterprise. To speak of "the scientific
enterprise" in such simple terms, however, obscures the differing ways
in which it has been portrayed over the past four centuries. Furthermore,
the relation of the knowledge gained through the scientific enterprise to
traditional theological statements has also been variously construed
over the past four centuries. Today it is well documented in books such
as those by Hooykaas, Russell, Brooke, Barbour, and others. There is
within the writings of such authors a general consensus. It behooves
anyone writing about the relationship of psychology and Christianity to

pause and ask what lessons we may learn from earlier attempts to relate knowledge from the scientific enterprise with the Christian faith. In so doing we may find guidelines to follow as well as identify errors to be avoided.

RELATING SCIENCE AND FAITH: SOME GENERAL POINTERS FROM THE PAST

Greek Influences on the Development of Science

In the centuries immediately preceding the sixteenth, an attitude toward the natural world began to crystallize that was to set the stage for the emergence of modern science. Two major formative influences gave rise to this new attitude: the Greek, or perhaps in the light of more recent research we should say Greco-Roman, and the Hebrew-Christian. Colin Russell[1] has portrayed these as two streams of thought that have flowed together over the centuries, interacting in numerous ways and producing reciprocal alterations upon each other. Others have warned that even to characterize them in these simple ways can be misleading. Hooykaas,[2] for example, cautioned that to speak of the Greek view of nature is misleading in that it fails to do justice to the wide spectrum of views that were held by Greek thinkers up to the third century B.C. At the risk of oversimplification, we may identify some of the common features of the Greek view of nature as follows.

Greek thinkers believed that the universe should be regarded as noncreated and therefore as existing from eternity. In this sense it was eternal and thus also divine or at least semidivine. On the Greek view, nature was indwelt by divine forms that provided a ready link between man and nature since the mind of man was believed to possess the same divine character attributed to the forms of nature. This belief, however, did not go unchallenged among other Greeks. Aristophanes, for example, parodied Theophrastus's doctrine "the air within us is a small portion of the God" when, as Guthrie reminds us, "In one of his comedies he brings Socrates on to the stage suspended in the air in a basket. Asked the reason for this strange proceeding, Socrates replied that to discover the truth about celestial matters, he must allow his mind to mingle with the kindred air." Even so, because it was assumed that both the mind of man and forms of nature were divine, it was thought that the one could read off or intuit the other. It was this tendency to impose patterns where in fact they were not readily found and to rely solely on reason in doing so that minimized the importance of observation and deduction. Thus, the tremendous achievements of the Greeks in the development of logical reasoning were in danger of becoming the very factors that would place limits on the developments of empirical science. The ancient Greeks believed that fundamentally the world should be understood, that there was no need to change it. The net result was that the magnificent intellectual achievements of the Greeks, destined to rule over Western thought for two millennia, had within them their own inherent limitations.

Probably three features of Greek thought in the end most consistently inhibited the development of a modern scientific approach. First, there was felt to be little need for empirical testing; contemplation allied to reasoning was sufficient. Second, the Greek view of nature regarded the universe and the various parts of it as indwelt by living forms, usually divine in character, and it was therefore perfectly natural to look for teleological explanations to the exclusion of any other types. Third, because on the Greek view the mind of man was rational, they elevated the processes of intuition and the use of reason above careful observation. As Guthrie put it when quoting Daremberg, "The philosophers tried to explain nature whilst shutting their eyes."[3]

Despite these shortcomings there were other features of Greek thinking that contained the germinal seeds for the eventual development of modern science. For the Greeks the world had order in spite of its apparent chaos. They clearly saw the worthwhileness of a body of knowledge about nature. They discovered and perfected a method of deductive reasoning. They enjoyed remarkable achievements in philosophy, logic, and mathematics, all of which were basic and essential tools for the rapid development of science. Just as their eye shutting retarded the growth of science, so their mind opening led to things perhaps equally important: metaphysics and mathematics. Finally, they made significant beginnings in astronomy, physics, and biology. In short, the main legacy of the Greeks as far as the development of science is concerned is found not in particular theories, but in their general attitudes of rational investigation of nature by means of logic, mathematics, and observation. Moreover, while they may not have felt any necessity for empirical testing that involved changing nature, some of them, according to Russell, emphasized that aspect of the empirical method in which observation plays a dominant role. Thus he cautions, "Even though Greek influence on science may not seem as monolithic as is often imagined, the very diversity of its effects testifies to its immense significance for the emergence of science."[4]

Views about the contribution of Greek thought to the eventual bursting forth of the intellectual and cultural activity known as the Renaissance have been revised somewhat over the past century. A hundred years ago it was generally agreed that Renaissance science was almost entirely dependent on its Greek origins. Thus, the scientific revolution was a product of Greek thought banishing the mists of medieval theology. Rationality had overcome superstition. Science had won round one of its fight with religion. That, says Russell, is a view few scholars in the field would accept today. A more balanced view, as Hooykaas and Russell have documented, would be to recognize the importance of Hebrew-Christian roots while not denying the Greek heritage of the sciences. As Russell has written, "Science arose in the West, not when Christian theology was submerged by Greek rationalism, but rather when Greek and other 'pagan' ideas of nature were shown to be inadequate in the new climate of biblical awareness brought about by the Reformation."[5]

Chronologically, of course, the Old Testament comes before the intellectual age of the Ancient Orient and Greece. It was with the rediscovery of the Bible and its message at the time of the Reformation, however, that a new impetus came to the development of science. This new impetus, together with all that was best in Greek thinking, was to produce the right mixture to detonate the chain reaction leading to the explosion of knowledge that began at the start of the scientific revolution in the sixteenth century and that is proceeding with ever-increasing momentum today.

The Hebrew-Christian View of Nature

The outstanding feature of this view is of a world totally dependent on God. This has implications that immediately contrast with several aspects of the Greek view. The world is noneternal; it was created by God (Gen. 1) and is dependent on him for its continuing, moment-by-moment existence (Heb. 1:3). God and nature are not to be identified with each other; they are to be sharply separated. God is eternal; nature is created and will one day pass away. The natural order is not divine; it is created. God made the firmament (Gen. 1:7); the world is an ordered one but not autonomous. Not only did God take the initiative in creating the world, but the world continues in existence only by reason of his sustaining activity in "upholding all things by the word of his power," as the writer to the Hebrews puts it (1:3). Whereas for the Greek the workings of nature were rationalistic and purposive, with that purposefulness firmly embedded within nature itself, in the Hebrew-Christian tradition purpose resides in God. Those who wish to discover the patterns of order in nature must have recourse to experience; they cannot discover these patterns by intuition or reason alone.

For the Hebrew, God alone is to be worshiped; nature is only his creation and to worship that is idolatry—and the Lord God will not tolerate idolatry. Finally, since the mind of man is part of the created order, it is thus nondivine and subject to error; it cannot infallibly intuit or read off from nature the inherent qualities of nature.

INTERACTING STREAMS AND THE RISE OF SCIENCE

By the seventeenth century puritan scientists were regarding science as an ally of true religion. In a spirit of optimism we find among the puritans of all shades great protagonists of the free science. Very conscious of the dangers of appealing to any authority other than that of revelation, they put their free science, "not adorned by great names but naked and simple," over against the superstitious cult of Aristotle.[6]

With the Enlightenment we find its great prophet Newton adhering to Baconian empiricist ideals in the face of the forces of rationalism and deism. Much of this, in Hooykaas's view, led to the Enlightenment becoming a secularized puritanism; the essential difference between the eighteenth-century Enlightenment and the puritan enlightenment was that to the puritans it was not freedom that led to truth, but truth that led to freedom. These different emphases also probably reflect more basic convictions. In an age of optimism, as the eighteenth century was, it was natural to develop an excessive faith in reason unless one's views on larger issues were constantly brought to the bar of revelation. The puritan view of man and his fallen state for their part constrained them to develop a much more realistic assessment of the place of unaided reason, that is, reason unaided either by revelation in matters of faith or by observation and experiments in matters of science. By the nineteenth century another widely accepted product of Aristotelian doctrine came under scrutiny and then under fire. It seemed natural, *reasonable*, to conclude from Aristotle's teaching that, since all living things are in some sense embodiments of eternal forms or unchanging essences, species are therefore fixed and unchanging. Now, however, with Darwin's teaching, Aristotelian biology was shaken at its very foundations. What if species are not fixed? What if there is a measure of change from generation to generation? What Newton had done to Aristotelian physics, Darwin was about to do to Aristotelian biology. With this challenge Darwin, like Newton, was to produce work that became the point of departure for a new worldview. Newton's intelligently designed machine would, under Darwin's influence, acquire the properties of a dynamic and progressive process.

Strangely perhaps to some of us today we thus discover that aspects of Darwin's views of man were recapturing a Hebrew-Christian emphasis on the nature of man. Nature, said Darwin, includes both man and his culture. By contrast, the Greek tendency was to separate man from the rest of creation and to give him and his mind an arrogant, aristocratic place, over against nature. Darwinian views also challenged any simple analogy of God as the "maker" of the universe, that is, as an absentee landlord who made the world and then left it to run autonomously.

SCIENCE AND FAITH: FRIENDS OR FOES?

If Hebrew-Christian thinking about the natural world positively facilitated the rise of science and if it is the case that Christians were so influential in the development of science, how did it come about that the popular view of the relation of science and religion is one of conflict? It is undoubtedly a widespread view but one that Russell believes is a widely held myth and certainly one that needs urgently to be demythologized. His own belief is that "the cumulative effect of twenty years of historical scholarship has been to demonstrate its mythical character."[7]

This common belief in a deep and enduring hostility between science and faith is sustained by the popular media. Russell believes that it has its origins in two books written in the late nineteenth century: *History of the Conflict between Religion and Science* by J. W. Draper[8] (1875) and *A History of the Warfare of Science and Theology in Christendom* by A. D. White[9] (1896). Both books achieved wide circulation, and yet Russell asserts that "today the historical views of Draper and White are totally unacceptable, not merely because of many factual aberrations, but much more because they represent a long demolished tradition of positivist, whigish historiography."[10] It is interesting and perhaps significant that both books were written from the New World. Russell argues that in both instances the conflict and warfare metaphors arose from within each writer's own personal and social circumstances and to that extent were largely culturally determined.

George Marsden[11] has documented how the events in the New World sometimes tagged "1859 and all that" came to be framed in metaphors of warfare. He poses the question, "How, then, did the conservative evangelical reaction to Darwinism come to be regarded as though it always had been an all out warfare, when for a half century the attitudes among some of the movement's most prominent leaders were, at least, mixed and ambivalent?" (139). Marsden's answer is the same as Russell's, and he attributes the strength and success of the warfare metaphor to those anti-Christian polemicists who "suggested that traditional Christians had always attacked modern science" (139). And thus, in their view, the inevitable clash of Darwinism with Christianity was but "another instance of a long standing war between faith and science." Thus, says Marsden, "soon after Darwin published, his defenders vigorously promoted this warfare metaphor," and foremost among those in North America were White and Draper, who "were prophets of a new age in which the scientific quest for truth would finally be freed from religious constraint" (140).

Marsden emphasizes how, particularly in North America, the relation between science and religion came to be framed in terms of metaphors of warfare: "The stereotyped story so convenient to those of us who lecture about modern culture, has been framed by the metaphors of warfare. According to this story, Darwinism marked the triumphant assault of modern scientific culture against the last remaining citadels of pre-modern religious culture" (135). Over against this he points out how necessary it is to remember the well-documented commitments of American evangelicals around the 1850s to a scientific culture. For example, he refers to the writings of Lewis Green, who in 1854 pointed out that "Christians had nothing to fear if astronomy discovered new worlds, geology new ages, or anthropology extinct races and species. Rather would the Christian welcome joyfully and appropriate each successive revelation" (134). Moreover, among American evangelical Protestants on the specific issue of Darwinism there were already distinguished advocates of mediating positions, usually designated "theistic evolution" or "progressive creation." Thus, immediately upon the announcement of Darwin's theory some conservative believers had already responded to the suggestion that evolutionary doctrine must undermine faith and the Creator. God, they said, controls all natural processes through his providential care. The questions raised by biological evolution are therefore in principle no different from those suggested by other natural phenomena such as photosynthesis. A fully naturalistic account of the process does not preclude belief that God planned and controlled it. So God may have used evolutionary processes as his means of creating at least some of our species.

Whether the creation of humans involves some divine intervention has been a matter of some debate among evangelical theistic evolutionists. A strict reading of Genesis, they agreed, however, does not preclude evolutionary developments. After all, already by the mid-nineteenth century most American evangelical scholars concurred that "the days of Genesis 1 could mean long eras sufficient to allow for the enormous amounts of time demanded by geological theories. Evolutionary doctrine as such, therefore, need contradict neither any theological dogma nor a faithful reading of scripture" (154, 155). In light of all this Marsden raises the natural question, "Why have creation scientists insisted upon a polarization, and why have such dichotomized views been so popular in America?" (157). In the context of our discussion in this present book his answers are particularly illuminating examples of how extrascientific matters may and at times do become more informative and influential than strict matters of science. The general local Christian climate and strongly held doctrinal beliefs having nothing to do with evolution per se or an exactitude in the reading of Scripture of a kind that other Christians and biblical scholars believe cannot be sustained. In the case of creation science Marsden specifically identifies premillennialism and some forms of what he calls "Protestant scholasticism" as these extra-scientific matters that were so influential and to a point continue to be so in the creation science–evolution debate.

As we shall be considering, from a variety of starting points, models of human nature suggested by modern science, we shall do well to remember and be sensitive to any extrascientific influences of a cultural kind, or of traditions that are not biblically based, which have in the past led us readily to accept particular models of humankind as being those that arise out of the study of Scripture. As we shall discover (chapter 6), it is noteworthy that as one looks at modern translations of the Scriptures, such as the Revised Standard Version or the New International Version, one frequently finds that those passages that had, in the past, been translated to convey the impression that the soul is some separate part of humankind, tagged on to another part named the body, have in general been removed and the passages have been retranslated accordingly. One widely accepted reference work, the *New Dictionary of Christian Theology*,[12] tells us that "soul (a word used sparingly in modern translations of the bible) is not a part of human nature but characterizes it in its totality, just as flesh and spirit do. A separate or different origin for 'soul' no longer enters the picture."

One important lesson from the past is that texts that were widely used at one time to contradict an apparently developing scientific view on a particular issue were later reassessed and the true force of what they were teaching was brought to the surface. For example, cosmology texts such as "Sun, stand thou still" (Josh. 10:12), "The sun rises and the sun goes down" (Eccles. 1:5), and "The world is established; it shall never be moved" (Ps. 93:1) were all held to support a geocentric view of the universe, which made the developing heliocentric theory of Copernicus untenable. This is but one example of a more general tendency to interpret particular passages of Scripture as if they were part of a twentieth-century scientific textbook.

MODELS OF THE RELATIONSHIP BETWEEN SCIENCE AND THEOLOGY

In addition to the conflict or warfare model, other models have been proposed for this relationship. One is that the domains of science and theology are totally independent. Such a model, however, simply does not fit the historical evidence, which, as we have indicated, points to a continuing series of interactions between science and theology over many centuries. Another view is to argue that if only scientists and theologians would formulate their statements more clearly they would realize that they were complementary rather than conflicting. This may be traced back at least to Francis Bacon (1561–1626). He spoke of two "books," the book of nature and the book of Scripture, each of which had to be read and understood. He further argued that because the Author of both was the same they could not ultimately conflict. According to this view, since each had a different purpose, it was idle to mix "philosophy" (science and divinity) and to seek scientific data in the pages of Scripture. Even so, there were areas where biblical and scientific evidence appeared to clash and when that happened the complementarity of the two was invoked. Calvin, following Augustine's ideas of "accommodation," asserted that the Holy Spirit accommodated his language to that of common speech to teach spiritual principles. On this view, for example, the days of creation statements about the structure of the cosmos or statements about the sun standing still or statements about a universal flood are susceptible to a nonliteral interpretation. The concerns of Scripture are spiritual and eternal and in this sense complementary to the purposes and concerns of natural science.

Brooke[13] believes that the "two books" approach oversimplifies the issues and that the passage of ideas from one domain to the other occurred steadily over the past four centuries. He notes a third position with which he himself is sympathetic, namely, that religious beliefs and scientific claims have in fact often mutually affirmed one another. In this regard he sees R. K. Merton's[14] classic sociological analysis supporting the argument that, as described earlier, puritan values did, indeed, facilitate the expansion of science in seventeenth-century England. However, Brooke's overall assessment is that "serious scholarship in the history of science has revealed so extraordinarily rich and complex a relationship between science and religion in the past that general theses are difficult to sustain. The real lesson turns out to be the complexities."[15]

Russell likewise feels that the complementarity model is inadequate in some respects. He also believes that it ignores the considerable network of relationships between science and theology already disclosed by recent historical scholarship. For this reason he suggests that there is a fourth possible model that takes these into account, which he calls symbiosis. This, he says, "recognizes that historically, scientific and theological thinking have owed much to one another and that their growth has been mutually promoted. It conforms with the widespread acknowledgment that much human knowledge is culture dependent, but it does not prejudice the independence of data either in the bible or in the natural world. It merely recognizes that in the interpretation of such data, theological and scientific ideas are often intermingled in one brain, as they are indeed in one society. Hence one might expect some degree of mutual influence; and such turns out to be the case."[16] We shall develop this way of thinking about the relationship between psychological knowledge and biblical teaching in our concluding chapter.

SCIENTIFIC PSYCHOLOGY AND CHRISTIAN BELIEF

Having noted in chapter 1 the close links, both historical and contemporary, which different branches of psychology have with physics, physiology, anatomy, biochemistry, neurology, and zoology, it seems sensible to bear in mind the lessons, at times very hard learned, from past attempts to relate knowledge derived through the scientific enterprise and that given through revelation in Scripture. Thus, as we begin to explore the models that are emerging from psychology in the late twentieth century, we have to be particularly sensitive to the temptation to foreclose issues, because at times the words in which contemporary psychology is expressed look and sound so similar to some scriptural statements about human nature. It is such areas that we have concentrated on in this book. For example, the evidence from neuropsychology of the ever-tightening link between mind and brain raises all sorts of questions about what is meant by the soul in the Bible and what the relation of the soul to the body is; the evidence from behavior genetics and neurogenetics raises a whole host of questions about human responsibility for actions; the whole area of personology raises questions about how the profound accounts of human needs and human motivation presented to us in Scripture are to be related to those psychological models that also purport to tell us about basic human needs. As regards the relation between human nature and animal nature we have to be sensitive to the temptation to make unbiblical and unscientific claims about differences between animals and humans because we believe that in so doing we are, in some way, defending the uniqueness of humankind. The current widespread discussions about consciousness, its emergence and to what extent it is the same and different in animals and humans, is an issue of this kind.

How best to view the relationship between the knowledge given to us through the scientific enterprise and knowledge through revelation in Scripture is something that we need to keep in mind as we deal with specific topics in succeeding chapters. In the final chapter we return to this issue and ask how best we may view the relationship between psychology in the late twentieth century and the teachings of Scripture.

THE OCCURRENCE OF WARFARE METAPHOR
IN PSYCHOLOGY–RELIGION INTERACTIONS

The warfare metaphor, used by some to characterize the relation between science and religion in the nineteenth century, though largely discredited by historians of science, has continued to appear from time to time in discussions of the relation between psychological science and religious belief in the present century.

It is not unusual to hear highly intelligent and well-informed people spontaneously repeat the claim that psychology, in general, and Freud, in particular, have "explained away" religious beliefs as nothing but wishful thinking—whistling in the dark of an empty universe to keep our spirits up. In this sense, at least, the warfare metaphor is alive and well and ready to be used as a shorthand way of portraying the ongoing relation between psychology and religion in the twentieth century. How accurate is this way of portraying the relationship? Does it fit with the facts of the story?

Broadly speaking, psychologists who have taken an interest in religion have concentrated on what we might call its roots and its fruits. Hearnshaw[17] identified four significant influences at the end of the nineteenth century that provided the basis for later psychological studies of religion: (1) Francis Galton's studies of the manifestations of religion (e.g., prayer); (2) studies of anthropologists, such as Sir James Fraser, of comparative religion and the origins of religion; (3) the writings of theologians such as W. R. Inge on mysticism and religious experiences; and (4) the beginnings of the systematic psychology of religion (e.g., E. G. Starbuck[18]). These in turn culminated in William James's classic, *The Varieties of Religious Experience* (1902).

It is noteworthy that none of the influences listed above seem to have been motivated by a desire to generate or perpetuate a warfare metaphor to describe the relationship between psychology and religion. Certainly, in the case of William James, the relationship was a clearly and strongly positive one as he sought to explore how psychology could deepen our understanding of the roots and fruits of religion.

As we move into the twentieth century the picture changes, so that by the time Sigmund Freud's radical views were becoming more widely known in society at large, the stage was set for a strong resurgence of the warfare metaphor. Despite Freud's own disclaimers that his accounts of the roots and fruits of religion were neutral as regards the truth value of specific religious beliefs, which, he agreed, must be decided on other grounds, nevertheless his own accounts were soon seen as explaining away religious beliefs and exposing the practices of religions as nothing but the persistence of an interim social neurosis that we must eventually grow out of.

In due course Freud's views on the origins of religion in *Totem and Taboo* (1919) and *Moses and Monotheism* (1938) were severely criticized as it became clear that many of the so-called facts on which he based his theories were shown by professional anthropologists to be incorrect; this did little in the popular mind, however, to bring his views into disrespect (e.g., B. Malinowski, *Sex and Repression in Primitive Society* [1927] and *The Foundations of Faith and Morals* [1936]). Freud had produced a good story and his influence in this, as in other areas, persisted long after his views were widely discredited and disregarded by scholars in related disciplines.

Much the same may be said about Freud's views of developed religion presented in *The Future of an Illusion* (1927) and *Civilisation and Its Discontents* (1930). Here, as we mentioned above, in Freud's terminology an "illusion" stands for any belief system based on human wishes. He was careful to point out that such a basis does not necessarily imply that the system is false; nevertheless, as far as Christianity was concerned, he clearly believed that it was. In that sense he championed and perpetuated the warfare metaphor.

Another major figure in psychology during the first half of the twentieth century was Carl Jung. For a time Jung was a close collaborator with Freud, though he subsequently developed his own views within the psychoanalytic tradition. Freud and Jung, as in matters psychological, ultimately differed radically in their views of religion. Whereas for Freud psychology pointed to religion as a neurosis that in time could be dispelled and the patient (the human race?) cured, for Jung religion was an essential activity of humanity. The task of psychology was not to explain away religion, but to try and understand how human nature reacts to situations normally described as religious. Freud's and Jung's contrasting views were aptly summarized by G. S. Spinks when he wrote, "For Freud religion was an obsessional neurosis, and at no time did he modify that judgment. For Jung it was the absence of religion that was the chief cause of adult psychological disorders. These two sentences indicate how great is the difference between their respective stand points on religion."[19]

While Freud and Jung captured the headlines and the public interest in what was happening at the psychology–religion interface in the first half of this century, there were others such as R. H. Thouless[20] who were writing on the same topic and in many psychologists' judgments making a much more lasting contribution, as evidenced by the 1971 reprinting of his book *Introduction to the Psychology of Religion*, first published in the 1930s. Thouless's approach was primarily constructive and a complete contrast with the warfare metaphor. Since the Second World War there have been several noteworthy attempts to offer new insights into religion through the eyes of psychology. Notable among these are G. W. Allport's *The Individual and His Religion* (1951), Michael Argyle's several books, including *Religious Behaviour* (1958) and (with Beit Hallahmi) *The Social Psychology of Religion* (1975). These, like Thouless's book, are not confrontational and bear no mark of the warfare approach. There are thus many excellent books on the psychology of religion that are not infused with the warfare metaphor but, while they are read by psychologists and others interested in deepening our understanding of the insights that psychology can offer into the part played by religion in our thoughts and feelings, they are not newsworthy because they are not confrontational. Such, however, was not the case with B. F. Skinner's views of religion.

If Skinner's views are perhaps the most widely publicized of the warfare genre in the second half of this century, this is because of his well-deserved reputation as the leading behaviorist psychologist of the past fifty years. Having achieved considerable success in the development of techniques for shaping and modifying behavior, Skinner went on to speculate about how such techniques might be harnessed to shape the future of society. He believed that similar principles, based on rewards and punishments, could explain how the practice of religion functions psychologically. "The religious agency," he said, "is a special form of government under which 'good' and 'bad' become 'pious' and 'sinful.' Contingencies involving positive and negative reinforcement, often of the most extreme sort, are codified—for example as commandments—maintained by specialists, usually with the support of ceremonies, rituals and stories."[21] He argued that the good things, personified in a god, are reinforcing, whereas the threat of hell is an aversive stimulus. Both are used to shape behavior. Underlying Skinner's approach is a reductionist presupposition. He speaks of concepts of God being "reduced to" what we find positively reinforcing. There is no doubt that Skinner provided ready ammunition for anyone wishing to perpetuate the warfare metaphor of the relation of psychology and religion.

If Skinner wished to champion the warfare metaphor, another distinguished figure in psychology in the second half of this century took quite a different view. Psychologist, neuroscientist, and Nobel Laureate Roger Sperry wrote not only of the bankruptcy of some forms of behaviorism but strongly advocated the benefits of a positive relationship between psychology and religion viewed as allies engaged in a common task. We must note at once, however, that Sperry's views of religion would sound very strange to conventional Christian believers. Typical of Sperry's[22] views is the following:

The answer to the question, "Is there convergence between science and religion?" seems from the standpoint of psychology to be a definite and emphatic "yes." Over the past 15 years, changes in the foundational concepts of psychology instituted by the new cognitive or mentalist paradigm have radically reformed scientific descriptions of human nature, and the conscious self. The resultant views are today less atomistic, less mechanistic, and more mentalistic, contextual, subjectivistic and humanistic. From the standpoint of theology, these new mentalistic tenets, which no longer exclude on principle the entire inner world of subjective phenomena, are much more palatable and compatible than were those of the behaviorist–materialist era. Where science and religion had formerly stood in direct conflict on this matter to the point even of being mutually exclusive and irreconcilable, one now sees a new compatibility, potentially even harmony with liberal religion—defined as religion that does not rely on dualistic or supernatural beliefs, forms of which have been increasingly evident in contemporary theology.

From the above quote, several things are clear. Sperry once used the warfare metaphor to characterize the relation between science and religion. He believes that as far as psychology is concerned that is now a thing of the past. However, he places his hopes in a liberal theology that makes no supernatural claims—hence my earlier warning to those who hold traditional Christian beliefs lest they are tempted to embrace too readily, lock, stock, and barrel, Sperry's views without careful scrutiny. What he has written is provocative and worthy of careful consideration, but his theological views bear little relation to the revealed truth of Scripture.

The Continuing Search for a Constructive Partnership

As we noted above, there remains the widespread impression in some quarters today that psychology has "explained away" religious experience and behavior and that religious beliefs are "nothing but" wishful thinking. In a way this is strange since two of the major figures in academic and applied psychology this century, whose enduring contributions are increasingly acknowledged, in fact held positive, sympathetic, and constructive views of religion. Both Gordon Allport in the United States and Sir Frederic Bartlett in Britain made a point of emphasizing the potential for a positive cooperative relationship of psychology and religion, at the same time underlining the limits of psychological inquiry, at least when practiced as a science.

Allport, a major influence on the development of theories of personality, wrote that "different as are science and art in their axioms and methods they have learned to cooperate in a thousand ways—in the production of fine dwellings, music, clothing, design. Why should not science and religion, likewise differing in axioms and method, yet cooperate in the production of an improved human character without which all other human gains are tragic loss? From many sides today comes the demand that religion and psychology busy themselves in finding a common ground for uniting their efforts for human welfare."[23]

Bartlett, often described as one of the precursors and architects of the cognitive revolution in psychology, wrote:

It is inevitable that the forms which are taken by feeling, thinking, and action within any religion should be molded and directed by the character of its own associated culture. The psychologist must accept these forms and attempt to show how they have grown up and what are their principal effects. Should he appear to succeed in doing these things, he is tempted to suppose that this confers upon him some special right to pronounce upon the further and deeper issues of ultimate truth and value. These issues, as many people have claimed, seem to be inevitably bound up with the assertion that in some way the truth and the worth of religion come from a contact of the natural order with some other order or world, not itself directly accessible to the common human senses. So far as any final decision upon the validity or value of such a claim goes, the psychologist is in exactly the same position as that of any other human being who cares to consider the matter seriously. Being a psychologist gives him neither superior nor inferior authority.[24]

Both Allport and Bartlett held a high view of the potential benefits of a developing science of psychology. They also recognized the distinctive approaches to the gaining of knowledge possible through the scientific enterprise—a view already well articulated by leading physical scientists of earlier generations.

If there were psychologists using the warfare metaphor who were antagonistic to religion, there were also Christians who were antagonistic to psychology. Hendrika Vande Kemp[25] has noted that "the anti-psychologists seem to regard psychology as offering alternative answers to the same questions answered by Christian theology and biblical revelation, questions concerning knowledge of God and salvation history and a proper human response to both. Psychologists, for the most part, are not interested in 'knowing God.' They are interested in what kinds of images of God persons entertain and what beliefs they embrace, and how their faith relates to practice—but these involve 'knowledge' of a very different sort." She continues: "The most conservative of the anti-psychologists, who reject all sources of knowledge other than authority, should be equally skeptical of empiricism (or science), rationalism (or philosophy), and mysticism (or phenomenology), as all involve 'excessive curiosity.' Since no form of psychology would be acceptable to them, there is little point in presenting an argument. One might challenge them, however, as to their exegetical method—it is hard to envision one that involves neither induction, deduction nor intuition."

While expressing her concerns about the anti-psychologists, Vande Kemp also indicated her unease about what she describes as the "simplistic epistemology" of Christian psychologists, such as Foster and Ledbetter, who nevertheless shared her opposition to the anti-psychologists. Vande Kemp criticizes Foster and Ledbetter's limited conception of the scientific enterprise. Vande Kemp's own description of the scientific enterprise and the way scientists work is very similar to that of physical scientists such as Euan Squires (see chapter 10). Thus she writes, "Scientists rely heavily on the testimony of past witnesses, as any introductory textbook will attest. Most scientists also rely on intuition, as a source of hypotheses or a creative explanation of unexpected findings, and in their development of new instruments. All contemporary scientists integrate reason and observation in the hypotheticodeductive method, in which hypotheses developed on the basis of observation are tested empirically (or experimentally) and used to build models and theories" (20).

As we shall see in more detail in chapter 6, there are other Christians who are deeply concerned about the seemingly exclusive adherence of some psychologists to the experimental method and to a positivistic view of science. They are concerned that something should be done to "humanize" psychology. Mary Van Leeuwen[26] comments on such an approach: "Human action, they say [i.e., the humanizers], cannot be understood merely by observation and description from an outsider's point of view. . . . Consequently methods are needed which will enable the scientists to understand, in active cooperation with the subjects, how the subjects see their particular situation." Commenting on Van Leeuwen's proposals, Foster and Ledbetter[27] note that "Van Leeuwen (1985) does not advocate a complete abandonment of the scientific method, but rather believes that we must be willing to modify our procedures to allow the person being studied to be more human." This in practice means to rely much more heavily on subjective reports. As Foster and Ledbetter go on to note, "We can accept this type of research within a broad definition of empiricism, but generalizations from these results would have to be severely limited due to the subjectivism introduced by the procedures. While Van Leeuwen (1982) correctly points out that rigorously controlled experimentation limits generalizability, it is also true that generalization from research using the methods she advocates should be even more restricted."

While Vande Kemp shares some of Foster and Ledbetter's concerns about the humanizers' of science attempts to recognize the limitations of an extreme positivist characterization of the methods of scientific psychology and the knowledge derived from it, she has her own preferred solution for dealing with this same problem. She labels it "philosophizing psychology." As a historian of psychology she is very aware of the past intimate and beneficial links between philosophy and psychology. Thus she has written, "I would personally recommend the 'philosophizing' of psychology. Contemporary psychologists would generate much more meaningful research if they were not afraid to align themselves with 'the old psychology' which was undifferentiated from philosophy. . . . A psychology which has no connections with philosophy and theory may not be capable of humanizing, despite our best intentions—and philosophy may be reluctant to welcome us back unless we broaden our thinking (and method) considerably."

Vande Kemp will be encouraged to note how up-to-date some of her proposals are. The September 1995 issue of the *British Journal of Psychiatry* included a paper by Michael Shepherd[28] entitled "Psychiatry and Philosophy." Shepherd notes (287) that "both psychiatry and psychology have attempted to sever their conjunction with formal philosophy, basing their claims to independence on the spirit of empiricism and scientific enquiry and condemning, in the words of a major textbook of psychiatry, 'attempts to solve the problems of psycho-pathology by philosophical short-cuts, instead of the relatively slow method of investigation with the disciplines of natural science' (Slater and Roth, 1969). This view echoes Claude Bernard's belief in determinism as the only justifiable scientific philosophy and his maxim that 'le meilleur systeme philosophique consiste a ne pas en avoir' (Bernard, 1865)."

Shepherd balances this trend by reminding the reader that "it is worth recalling that no 'philosophical short-cuts' are to be found in the work of the two outstanding medically qualified men who can be credited with both an intimate knowledge of the psychological sciences and a worldwide reputation as philosophers. They reached the same conclusion in slightly different ways." He notes that "to the psychologist/philosopher William James psychology was 'the ante room to meta-physics (James, 1887)' and metaphysics was no more than 'an unusually stubborn effort to think clearly.' To the psychiatrist/philosopher Karl Jaspers 'a thorough study of philosophy is not of any positive value to psycho-pathologists, apart from the importance of methodology . . . but philosophical studies can protect us from putting the wrong question, indulging in irrelevant discussions and deploying our prejudices' (Jaspers, 1963)."

The major contribution that closer links with philosophy can afford the science and practice of psychology (and psychiatry) is the constant reminder of the need to examine and lay bare the otherwise often hidden and undeclared assumptions and presuppositions influencing the questions being asked, selecting the methods appropriate to answering those questions, and interpreting the results of any empirical/experimental projects carried out. In the context of psychiatry, as Shepherd pointed out, this was well expressed by the late Sir Aubrey Lewis, one of the leading British psychiatrists of this century, when he asked how far a psychiatrist's general philosophy of life can be kept apart from his clinical practice. Thus Lewis wrote, "Nobody in psychiatry can do without a philosophical background, but very often it is an implicit and not an explicit one. This matter has received much less attention than it deserves. Philosophical influences, social influences, religious influences, ideological influences, all play their part in molding the mental outlook of psychiatrists."[29] We would add that precisely the same statement could be made of psychologists.

To be effective, any closer links between philosophy and psychology will require psychologists to make sure they are more aware of the history of their discipline and better acquainted with relevant aspects of philosophic writings. At the same time, effective closer links of psychology with philosophy will, as Francis Crick has pointed out, impose even greater demands on philosophers. A casual acquaintance with what is happening in psychology and neuroscience simply will not suffice. A sustained detailed knowledge will be required if the views of the philosophers are to be taken seriously by psychologists, psychiatrists, and neuroscientists.

TAKING STOCK

1. There are lessons that we, as psychologists, can learn as we recall earlier attempts to relate the knowledge that comes to us through the scientific enterprise with that which comes in other ways, including through religion. This becomes evident as we notice that there are areas of contemporary psychology with close links, historically and today, with physical and biological sciences. By taking note of these lessons we shall be better able to avoid repeating past errors. We, of course, share many Christian beliefs with our forebears, who sought, in their generation, to relate, for example, the accumulating knowledge in cosmology, physics, and geology to what they read in Scripture about the world in which we live. Then, as now, according to some interpretations of the biblical statements, there appeared to be conflicts with what scientists were discovering. What was true of cosmology, physics, and

geology in the past has obvious parallels with psychology and neuro-science today.

2. Despite clear historic evidence of an early alliance between men of science and men of faith, including the recognition that "the two books" were describing the same reality, though from different viewpoints, there nevertheless remains, in the popular mind, a warfare metaphor to portray the relationship of science and faith.

3. Some of the most distinguished of the early psychologists, such as William James, would have no part in the warfare metaphor. Nevertheless, with the increasing and, in popular culture, enduring influence, of Sigmund Freud (if not in academic psychology) the impression is still widely held by many people that, for example, psychology has explained away Christian beliefs and has accounted fully for the motivation behind religious behavior. This view has been reinforced in the middle of the twentieth century by the distinguished behaviorist psychologist B. F. Skinner with his "nothing buttery" account of religious beliefs and behavior.

4. Closer scrutiny of some of those who have had an enduring influence on twentieth-century psychology indicate that, in contrast to Freud and Skinner, their approach toward religion was essentially positive. Thus we noted how Gordon Allport, a major influence on personality theories, Sir Frederick Bartlett, influential in the cognitive revolution, and Roger Sperry, a leading neuropsychologist, all expressed clearly positive views toward religion. We also noted that some of the major textbook writers, such as Norman Munn in the 1950s and David Myers today, have expressed positive attitudes toward the Christian faith.

5. Because of the diversity of the subject matter of psychology at the end of the twentieth century, as set out in chapter 1, we find that it is far from easy to formulate, in simple terms, how best to characterize the relation between psychological statements and religious beliefs.

6. We all have presuppositions, and one of the essential first moves if we are to avoid false conflicts is to bring such presuppositions out into the open. In this way we are frequently able to discover hidden roots of some of the supposed conflicts between psychology and Christian belief. Often they turn out to have nothing to do with psychology as such but rather with the basic beliefs and values of the psychologist.

NEUROPSYCHOLOGY

Linking Mind and Brain

The distinction between diseases of "brain" and "mind,"
between "neurological" problems and "psychological"
or "psychiatric" ones, is an unfortunate cultural inheritance
that permeates society and medicine. It reflects a basic
ignorance of the relation between brain and mind.
—Antonio Damasio, *Descartes' Error*, 1994

THE CHANGING SCIENTIFIC PICTURE

THE PAST TWO DECADES have seen some of the most exciting developments ever witnessed in neuroscience and neuropsychology. Andrew
Kertesz,[1] in his editorial foreword to a recent (1994) book on localization
and neuroimaging in neuropsychology, writes, "Advances in neuroimaging in the past ten years have been nothing short of spectacular. These
changes have been closely followed by theoretical and empirical progress
in neuropsychology and cognitive science." It could be argued that
together they are pointing to a view of man in which every advance in
neuroscience seems to tighten the link between mind and brain. What is
the historical context of these developments? What are the main features
of the converging lines of scientific evidence and what do they imply?
What sort of an emerging picture of man do they suggest, and how do we
relate this to the salient features of a biblical, Hebrew-Christian view of
man? Since we believe that all truth is one, we believe that scientific and
biblical truth (together with insights from literature, art, and philosophy)
can give us a fuller and more accurate composite picture of humankind.

Before the Eighteenth Century

If you pause and reflect for a moment, the "obvious" place to localize the mind, if it is to be localized at all, is in the heart. When you think exciting thoughts there is a thumping in the chest. When you think peaceful thoughts your heart is quiet. From what is called a phenomenological point of view, then, it seems "obvious" that the mind resides in the heart. Down through the centuries limited observations seemed to support different theories of the mind–body relationship. In the fifth century B.C., Empedocles reasserted the notion that the soul (the Greek word for the mind) was found in the heart and in the blood, a theory labeled "the cardiovascular theory." His views, however, did not go unchallenged. At the same time Alcmaeon of Croton asserted that mental functions are to be located in the brain. His view was labeled "the encephalic view." These two theories were destined to compete with each other for two thousand years.

The great physician, Hippocrates, who lived sometime between 460 and 360 B.C., adopted the brain or encephalic theory of mind. One of his texts deals extensively with epilepsy and, as is well known, bears the famous title "On the Sacred Disease." It makes the brain the interpreter of consciousness as well as the mediator of feelings. It argues that epilepsy is not really a sacred disease but a perfectly natural and understandable disease with natural causes.

In the fourth century B.C., Plato and Aristotle exemplified the continuing conflict between the encephalic and cardiovascular theories. Plato seems to have wanted it both ways, locating the immortal soul in the "marrow" of the head, which presumably is the brain, but locating the passions between the neck and the midriff. He also put the appetites between the midriff and the navel. Aristotle for his part quite unambiguously localized the soul in the heart. He had reasons for his views and he still had a role for the brain. Being a good biologist he decided it must serve some function. Noticing that it was moist and cool to the touch, he concluded that it refrigerated the blood. Aristotle's views were passed on through the Stoic philosophers to one of the early church fathers, Tertullian, while the encephalic theory continued to survive through one of Rome's outstanding physicians, Galen.

Galen was a great anatomist and his brain dissections provided new anatomical data that strengthened his views. He was very impressed with the size and location of the ventricles in the brain and concluded that the network of ventricles was where the "vital spirits" or the "animal spirits" were located. Shortly after Galen died the Germanic invasions occurred in Western Europe, which consequently lost its knowledge of the Greek classics (which the Romans never greatly admired anyway).

In the fourth century A.D., Nemesius, a bishop of Emesa in Syria, produced a new theory of the physical basis of mind. He claimed that he was a loyal follower of Galen, but actually took Galen's views further. He distinguished three different mental faculties—sensation and imagination, thought and judgment, and memory—and he localized these in the different ventricles of the brain. The encephalic and cardiovascular theories, however, were not lost. Intellectual exchange, primarily in Spain, reintroduced the ideas of Aristotle and Galen to Western European thought and soon three groups of partisans were formed supporting, respectively, the encephalic, cardiovascular, and the ventricular theories of the mind–body relationship.

It was left to Vesalius in the early sixteenth century to strike the first major blow against the ventricular theory. He did this through his dissections of the human body, which had previously been forbidden on theological grounds. His argument was simple: He dissected not only humans but also apes, dogs, horses, sheep, and other animals and found that they all possessed ventricles in the brain. Yet he had been told that man was essentially different from all the animals because man possessed a soul that resided in the ventricles and all the other animals did not. At the same time, the growing body of anatomical and physiological knowledge lent little support to the cardiovascular theory and Harvey's analysis of the circulation of the blood further discredited it. By the time Shakespeare was writing his plays there were three different theories in circulation. It is the same today as we smuggle our views of the mind into our everyday expressions. We talk about somebody being "switched on" or "switched off," hinting at the computer analogy of mind. We talk about somebody being "conditioned" to do so and so, hinting at Pavlov's physiological model of the mind. The same was true in Shakespeare's day.

A Century of Change 1783–1874:
Four Illustrative Cameos

June 16, 1783 — Samuel Johnson

By the year 1783, the famous English author and lexicographer, Dr. Samuel Johnson, was already markedly overweight. In his diary he records how he spent the afternoon of June 16 sitting for a portrait. The artist was the somewhat untalented sister of Sir Joshua Reynolds. (It was said that her paintings made most people laugh and her brother cry.) At the end of the afternoon sitting, Dr. Johnson walked a considerable distance from Frances Reynolds's studio to his home. According to his own account of what happened next, he went to sleep at his usual hour but awoke around three o'clock the following morning to discover, to his horror and surprise, that he could no longer speak. He records how he immediately tested his mental faculties by trying to compose a prayer in Latin verse. Having succeeded in doing this, he then tried to loosen his powers of speech by drinking a little wine, thereby violating his recently acquired habits of temperance. The wine had an effect, but rather than releasing his speech it put him back to sleep.

When he reawoke after sunrise he still couldn't speak. He found, however, that he could understand what others said to him and he could still write, although his penmanship and composition were somewhat defective. He summoned his physicians who, having examined him, prescribed the accepted treatment of that time. It was to inflict blisters on each side of his throat up to the ear, one on the head, and one on the back, together with regular doses of salts of hartshorn (ammonium carbonate).

He was fortunate to be under the care of one of London's leading physicians, Dr. Heberden, who predicted a speedy recovery. His confidence was justified. Indeed, the therapeutic procedure was so successful that Dr. Johnson's speech began to return within a day or two, proceeded smoothly over the next month, and even the mild disorders in writing lessened. While he was left with a slight difficulty in speaking, it was to other causes that he finally succumbed later the next year. The point of relating this incident is to note that in the eighteenth century the leading physicians seemingly saw no link between the ability to speak and what was going on in the brain. Instead, they "treated" peripheral structures located in the neck and throat, believing that here was the physical substrate of speech. Brain events and mind events were not linked.

February 21, 1825

On February 21, 1825, the French physician Dr. J. Bouillard read a paper at a scientific meeting in France in which he argued from his clinical observations of brain-damaged patients that speech was localized in the frontal lobes. In this he supported the views of the distinguished anatomist and phrenologist Gall. Shortly afterwards, in 1836, Marc Dax read a paper at a meeting in Montpellier, also reporting a series of clinical cases that he believed demonstrated that speech disorders were linked to lesions of the left hemisphere.

September 13, 1848 – Phineas Gage

It was summer in New England. A twenty-five-year-old foreman working for the Rutland and Burlington Railroad Company and described by his employers as "most efficient and capable" was preparing to detonate an explosion in order to remove rock obstructing the path of the railroad.

At a crucial moment he looked away when someone called over his right shoulder. It was only a brief instant but Phineas Gage turned back and put in his iron bar to begin tamping the powder, not realizing that his assistant had not poured in the sand beforehand. A deafening explosion and the bar, manufactured to Gage's exact specifications—weighing 13 1/4 pounds, 3 feet 7 inches long, and tapered to a point 1/4 inch in diameter—entered Gage's left cheek, pierced his skull, traversed the front of his brain, and exited at high speed through the top of his head. The rod landed more than a hundred feet away, covered with blood and brains. Phineas Gage was stunned! But the amazing thing was, he was still awake. He made a remarkable recovery, but his personality had undergone a dramatic change. His likes and dislikes, his aspirations, his ethics and morals all changed.

The point of recounting this incident is to indicate that while earlier studies of neurological damage had begun to show that the brain may be the foundation for language, perception, and motor control, Phineas Gage's experience suggested that there may be systems in the human brain which, if damaged, may alter the personal and social dimensions of normal life. It looked as if previously acquired social conventions and ethical rules were lost as a result of selective brain damage, even though basic intellect and language remained essentially intact. There was, in fact, a dissociation between the intactness of several aspects of mind, attention, perception, memory, and language and the degenerated nature of his personality and character. The debate raged around whether and to what extent the damage caused to Gage's brain was localized and the degree to which such localization was linked to his character change. In later years one of the leading phrenologists, Nelson Sizer, concluded that the iron bar had passed "in the neighbourhood of Benevolence and the front part of Veneration." The phrenologists thus believed that there were centers that were brain organs and centers that were the substrate for proper behavior, including kindness and respect for others, and that in the case of Gage these were remarkably selectively injured. With hindsight it is clear that there is no question but that Gage's personality change was brought about by a circumscribed brain lesion in a specific site. The message from Gage's case was that to observe social convention, to behave ethically, and to make proper decisions required the integrity of specific brain systems. The question remained, By what plausible means could destruction of a brain region change personality? Antonio Damasio[2] in his book *Descartes' Error* concludes his description of Phineas Gage's experience with the very provocative question, "Is it fair to say that his soul was diminished, or that he had lost his soul?" We return to this later.

1861 – Paul Broca

Paul Broca, an anthropologist and physician, heard Bouillaud's son-in-law report the case of a patient who stopped speaking when pressure was applied to the anterior lobes of his brain. Soon afterwards, he himself saw a patient who had lost his speech and could say only one word and utter oaths. The results of the postmortem on this patient indicated damage to the left frontal part of the brain. It is usual to credit Broca with describing this syndrome, which consisted of an inability to speak despite an ability to understand language in the normal way. He was also the person who first elaborated the idea of left hemisphere cerebral dominance of language.

The experiences of Samuel Johnson and Phineas Gage and the clinical observations of Bouillard, Dax, and Broca vividly illustrate how, in the space of less than a hundred years, a radical change took place from the view of Dr. Heberden, Samuel Johnson's physician, which assumed that brain events and mind events were not linked, to a view that saw a clear link among the brain, language, and intellectual functions generally, but also the hints of a link between brain and personality, including social and ethical behavior. But the move to more localizationist views did not go unchallenged. For example, Pierre Flourens (1794–1867), a pioneer in techniques of ablation for investigating brain function, published findings that are usually taken to imply that psychological functions are *not discretely* localized in the cerebral cortex. This view was championed a century later by Karl Lashley in his famous monograph "In Search of the Engram."

1874 On

The next century, from 1874 on, began with the publication of Carl Wernicke's monograph entitled "The Aphasic Syndrome." This syndrome was different from that described a few years before by Broca. The striking feature of the aphasia described by Wernicke was that while the patient could express speech, the understanding of speech was severely impaired. Wernicke's thinking about his clinical findings contained a strong emphasis on brain centers and the connections between them, a view that went out of fashion between the two World Wars.

Certainly the history of thought on aphasia, over the past 150 years or more, illustrates the continuing debate about how mental functions are related to brain structure. Thus, one group of workers on aphasia, taking their lead from the early phrenologists, maintained that specific mental functions were subserved by separate areas of the brain. Those who opposed this localizationist view believed that mental capability reflected total intact brain volume. While Broca and Wernicke lie in the localizationist tradition, Hughlings Jackson and Kurt Goldstein represent the so-called holistic approach to aphasia.

For a time, however, the localizationist approach was abandoned in favor of a more holistic approach. Henry Head (1926) was dissatisfied with the classical neurologists' attempts to deduce schemes from clinical observations, believing that they were, as he put it, "compelled to lop and twist their cases to fit the Procrustean bed of their hypothetical conceptions." He attempted to bring some order to the field by devising a standard list of tests to be used in the study of aphasia, an idea developed by Weisenberg and McBride (1935). Earlier (1933), Weisenberg and McBride had made the important discovery that individuals who do not understand spoken language, although their hearing is intact and they can identify nonverbal sounds (e.g., a ringing telephone), may have damage in two different locations. Around the same time, the influence of Karl Lashley, who published his paper "In Search of the Engram" in 1938, is usually seen as significant. Lashley proposed a theory of mass action, contending that the behavioral result of a lesion depends more on the amount of brain removed than on the location of the lesion.

During the second half of the twentieth century and, in particular, immediately after the Second World War, there was a reawakening of interest in the brain–behavior relationship, and, as often happens in science, it was not so much the discovery of new ideas but the rediscovery of old ones. In this case it was the views of some of the nineteenth-century neurologists, combined with the development of the new behavioral techniques of the experimental psychologists, which were to give impetus to the development of neuropsychology.

Today there are several approaches to the study of brain–behavior relationships. The most prominent method naturally succeeds the work of the early neurologists. It is to observe carefully the effects of damage to specific areas of the brain and, where appropriate, to measure changes in mental ability and behavior. These techniques have also been used in animal studies. As we shall see later, it is noteworthy that their results have been extremely important in the development of human neuropsychology. The reason is obvious. In studying human patients one must, for ethical reasons, accept what comes and work within the limits of any ill-defined brain damage. By contrast, in animal studies, the locus and extent of lesions can be much more precisely defined and linked with behavior changes.

Converging Lines of Scientific Evidence

We see, then, that this century has witnessed a reemergence of attempts to understand the link between mental activity and brain structure and function. Today we are intensively engaged in trying to gain a better understanding of, for example, the psychopathology and neuropathology of Alzheimer's disease, Parkinson's disease, and schizophrenia. Such attempts focus on links between the disordered state of the minds of Parkinson's, Alzheimer's, and schizophrenic patients and how these relate to what we are discovering about changes in the structure and biochemistry of parts of their brains.

A good example of neuropsychological work is the studies of the specialized functions of the two cerebral hemispheres over the past thirty years. The surgically split-brain patients studied by Sperry and his colleagues afforded a new way of looking at the distinct abilities of each cerebral hemisphere. Their studies, along with the accumulating evidence from the effects of pathology on the two cerebral hemispheres and from investigations of how the two sides of the brain process information in normal people, has built up an impressive picture of localization of function within the brain. Such localization is not confined to particular areas of the brain but also to certain groups or columns of cells within particular areas. From the work of Hubel and Wiesel on, evidence for specificity of function has steadily increased. So today when patients present with prosopagnosia (the inability to recognize faces), we not only have a good idea of which parts of the cerebral cortex have been affected, but we know, from controlled studies of single cell recording in alert and awake monkeys, which particular columns of cells are likely to be involved in the processing of facial material. Similarly, from some of the recent and exciting reports by A. R. Galaburda and his colleagues in Boston we are now beginning to tie down certain forms of dyslexia to very small, circumscribed lesions in the brains of people suffering from that disability.

The link between mind and brain can be taken to another level by reminding ourselves of the intimate connection between altered behavior and disordered brain chemistry. The example that comes readily to mind is the so-called dopamine hypothesis of the basis of some forms of schizophrenia.

We see, then, that the general thrust of a massive amount of research in neuroscience and neuropsychology points increasingly to the tightening of the link between mind and brain. When something goes wrong with the brain there is a very high probability that, using sufficiently sensitive techniques, we shall be able to detect abnormalities of mental function. And it is not only mental processes that are disturbed. As the dramatic cases of Phineas Gage and Antonio Damasio's patient Elliott show, it is also personality and character that may be changed.

It is interesting, and perhaps significant, that the dramatic changes in Phineas Gage's personality following his accident have only recently been followed up in detail and with thorough investigations by eminent neurologists such as Antonio Damasio at Iowa. In reflecting on Gage he wrote,[3] "Gage's story hinted at an amazing fact: Somehow, there were systems in the human brain dedicated more to reasoning than to anything else, and in particular to the social and personal dimensions of reasoning. The observance of previously acquired social conventions and ethical rules could be lost as a result of brain damage, even when neither basic intellect nor language seemed compromised. Unwittingly, Gage's example indicated that something in the brain was concerned specifically with *unique human properties,* among them the ability to anticipate the future and plan accordingly within a complex social environment, *the sense of responsibility* toward self and others, and the ability to orchestrate one's survival deliberately, *at the command of one's free will."* He later writes, "There is no question that Gage's personality change was caused by a circumscribed brain lesion in a specific site."

But, as Damasio has shown from two decades of careful research, there are modern Phineas Gages who can easily be missed and misdiagnosed. He described one in great detail. The patient, whom he calls Elliott, "showed no sign of impairment when he was given standard intelligence tests."[4] It was easy to conclude that his problems were not the result of "organic disease" or "neurological dysfunction" but were rather, so it was superficially concluded, merely "mental trouble" amenable to psychotherapy." Not surprisingly to some of us, after a series of sessions of psychotherapy that proved unsuccessful, Elliott was, fortunately, referred to Damasio's neurological unit. Of this incident Damasio comments, perceptively, "The distinction between diseases of 'brain' and 'mind', between 'neurological' problems and 'psychological' or 'psychiatric' ones, is an unfortunate cultural inheritance *that permeates society* and medicine. It reflects a basic ignorance of the relation between brain and mind."

While to refer to "a basic ignorance of the relation between brain and mind" is a fair comment on a current state of affairs, it remains a deceptively simple way of characterizing a very complex field of scientific research. Those at the forefront of such research engage in lively debates among themselves about just what they mean by, for example, localization of cognitive functions, about what is the appropriate level of analysis of the neural substrate of particular functions, about how best to analyze and specify the levels of processing occurring between and within these neural levels of analysis and how such levels of analysis and processing are interrelated. We shall briefly review these issues to give readers a flavor of current concerns and debates.

Some Key Concepts

Localization

Studies of the possible localization of mental events in the brain look set to take significant steps forward as psychologists use new techniques to monitor the selective activity of different parts of the brain while cognitive tasks are being done. Underlying these approaches is a hypothesis: Performing a cognitive task depends on the integrated functioning of numbers of localized elementary operations. Because many such local operations are involved in any cognitive task, the activity across distributed brain areas must be orchestrated into a coherent whole. This orchestration is not performed by any single area in the brain; its operations are strictly localized. This way of thinking about localization fits well with some of the connectionist and network models currently held.

Michael Posner's studies of reading and listening provide a good example. Using the brain-imaging technique known as position emission tomography (PET scan), he observed brain processes that were active during the reading of a single word. He discovered that different areas of the brain were activated depending on whether subjects were passively looking at nouns presented visually or actively generating an associated word. So, presented with the word *hammer* they would say *hit* or *pound* or a similar word. Another task was to say whether two words presented simultaneously rhymed (e.g., *pint—lint* or *row—though*). Posner and his colleagues discovered that different parts of the brain were selectively active depending on the nature of the cognitive task being done. So, once again, we have evidence of the mind–brain link but now suggesting a distributed rather than narrowly circumscribed form of localization. The basic issue, however, remains the same: How do we think about this intimate relationship between mind and brain so as to do justice to both aspects of the unified event? Reductionism is too simplistic. While it may begin to satisfy as an explanation for tasks where subjects are told what to do, it will not suffice in other situations where the subjects' own choices are revealed in selective brain activity. Mind and brain both matter.

Levels of Analysis

The seemingly simple and automatic task of recognizing someone's face turns out, on analysis, to be extremely complex. When we look at an object we automatically and unthinkingly process a lot of information about it. What is the nature of its surface? What is its shape and size? We also normally readily distinguish an object from its background. What part does shading play in this? What part do edges contribute? Each of these seemingly simple questions turns out to be very complex. They are asked concurrently by visual neuroscientists, psychophysicists, and cognitive psychologists. The particular question that any group asks as they study the same phenomenon will differ depending on their specialized techniques and self-imposed research objectives.

The late David Marr took the notion of levels from computer science and applied it to problems in the study of vision. He pointed out that there were at least three distinct levels of analysis possible in any investigation and that each was important. At the highest level there were the computational problems that could be tackled in terms of an abstract analysis of what was going on. At this level, questions could be asked about the main constituents of the task being studied. Second, he identified a level of analysis that sought to specify in a formal way how you can ensure that, with a given input, there will be a correct output (the level of the algorithim). Finally, he believed that a further analysis was required: the level of how the processes going on were actually implemented. What sort of physical material was doing the job and how did it do it? At the second level, the level of the algorithm, we see that scientists work independently of any particular kind of physical implementation of the task. That may be satisfactory for one group of scientists, but the psychologist and cognitive neuroscientist wish to know how human beings *actually* carry out particular cognitive operations and how the central nervous system is actually built and works. Indeed, a knowledge of how the brain is actually wired and works can be of crucial importance in devising plausible algorithms at the second level of analysis.

Once one gets down to the third level of analysis, asking what sort of physical material is doing the job and how the processes are actually being implemented, one is confronted with a further set of levels of organization as one considers the actual structure of the brain and the central nervous system. The scale of the physical components in the nervous system varies from the molecular up to pathways and systems extending over a meter. Neuroscientists and neuropsychologists work at all of these levels.

Levels of Processing

Neuropsychologists and neuroscientists also talk about levels of processing. This notion is best illustrated by considering how the information on this printed page actually gets processed. First, there is a pattern of light and dark patches falling on the retina of your eyes. Basic processing of this input goes on initially at the retinal ganglia level, where several computations are performed on the physiological signals combining the information from a number of different photoreceptors. Thus, by the time the sensory signals leave the eye on their way to the brain, a good deal of processing has already been done. The retinal neurons that project from the eye travel to a number of distinct areas in the brain. They do not form a set of parallel lines of information projecting together from one complex processing station to another, but instead diverge to very different processing targets right from the outset. The two largest pathways from the eye to the brain in mammals are the retinotectal and the retinogeniculate. The first terminates in the optic tectum of the midbrain, named the superior colliculus in mammals. This is interconnected with a large number of other brain structures. The retinogeniculate projection, terminating in the lateral geniculate nucleus of the thalamus, is the most prominent visual pathway in primates. There are a number of other retinal projections not nearly so well studied as the two others. At successive levels further processing of the input signals occurs. To complicate matters even further, we discover that, at various processing levels, pathways go back downstream to centers at lower levels—so-called feedback projections. We do not yet understand the functions of these feedback pathways except that it is clear that what is happening at the highest levels can and does affect importantly what is coming upstream from the lower levels.

The Significance of Levels

What this discussion of levels means is that if, for example, you ask the deceptively simple question, How do I recognize someone's face? the answer you receive will depend very much on the level of analysis at which you pose the question. It will also depend on the particular interests of the psychologist or neuroscientist undertaking the investigations. What seems generally accepted in the community of cognitive neuroscientists is that we need knowledge at all these levels if we are to begin to understand the complex processes occurring as someone undertakes the simplest of cognitive tasks.

NEURAL NETWORKS AND CONNECTIONIST MODELS OF BRAIN FUNCTIONING

At the highest levels of mental functioning, where choices are made, some cognitive neuroscientists think about what is happening in the brain in terms of webs of interacting networks, representing whole systems of processing at work. They believe that it makes sense to think

about the brain as a mass of simple processing units and interconnections. Mental processes are then thought to arise through the myriad
interactions of such units. Today "neural networks" have become one of
the most actively researched areas of cognitive science. So-called connectionist network models are essentially simplifying models. While
some try to take account of what is actually known about the structure
and function of the nervous system, they all believe that the main constraints on their model building are computational.

Connectionist models, or neural networks, arose as cognitive psychologists drew ideas and inspiration from computational science. Connectionist models encompass many different forms. Their primitive building
blocks are simple processing units modeled abstractly on the neuron.
These are arranged in layered networks that are densely interconnected.
Although single- and double-layer systems are relatively simple to analyze
and fairly powerful, the concentration today is on developing potentially
more powerful (and complex) multilayered networks. The processing
units influence each other's values through connections that carry a
numerical weight or strength.

Today talk of neural networks has, in the minds of some people, an
unjustified aura or mystique. Some believe that the very term *neural networks* is regrettable, others that it is a misleading misnomer, since the
properties of the units and the interconnections may have little similarity with the properties of actual neurons and their interconnections.
Neural networks may show us what is possible but not necessarily what
is the case. As one recent reviewer in *Neuropsychologia* expressed it,[5]
"The 'Neural Network' movement has bifurcated into two separate
fields: 'Artificial Neural Networks' and 'Computational Neuroscience.'
The former deals with algorithms without taking into account the constraints due to biological reality, the latter prefers 'bottom-up' models
based on detailed neurobiological data." The same reviewer, Peter Erdi,
concluded his review as follows: "It seems to be a premature question to
decide whether or not quantum physical processes are really indispensa-
bly relevant for understanding the 'essence' of neural and mental
processes."

There are other models, sometimes called realistic models, which make
predictions about specific aspects of nervous system dynamics. These
models of actual neural networks are motivated by biological constraints
and what we actually know about the physiology and anatomy of nerve
cells. The hope is that the connectionist and realistic models will gradually converge to give a more coherent account of the mind–brain link.

Progress in scientific research is not easy even under ideal conditions.
There is so much to read and keep abreast of even in a relatively narrow
field that it is not surprising that, in general, scientists confine them-

selves to circumscribed topics. Even so some of the most exciting developments take place at the interface between specialist areas. That is true of the border between neural network research and that dedicated to realistic models of brain functioning. We[6] expressed this as follows in the preface to a recent report of a Royal Society meeting on natural and artificial low-level seeing systems, when we wrote, "However broad-minded and imaginative they may be, scientists are inevitably blind to much that is over the borders of their own special field, not for lack of interest or initiative but because they could not be expected to pick out the bridge-heads on the other side of the divides. The purpose of this meeting at the Royal Society was to bring together the computer vision specialists working on moving vehicles and flow fields with researchers on low-level natural visual systems working on active vision, having seen that one side should interest the other, in the hope that each can learn from the other and in the expectation that newcomers to this field can examine both sides, make a new synthesis, and take off in new directions." For anyone wishing to understand just how fast research in this field is progressing, we recommend this publication. It is not easy reading but demonstrates how the results of research carried out on invertebrate visual systems, of flies and bees, are being modeled in neural networks by computer experts and engineers.

MAKING SENSE OF THE EVIDENCE

It is clear that we do not expect to construct a single model that will cover all the levels of neural organization discussed above. The fact that what is happening at one level may be explained in terms of what is happening at a lower level does not mean that the higher-level model or theory is now useless or that the higher-level phenomenon no longer exists. Explaining what is happening at one level is not the same as explaining away the phenomenon under investigation. A fair assessment of these new advances in model building by cognitive neuroscientists would be that they are potentially exciting and rewarding but that in some quarters enthusiasm at times outruns achievement. Time will tell their true worth. The point for our present discussion is that tomorrow's theories will surely offer models of mental events embodied in the physical brain.

It is one thing to outline the increasing evidence for the tightening of the mind–brain link but it is important to remember that the mind–brain unity does not function in a vacuum. The physical and social environments in which we live affect the mind–brain unity that we are. Thus any attempt to understand the complexities of the mind–brain link needs to be set in the context of the clear recognition of the importance of the environment.

Lipowski, a distinguished Canadian psychiatrist, has argued that neither brainless nor mindless psychiatry can do justice to mental illness
and the treatment of patients. He has emphasized that "a person, viewed
as a mind/body complex, is in constant interaction with the environment. It follows that both study of mental illness and clinical practice
need to take into account the psychological, the biological and the social
aspects. These three aspects are not mutually reducible and are indispensable for the understanding and treatment of the individual patient."[7]
A recent review article in the *British Journal of Psychiatry*[8] reached an
essentially similar conclusion: "A multi-modal research program is
required in the search for a comprehensive model of psychopathy that
can guide both research efforts and clinical interventions" (151).

This view is echoed and further underlined by Antonio Damasio:[9]
"Does this mean that love, generosity, kindness, compassion, honesty,
and other commendable human characteristics are *nothing but* [my ital-
ics] the result of conscious, but selfish, survival-oriented neurobiological
regulation? Does this deny the possibility of altruism and *negate free
will* [my italics]? Does this mean that there is no true love, no sincere
friendship, no genuine compassion? That is definitely *not* the case [his
italics]. . . . Realizing that there are biological mechanisms behind the
most sublime human behavior does not imply a simplistic reduction to
the nuts and bolts of neurobiology."

It is evident that there is more than one way of interpreting the evidence on the tightening of the mind–brain link. Until relatively recently,
the gap between single-cell studies by neuroscientists and cognitive
studies by psychologists seemed so large as to be virtually unbridgeable
—at least in the foreseeable future. There were, and still are, some neuroscientists who believe that the only way to make progress is to concentrate exclusively on the study of the most basic processes of neural
functioning—what is sometimes called the bottom-up approach. Other
scientists are equally convinced that the only way to make real progress
is to concentrate on gaining a deeper understanding of mental processes
at the level of investigation of cognitive psychology—a top-down
approach.

The need to recognize and do justice to what is happening at the higher
levels of analysis was one of the factors that so impressed the Nobel Laureate brain scientist and psychologist Roger Sperry that he could declare
that a major revolution in our thinking about mind and brain has taken
place in the past two decades. He commented: "We do not look for conscious awareness in the nerve cells of the brain, nor in the molecules or
the atoms in brain processing." He detected among neuroscientists "a
move away from the mechanistic, deterministic and reductionistic doctrines of the pre-1965 science to the more humanistic interpretations of

the 1970's." As we shall see later, while Sperry's own formulation of the mind–brain relationship is not without its problems, the fact remains that after working at the leading edge of the discipline he firmly believes that it is simplistic to try to reduce humans to "nothing but" physical-chemical machines. As he put it recently, "The new model adds downward to the traditional upward microdeterminism and is claimed to give science a conceptual foundation that is more adequate, valid and comprehensive."[10]

A range of options face us as we consider how best to characterize the complex interactions between mind and brain. It is not unusual for the science to come coupled with a particular set of metaphysical assumptions, not always openly declared. Those with a religious commitment may espouse some form of dualism. Sir John Eccles is one proponent. On this view mental events act causally on the brain, at times preceding the corresponding brain activity. Others choose to simply identify mind with brain. Such views come linked to materialist presuppositions. Leading behaviorists of an earlier generation, such as B. F. Skinner, seemed to espouse such views. They may argue that mental events are products of physical events but have no causal efficacy. Such views are labeled epiphenomenalist. It is a feature of all varieties of materialist views that they give ontological priority to matter, in this instance brain, rather than mind.

Yet others believe that the best way of thinking about mind–brain links is psychophysiological parallelism. On this view there are two parallel streams of events. Physical events cause further physical events and mental events cause further mental events. The physical and mental events are tightly coupled in time.

The view we have taken here was labeled by Donald Mackay comprehensive realism. On this view mental activity and correlated brain activity are seen as inner and outer aspects of one complex set of events that together constitute conscious human agency. The two stories that may be written about such a complex set of events, the mental story and the brain story, are said to demonstrate logical complementarity (see chapter 12 for further discussion of this). The irreducible duality of human nature is, on this view, seen as duality of aspects rather than duality of substance.

Thus, the tightening of the link between mind and brain we have discussed earlier does not in any way minimize the importance of the mind or of mental activity in general. It does not mean that the mind is a mere epiphenomenon of the physical activity of the brain. The mind determines brain activity and behavior. But in complementary fashion the mental activity and the behavior depend on the physically determinate operations of the brain, itself a physicochemical system. When that system goes wrong or is disordered, there are changes in its capabilities for running the system that we describe as the mind or as mental activity. And, likewise, if the mind or the mental activity results in behavior of particular kinds, this in turn may result in temporary or chronic changes in the physicochemical makeup and activity of the brain, its physical substrate. Thus, this ever-tightening link does not minimize the importance of the mind or the brain in this unitary complex system.

We are, therefore, thinking of mental activity as embodied in brain activity rather than as being identical with brain activity. To go beyond this view and to adopt what is called a monist identity view is to confuse categories that belong to two different logical levels, as we saw above when we described the levels of analysis approach of today's cognitive neuroscientists. There is nothing within brain science or psychology that offers any justification for asserting that a monist identity view is more compatible with the evidence than the view we have outlined here. Sperry[11] put it well: "The laws of biophysics and biochemistry are not adequate to account for the cognitive sequencing of a train of thought." J. Z. Young[12] was making a similar point when he wrote, "For the present we shall use the terminology that the brain contains programs, which operate as *a person* makes selection among the repertoire of possible thoughts and actions." Note it is the person who makes the selection *not* the brain. One of the points that we have continually to be aware of is the danger of confusing talk about brains or machines and talk about persons. It is conscious cognitive agents who think. It is people, *not* brains, who make choices. Damasio[13] echoes this view: "To understand in a satisfactory manner the brain that fabricates human mind and human behavior, it is necessary to take into account its social and cultural context. And that makes the endeavor truly daunting."

One cannot emphasize too strongly the dangers of sliding into a form of thinking about human beings that relegates the conscious cognitive agent to second place, as Lipowski[14] put it, of adopting "the reductionistic gospel." The point simply is that all our knowledge of brains and minds and computers comes only through our experience and activity as conscious agents. It is only in and through that experience that we gain scientific or any other kind of knowledge and that means that the conscious agent has what philosophers call ontological priority. As Donald Mackay put it some years ago, "Nothing could be more fraudulent than the pretense that science requires or justifies a materialist ontology in which ultimate reality goes to what can be weighed and measured, and human consciousness is reduced to a mere epiphenomenon."

No amount of use of analogies, however, of this or any other kind, can, for the time being, remove the sense of awe that we feel as we reflect on our own experience as embodied conscious agents with all capacities necessary to interact in dialogue with other conscious agents. The sense of mystery, for us at least, remains untouched by any amount of brain science.

TAKING STOCK

1. Human curiosity about how the mind is related to the body, and, more specifically, to the brain, has left a rich legacy of possible models from Plato and Aristotle, through Galen and Nemesius, to Descartes. Most, but not all, have leaned toward some form of dualism.

2. Views expressed in the academy in any particular era are often seen reflected in common speech from Shakespeare's "tell me where is fancy bred or in the heart or in the head," to, in today's computer age, reference to someone being "switched on."

3. In the past two hundred years the scientific data have pointed steadily and decisively toward the intimate link between mind and brain.

4. The overall picture remains very complex, with research progressing simultaneously at several different levels from the molecular to that of neural networks.

5. Personal presuppositions easily enter into wider interpretations of what all the new data mean for models of persons. Some espouse a dualist view, some an identity hypothesis, others a psychophysiological parallelism. Our view is of a comprehensive realism as proposed by Donald Mackay. On this view the irreducible duality of human nature is seen as duality of aspects rather than as duality of substance.

CHAPTER 4

NEUROPSYCHOLOGY AND SPIRITUAL EXPERIENCE

The biblical view is that human identity is of a creature
rooted in the processes of a physical body.
—Glenn Weaver, *Senile Dementia and Resurrection Theology*, 1986

I believe that the man who (because of some biochemical
problems in his brain and constitution) feels ill with depression
has as little to blame himself for as a diabetic who feels ill.
—Gaius Davies, *Genius and Grace*, 1992

IN THE WESTERN WORLD TODAY the media daily bombard us with news telling of advances in medical science, including the treatment of some high-profile illnesses affecting the mind such as schizophrenia and Alzheimer's disease. One beneficial result is that the days are long past when, if someone claimed divine possession or divine powers, he or she was immediately put up on a pedestal and the claims were uncritically taken seriously. Today when abnormal behavior occurs it is quickly recognized as evidence of mental illness and not divine possession. It was not always so. What today's general public is perhaps not so well aware of is that some of the significant scientific advances point to the possible neural substrate of conditions such as schizophrenia. Witness, for example, the recent publication of volumes such as *The Neuropsychology of Schizophrenia* and *The Cognitive Neuropsychology of Schizophrenia*. These volumes are illustrative of the fact that today some forms of schizophrenia increasingly are being viewed as neurological disorders. Researchers in this field seek to understand how abnormalities of the brain produce the characteristic signs and symptoms of this most distressing and mysterious of mental disorders. Researchers want to know where any brain abnormalities are located, how they develop, how we can detect them, and what specific clinical and cognitive consequences they may have for patients. In November 1995, the science journal *Nature*[1] published a report by a team of U.S. and British researchers, using a special imaging technique called PET scanning that enabled them to scan the brain of a schizophrenic man every ten seconds when he was hearing voices. One of the researchers, neurologist David Silbersweig, noting how their research had enabled them to pinpoint brain circuits that seemed to control the auditory and visual hallucinations of schizophrenics, commented, "We've identified the areas that are responsible for the brain creating its own reality." As importantly, their results helped eliminate an alternative theory about what was happening, namely, that hallucinating patients are talking to themselves. The brain scan data, in fact, found activity in the areas responsible for hearing but not those involved in speech. These, then, are examples of further rapidly increasing knowledge of the mind–brain link. They also focus on some of the more intractable problems that we face as we seek to relieve the plight of the mentally ill.

A Spiritual Dimension to Neural Degeneration?

Over against the welcome knowledge that there are advances in our understanding of some forms of brain disorder that formerly were claimed to show divine attributes, such as epilepsy and schizophrenia, we still face very real problems with other common brain disorders that have distressing implications for the spiritual lives of Christian believers. What is not so readily recognized is that within the Christian community there are those who are suffering spiritual distress because what begins as neural degeneration in the brain leads to psychological disordering of the mind and that this in turn may have profound spiritual consequences. In this chapter we illustrate this point by considering specific examples where we are beginning to understand something of the tight link among neural processes, psychological states, and spiritual awareness.

Alzheimer's Disease

With the average age of the population increasing, more people are living longer; as a consequence, more elderly people are suffering from Alzheimer's disease. Like the rest of the body, the brain is affected by the passing of the years. We all experience an occasional lapse of memory but in some that turns into something much worse—senile dementia. Senile dementia may affect as many as 5 percent of those over sixty-five and 30 percent of those over eighty. Dementia is a consequence of a variety of diseases, of which Alzheimer's is by far the most common.

Intensive research has already established that many of the symptoms of Alzheimer dementia are caused by damage to the nerve cells in the brain, some of which can be visualized using modern scanning techniques. So-called neurofibrillary tangles develop in the brain. These fiberlike structures appear to wrap around one another in helical fashion. Senile plaques are also present in the brains of Alzheimer patients. These plaques represent groupings of antibody material surrounded by the fragments of destroyed nerve cells. Another change observed in brain cells is evidence of granulovacular deterioration. This shows up as bubble-like areas within each cell filled with granular material. In addition to these structural changes there are accompanying neurochemical changes. The change most often reported is a deficiency of the neurotransmitter acetylcholine. One of the results of this depletion is that previously patterned circuits of nerve signals become scrambled so the brain can no longer sustain its normal psychological functions.

These changes in brain structure in turn have predictable psychological consequences. The major symptom is loss of memory, which in turn leads to confused language, thinking, and perceptual recognition. Other upsets also occur in perception, feelings, and motor activity. When these symptoms first appear after the age of sixty-five, the condition is usually referred to as senile dementia. The symptoms of Alzheimer's disease, developing at this stage in life, typically follow an insidious course. Close friends and relatives as well as the patients themselves are often unable to say just when the symptoms first appeared, but once the condition has been recognized it progresses steadily toward severe disorganization and death.

As Alzheimer's disease progresses it is frequently possible to observe three distinguishable stages. Not too obvious to begin with, because it happens to us all at times, is forgetfulness. It becomes more difficult for patients to recognize relatives and friends. They also tend to misplace things, cannot remember the names of people they have recently met, become quickly confused in unfamiliar places, and have difficulty concentrating when reading or watching television programs. They may also begin to care less and less about their personal appearance and be careless in their work. As they become aware of their difficulties they often begin to struggle to develop ways of covering up these problems and for a while do so quite well. When alone, however, they often become deeply aware that something is wrong, that they are losing personal control. In turn, this gives rise to anxiety and depression. In the next stage, they become increasingly confused. Difficulties already recognized increase and more marked changes in concentration and recent memory become apparent. Patients find that no sooner have they read something than it is forgotten; appointments just made are forgotten, and as a result it becomes increasingly difficult to maintain a job. Even familiar names cannot be recalled and one's own address may be forgotten. Patients forget what time it is and where they are. It becomes difficult to find the next word when speaking and things, including errors just made, are quickly forgotten. From being anxious and depressed they now become emotionally unresponsive. With all these changes they withdraw more and more from social contacts and tend to spend most of their time at home, restricting themselves to familiar activities.

Finally comes what is traditionally labeled dementia. Because at this stage they are apt to wander away and are incapable of initiating basic self-care, patients can no longer safely be left alone. They need to be dressed, washed, fed, and helped with bowel functions. They think continually about a few memories from the far distant past. These seem to survive and are much more accessible than memories of recent events. As they become more and more dependent on their caregivers they often become paranoid, making false accusations about assaults on their person. The result is psychotic-like delusions and hallucinations. Finally may come seizures and ultimately coma and death.

The general public is usually aware that senile dementia is a product of deterioration of the brain. They see it primarily as a health problem. If they are Christians they may be aware of its potential spiritual significance. They may, however, believe that the disorganization of psychological processes evident in dementia doesn't really affect awareness of one's relationship with God. This relationship, so it is said, is maintained through ways and channels that transcend the experience of the body. In effect, a simplistic medical compartmentalization of senile dementia takes place that certainly doesn't fit the experience of demented patients. Nor does it fit the holistic understanding of what it means to be a person, as given us in the Bible and as we briefly outline in chapter 6. We believe that a biblically based theology can lead to a better, more compassionate understanding of the harrowing spiritual journeys of many of these patients. It can also help us realize afresh the collective relationship that we and they have in the great hope for them and us—the hope of resurrection in Jesus Christ.

A Case Study

Some years ago Glen Weaver[2] pointed out that the Psalms, in many Christian traditions, occupy a central place in liturgies and serve to draw believers away from the pains of life to contemplate God. Thus he says, "When we construe the psalms primarily in this fashion, we tend to read them very selectively. We select for frequent reading only those passages that fit our preconceptions about worthy praise, for example, creation psalms (8, 19, 139), liturgical psalms (24, 46, 122), songs of thanksgiving (34, 40, 116), hymns of praise (100, 103, 107), songs of trust (23, 91, 121), and wisdom psalms (1, 37, 73). In so doing," he goes on, "we comfortably assign the psalms a liturgical and didactic function in the sanctuary but overlook their potential for providing a practical theology to deal with some of the most devastating problems in counseling and mental health care."

Weaver, expanding on this theme, returns us to the importance of the biblical, holistic view of persons. He writes: "The psalmist through and through affirms an understanding of human personhood that appears throughout the Old Testament . . . that humans were created *unified* beings. The Hebrew text of Genesis 2:7 states that when God breathed the breath of life into the dust of the earth, the human being became 'nephesh.' This Hebrew word is translated 'soul' in the King James Version, but is given a variety of translations in more recent versions: 'being,' 'creature,' and 'man began to live.'" The biblical view is that human identity is of a creature rooted in the processes of a physical body. "Nephesh," argues Weaver, "is not separate from the body, but includes the body and expresses the vitality of experience that it allows." He also goes on: "The human 'nephesh' also refers to the continuing relationship of our identity to God. God's act did not plant some divine entity in a body which then gave persons a generic claim to eternal existence. 'Nephesh' is not a divine form or force that humans have within. 'Nephesh' is what happened when God brought into existence the whole of a specific person, Adam. Adam's existence, and the existence of any other specific person whom he represents, remains completely dependent on the moment by moment breath of God that upholds that life." But, Weaver points out, "the breath of life may be removed. . . . Since one's identity is fully engaged in the body (there is no separate entity called 'soul'), the physical death of the body suggests the end of personal identity and falling out of relationship with God." Weaver goes on to say that "both in the Old and New Testaments, Jewish writers connect sin with the reversal of the ordering process of creation and a return to the chaos of the deep. In that most Jewish of the New Testament writings, the Book of Revelation, John envisions Satan rising from the abyss of chaos—the pit of disorder and non-existence—into which Satan will again be cast at his final defeat. Any process which threatens the created order must reflect sinful forces which separate us from God." The psalmist, he says, perceives just this return to chaos in the physical death of the body.

Weaver then emphasizes that "Hebrew men and women experienced personal identity as they lived in community with other persons." "God," he writes, "was revealed through historical events which established covenant with the people. The worship acceptable in God's sight was worship which emanated from the collective life of the people. They expressed their obedience in working the fields when they gathered one-tenth of their goods for support of the priesthood, and in rituals of family life (circumcision, marriage, passing blessings from one generation to another)." Thus, he writes, "as Psalm 42 puts it, to be separated from this experience of collective worship was to be separated from God and to sense one's identity slipping away."

Thus, what characterizes the progression of Alzheimer's dementia, the slow physical deterioration and loosened social relationships, has a profound spiritual significance, for they can leave the individual with the conviction that he or she is separated from God. Weaver notes that it is remarkable that the laments that so vividly portray this human despair dominate the Psalter, which is Israel's book of praise. Their presence, he says, reflects complex struggles to understand a God who could only be the just, loving, sovereign Lord, yet who stood witness to such violation of his purposes for human beings. And then, most significantly, he goes on to say, "If the individuals who faced death were held responsible for unleashing the chaos of the deep, the lament would have a different form. It would then be a prayer of repentance. Such is not the case. The psalmists struggle with the apparent evidence, manifested by God's wrath, that the petitioner has sinned, but they do not accept the conclusion. In fact many of the laments locate the forces of chaos in an unspecified group of enemies who assail one's person. . . . We hear echoes of Job's message," he writes, "that the mystery of suffering cannot be equated simply with personal sin."

Weaver illustrates graphically and movingly the effects of Alzheimer's on the spiritual pilgrimage of one devout Christian lady. He points out how, after a life of regular attendance at church services as the member of a congregation where she was known as a gentle and concerned Christian with a deep concern for her fellow Christians, she began to develop the tell-tale symptoms of forgetfulness. As she did so she struggled with the problem by writing copious lists of names and addresses to help her remember the people whom she knew and whom she wished to remember in her prayers. She struggled but fought a losing battle.

Her letters became verbose and lost more and more of their content. All this, in turn, made her anxious; anxiety led to depression and the pattern of her changes fit the classical textbook description we have given above. But, as Weaver points out, there was much more to her experience than any textbook could convey. She was deeply troubled about her relationship with God. She felt that she was personally responsible for falling from her close walk of discipleship by deserting her friends through friendship and prayer. She even concluded that because of her lack of faithfulness God was placing her aside because she was no longer fit for his service. As she continued and progressed through the confused stage, she began to lose control of her natural processes and, away from the security provided by her home and her husband, she would wander at night violating the commands of her nurses and then describing bizarre sexual disturbances in an explicit manner. She came to believe that she had committed sins that surely provoked God's wrath, and the continued deterioration of her condition and the fact that the doctors could not help her confirmed her thoughts even more. In due course she lost interest in her daily devotions and prayer. Indeed, her whole situation was almost that typified in the psalms of lament. She was indeed crying from the depths of chaos.

All of this, says Weaver, underlines why the resurrection of Jesus Christ must be the centerpiece of our Christian faith. For Christ's death involved a struggle with and victory over all the powers of chaos seeking to undo the order of God's creation, including human *nephesh*. Above all, the resurrection must be part of the result of Christ's death and struggle with chaos. The direction of earth's history, says Weaver, was reversed from movement toward disillusion to the final fulfillment of the purposes of God. To quote from Weaver, "The key to this reversal was the renewal of the image of God in this world and the pattern originally intended—a new person fully engaged in the body which chaos cannot overcome. In 1 Corinthians 15, Paul applies this message of cosmic victory to the lives of believers. In keeping with the Old Testament's theology of persons, he argues that 'if there is a natural body, there must also be a spiritual body.' Human *nephesh* finally cannot be anything but embodied existence. However, this body will be 'spiritual.'"

Weaver concludes that "the lament of Psalm 88 has been heard. There can be fewer clearer experiences of engaging in this battle with the forces of the abyss of chaos than the long pilgrimage experienced in Alzheimer's disease. Perhaps this foretells an even more intimate identification with the victorious suffering Lord at life's end. The church to be sure," he goes on, "has the mission and the power to renew the creation." And what he is saying is that the neuropsychological insights already gained by the careful study of Alzheimer's patients should remind the Christian church that it may help accomplish the mission of renewing the creation by doing all that it can to uphold the identities, the *nephesh,* of persons experiencing the ravages of Alzheimer's dementia. In so doing, believes Weaver, "the church can bring to fulfillment the Old Testament vision that one's identity is established, redeemed and maintained in a collective experience of a people living in a covenant with their God." If this message were remembered, then the biblical emphasis on a personal faith would not be allowed to become identified with individualism to the downplaying of true fellowship and community in the body of Christ.

The specific psychological changes that we noted earlier in Alzheimer dementia, brought out clearly by the research of neuropsychologists, can and should be attended to by the development of appropriate strategies by the caring Christian church. Thus, Weaver suggests that those who care for Alzheimer's patients should take time to learn as much as possible about the form of a particular patient's memory processes in the past. What sorts of cues did the patients find most valuable in organizing material for memory storage (faces, voices, colors, etc.)? When patients experience a new event, draw special attention to those cues and, when negotiating a recollection later, introduce those cues in a systematic way into the conversation. In the earlier stages of the disease, this technique can keep the patients involved in present experiences. It may also prepare them to accept the process of negotiation more easily when most of it must be initiated by caretakers later. There are many other detailed hints that emerge from the neuropsychological evidence, but this is neither the time nor the place to list them. The point is simple: With neural changes there are psychological consequences and these, in turn, affect spiritual awareness. The knowledge that God has given and will continue to give us through sustained neuropsychological research into these and other human conditions can and should be properly used to relieve the distressing pilgrimage of the typical Alzheimer patient, particularly for the Christian who experiences an increasing feeling of separation from God.

THE NEUROPHYSIOLOGY AND NEUROPSYCHOLOGY OF CONVERSION AND MYSTICAL EXPERIENCES

The possibility of linking changed spiritual awareness with the neurological state highlighted by Alzheimer's disease is not new. Several decades ago, the British psychiatrist William Sargant[3] had speculated about hypothetical changes in brain processes occurring at the time of sudden religious conversion. Sargant had been much impressed by the Russian physiologist Ivan Pavlov's work on classical conditioning and had been intrigued by Pavlov's explanation of the physiological mechanisms underlying such conditioning. Pavlov had claimed to identify four main constitutional temperaments in his experimental dogs and chose to label them, as Hippocrates had done, for the main temperamental types in human beings.

It then was a short step from labeling an animal as having, for example, a strong excitatory or a strong inhibitory temperament, to identifying what was going on in the brains of these animals in terms of inhibition. When these ideas were applied to human behavior, attention focused on so-called transmarginal inhibition. This, said Sargant,[4] "once it sets in, can produce three distinguishable phases of abnormal behavior—the equivalent, paradoxical, and ultra-paradoxical phases. And finally, stresses imposed on the nervous system may result in transmarginal protective inhibition, a state of brain activity which can produce a marked increase in hysterical susceptibility (or, more rarely, extreme countersuggestibility) so that the individual becomes susceptible to influences in his environment to which he was formerly immune."

Sargant's too hasty and uncritical dependence on Pavlov proved mistaken. The late professor Oliver Zangwill of Cambridge, a distinguished neuropsychologist, when reviewing Sargant's earlier book in the *British Medical Journal* wrote, "Few neurophysiologists brought up in the post-Sherringtonian climate have found it possible to take Pavlov's theories—as opposed to his facts—seriously. . . . This does not mean that Pavlovian theory is necessarily wrong or lacking in heuristic value. It does however mean that it is esoteric, controversial and hence perhaps an insecure foundation for Dr. Sargant's psychological super-structure." What Zangwill wrote of Pavlov, others have since written of Sargant's views. While in his two books Sargant has undoubtedly assembled an impressive and well-documented survey of ecstatic religious behaviors from around the world, he has not, as a lay reader of his books may be forgiven for believing, even begun the task of formulating plausible brain mechanisms underlying such behavior.

If Sargant's attempts to link neural processes with changed psychological states, which in turn are associated with heightened spiritual awareness, were unsuccessful, it does not follow that other attempts may not, in due course, be more successful. Attempts to explore the association of some forms of religiosity and the occurrence of mystical experiences with their possible neural substrates have continued sporadically over the past twenty-five years. Many who write on the topic begin with the apostle Paul's Damascus road experience and quickly move on to point out that the "religiosity" of the typical epileptic patient has been recognized since the time of Esquirol[5] (1838) and Morel[6] (1860). Early attempts to explain this association favored an environmental explanation, noting the tendency for the epileptic to find himself in social isolation and to suggest that one way of coping with his predicament was to turn to the consolation that religion may bring. Negative evidence concerning the relationship between epilepsy and religious hallucinations is often left uncommented on. For example, the classical studies of temporal lobe epilepsy by Penfield and Jaspers[7] did not report a single case associating religious hallucinations with epilepsy. The same could be said of surveys in the 1950s and 1960s undertaken by a variety of distinguished neurologists. Despite this negative evidence it remains conventional to discuss the sudden conversion of the apostle Paul in terms of a diagnosis of epilepsy. It is reported that at the time of his sudden conversion on the Damascus road, Paul fell down and reportedly experienced visual and auditory hallucinations with accompanying transient blindness. By confusing their categories, this has led a number of authors to argue that Paul's conversion was the result of an epileptic seizure rather than a mystical experience. Others reject this view on the grounds that Paul did not show the subsequent mental deterioration that would normally be associated with a major epileptic episode. Thus, some would suggest that Paul's hallucinations were understandable because he was an extremely tired traveler who had possibly been neglecting his physical health and was struggling with the heat of the day.

In this context Kenneth Dewhurst and A. W. Beard[8] have documented the experiences of other notable Christian mystics down through the centuries and have speculated about the etiology of their experiences. They remind us that Robert Thouless[9] makes mention of the fact that the mood of exultation may stimulate the expression of religious sentiment immediately before an attack of epilepsy. Thouless, as an example, quotes Dostoyevski's Prince Mishkin in *The Idiot*. Prince Mishkin describes the experiences of the aura that preceded his epileptic seizures: "In his attacks of epilepsy there was a pause just before the fit itself . . . when suddenly in the midst of sadness, spiritual darkness, and a feeling of oppression, there were incidents when it seemed his brain was on fire, and in an extraordinary surge all his vital forces would be intensified. The sense of life, the consciousness of self were multiplied ten fold in these moments, which lasted no longer than a flash of light; all torment, all doubt, all anxieties were relieved at once, resolved in a kind of lofty calm, full of serene, harmonious joy and hope, full of understanding and the knowledge of the ultimate course of things."[10]

Dostoyevski was an epileptic and offers his analysis of these experiences in the thoughts of Mishkin:

Thinking about this moment afterwards, when he was again in health, he often told himself that all these gleams and flashes of superior self awareness and, hence, of a "higher state of being," were nothing other than sickness . . . and so, were not the high state of being at all but on the contrary had to be reckoned as the lowest. And yet he came finally to an extremely paradoxical conclusion. In "What if it is sickness?" he asked himself, "What does it matter if it is abnormal in intensity, if the result, if the moment of awareness, remembered and analyzed afterwards in health, turns out to be the height of harmony and beauty, and gives an unheard of and until then undreamed of feeling of wholeness, of proportion, of reconciliation, and an ecstatic and prayer like union in the highest synthesis of life?" . . . If in that second—that is, in the last lucid moment before the fit—he had time to say to himself clearly and consciously: "Yes, one might give one's whole life for this moment!" Then that moment by itself would certainly be worth the whole of life."[11]

David Bear and Paul Feddio,[12] in their attempt at a comprehensive quantitative analysis of the behavior of temporal lobe epilepsy patients in between seizures, reported that those patients in whom the epileptic focus was in the left hemisphere "showed a predilection for ideative, contemplative and perhaps verbal expressions of affect as represented in cosmologic or religious conceptualizing." In a later paper, however, Bear[13] presented an important critical analysis of the difficulties in the kind of research that attempts to link psychiatric descriptions with specific physical parameters of brain functioning. For example, he writes, "To attempt to correlate objective physical parameters with such a poorly defined descriptive term (in this instance schizophrenia) is methodological suicide, since the psychiatrically designed index groups would be neither standard nor homogeneous" (76). And he continues: "A scientific alternative . . . is to specify a physical variable (neuroanatomical, physiological, pharmacological) and to treat the behavioral state as the dependent variable to be described" (77). Following this procedure, he then goes on to explore the association between identifiable behavioral effects and the localization of neurological processes in temporal lobe epilepsy. He notes that "multiple case reports suggest, for example, that patients may undergo frequent religious conversions, keep extensive diaries and autobiographic texts, or develop pervasive moralistic feelings." He continues: "These behaviors need not be seen as psychopathological and would not necessarily lead to psychiatric attention, but a cluster of such features, if shown to occur regularly in association with temporal lobe foci, might elucidate the nature of an underlying neuropsychological process" (79). His analysis of the behavior exhibited by temporal lobe epilepsy patients studied led him to conclude that these patients exhibited "a combination of circumstantial concern with details, religious and philosophical interests, and intense, sober affect—a characteristic of virtually every patient, distinguishing them on an individual basis from each of the contrast subjects." And he continues: "Thus objects and events shot through with affective coloration may be incorporated into a mystical or religious view of the world" (87).

Ten years after the study by Bear, a report appeared in the *Journal of Nervous and Mental Disease* by David Tucker, Robert Novelli, and Preston Walker.[14] They carried out a careful study of seventy-six people with a primary diagnosis of complex partial seizures with a unilateral temporal lobe focus and studied them for the presence of hyperreligiosity. Fifty-one subjects had a left temporal lobe seizure focus and twenty-five had a right temporal lobe seizure focus. Noting the work by Bear and Feddio, they observe that these authors hypothesized "that repeated seizure discharges in the temporal lobes resulted in the establishment of increased functional connectivity between temporal neocortex and limbic structures. This sensory limbic hyperconnection in turn results in increased limbic excitation during routine daily experience compared with that of non-epileptic patients." And they note, as we have done earlier, that Bear and his colleagues found religious preoccupations to significantly differentiate temporal lobe epileptics from a mixed psychiatric sample.

David Tucker and his colleagues go on to say that it was the purpose of their study to test the hypothesis that excessive religious preoccupation is a consistent interictal (between seizures) personality trait of individuals with temporal lobe epilepsy. They did this by using an independent sample as well as an independent measure of religiosity compared to that used by Bear and Feddio. Their conclusions are clearcut; they state: "The results of this study fail to support the hypothesis that individuals with TLE are characteristically hyper-religious during the interictal state. There were no significant group differences between the left versus the right TLE groups, nor were there any significant group differences between the two TLE groups versus the two comparison groups." More generally, at the end of their paper, they make the following perceptive comments about studies of this kind: "Although explaining behavior in terms of a neural substrate is the goal of the behavioral neurosciences, the proposition that recurrent temporal lobe seizures will result in a specific personality type has profound social implications. Hence, a conservative approach and independent replication are essential. These data indicate that hyper-religiosity is not a consistent interictal trait of individuals with temporal lobe epilepsy. Further, although hyper-religiosity and temporal lobe epilepsy may co-occur in a few individuals, it does not appear to be a direct causal relationship between repeated seizure discharge in the temporal lobes and hyper-religiosity"

(183). It is against this background that we may now move on to look at some of the studies carried out by Persinger and his colleagues.

Persinger's approach links naturally with some of Sargant's views but, more obviously, with the work on temporal lobe epilepsy and religiosity just reviewed. He argued that many sudden conversions are the result of abnormal circumstances leading to ecstatic experiences associated with a malfunctioning brain. An obvious linkage was with epileptic episodes.

Persinger[15] noted that the incidence of reported mystical religious experiences in association with seizures in temporal lobe epilepsy (variously labeled "complex partial epilepsy" or "psychomotor epilepsy") is (as we have seen) well documented in the clinical literature. (Though, as we have seen, not all studies support this.) The focus of the seizure activity usually begins in the brain stem, and it is for this reason that the aura experienced is associated with dramatic changes in mood, felt variously as euphoria, anxiety, or fear. In addition, there are frequently feelings of strangeness, hallucinations, and delusions. The combined effect of these events is endowed by the patients with a deep personal significance. For this reason it is not surprising that the overall events take on a strong religious flavor.

Starting from an analysis of the recurring characteristics associated with such seizures, the next step was to characterize the salient features of the so-called epileptic personality. These are features that are not confined to the times surrounding seizures but are seen as more enduring "normal" characteristics of such individuals. The defining list usually includes being unusually emotional, obsessional, and humorless, and tending to be paranoid. All of these are, in turn, said to be associated with a philosophical or religious disposition. One investigator of these individuals (Bear) has, as we saw, described them as "holding deep religious beliefs, often idiosyncratic" and as undergoing "multiple conversions" and experiencing "mystical states."

The next step was to propose a possible neuropsychological model of the brain processes underlying these seizure events. Persinger followed Bear's model, noting that it was congruent with other known functions of different parts of the brain. He believes that the personality type, as described above, results from the seizures producing a hyperconnectivity between cortical brain areas involved in conscious thought and limbic brain areas that mediate emotional experience. The general picture presented by Bear is, as we saw, certainly supported by some of the clinical literature on epileptic patients, though as we have noted not all investigators have reported the personality profile as described by Bear with their epileptic patients. Even so, it is fair to say that Bear has proposed a plausible model for neural events associated with some religious conversions and general religiosity in some individuals.

This story was then taken further by Persinger and his colleagues,[16] who explored whether a model along the lines of Bear's might be extended to include more or less religious people in the normal (seizure-free) population. Persinger's basic idea is that some normal people, who report mystical or paranormal religious experiences, are in fact suffering "microseizures." By this he means slightly abnormal electrical discharges of the limbic, emotional brain, sufficient to produce a mystical experience. An interesting idea to be sure, but what is Persinger's evidence?

Persinger constructed a personality inventory designed to measure the prevalence, in normal individuals, of temporal lobe seizure-like experiences. He labeled it the Personal Philosophy Inventory. This included items designed to register any experiences resembling those documented in seizures associated with temporal lobe epilepsy, the so-called complex partial epileptic signs (CPES). Persinger and Makarec[17] reported finding a high correlation, in a population of college students, on scores on their CPES questionnaire and the frequency of reporting "paranormal" (mystical, with religious overtones) experiences and "a sense of presence." Moreover, Persinger reported that those individuals who reported such paranormal experiences and scored highly on their CPES questionnaire also evidenced a relatively high incidence of abnormal temporal lobe brain wave activity. Persinger concluded that there is a continuum of functional hyperconnectivity between limbic and cortical areas in "non-seizure" patients and that this predisposes some individuals to mystical and religious experiences.

Persinger's approach certainly warrants further exploration, though as it stands it suffers from a number of obvious, and some not so obvious, weaknesses. First, the experiences of seizure patients are almost always bizarre and out of the ordinary, and are quite unlike those habitually reported as typical of Christian conversions. Typically, the latter are described as conscious, deliberate decisions often made in nonemotional circumstances and with none of the accompanying bright lights and mystical overtones of epileptic patients. Second, on close scrutiny Persinger's CPES questionnaire items turn out to be in large measure another way of asking the same individuals about unusual mystical or religious experiences, and it is with the incidence of these that the scores on the CPES are being correlated. It is no surprise, therefore, that if you ask the same questions in two different ways, the results will show a high correlation between the responses given. The results could hardly be otherwise! Of more interest was the report of abnormal brain activity in normals scoring high on the CPES. That is certainly interesting and warrants an attempt at replication. Whatever the outcome of such a replication, it remains highly likely that the incidence of religious conversions in the general population far outstrips the incidence of abnormal brain activity. To foreshadow our later comments we may simply note here that the God of the Christian is just as capable of communicating through normal brain activity as through abnormal brain activity, and indeed would seem to do so habitually. Warren Brown,[18] an experienced neuropsychologist and electrophysiologist, with Carla Caetano, offered a very fair and balanced assessment of Persinger's and related ideas and studies:

> Religious experience associated with brain seizures (or drugs), although undeniably a contributor to the conversions of some individuals, have a number of weaknesses as a general neuropsychological model of religious conversion. Most importantly, the accounts of mystical/religious experiences in the clinical epilepsy literature are not characteristic of *typical* Christian (or other) religious conversions. Seldom do individuals describe their religious conversion in terms confusable with seizures, i.e., as based on paranormal experiences having a sudden onset and perceived as discontinuous with one's ongoing stream of consciousness.
>
> The proposition that religious experiences in the normal population are related to "microseizures" seems to rest on a tautology, i.e., unobserved "microseizures" are hypothesized on the grounds that individuals with paranormal religious experiences score high on the CPES, which itself includes questions regarding significant paranormal experiences. There is little evidence to directly support the notion that the CPES is diagnostic of subclinical temporal lobe seizure events among apparently normal individuals. The Personal Philosophy Inventory and CPES are more likely to be simply different ways of asking individuals about unusual religious experiences.
>
> From a theological point of view nothing is accomplished by establishing that a particular conversion may have been related to abnormal brain activity; that is, the epistemological problem of the *truth* of the content of the experience is not solved. Imagine, for example, that you have the strong impression that someone is standing behind you but also know that you are having a seizure. It is still necessary to confirm or disconfirm the possibility that someone is there by turning and looking. The fact of the seizure does not bear on the fact that someone may well be standing behind you. In the case of St. Paul, if the Damascus road experience happened to involve a seizure it would have little relevance to the theological question of the truth of what he preached, taught and wrote (153–54).

THE BIOPSYCHOSOCIAL ROOTS OF SOME DISTRESSING SPIRITUAL EXPERIENCES — SOME SALUTARY CASE HISTORIES

We have considered ways in which known changes in the brain, occurring in people toward the end of their life span and who suffer from Alzheimer's disease, may significantly change their spiritual awareness. We have also examined some attempts to understand possible brain processes mediating the events of religious conversions in particular or heightened religiosity in general. There are, however, many Christians who will not suffer from Alzheimer's disease, whose Christian life began undramatically and yet decisively, and who could not be described as having experienced a sudden religious conversion and have experienced no dramatic mystical states. Most of us in that category will nonetheless be subject to "the changes and chances of this fleeting world." We shall be thankful for times when spiritual realities have been especially salient, while remembering other times when it seemed hard to be aware of the presence of God and we were all too conscious of doubts and discouragements. Some of the outstanding men and women of God, whom all acknowledge have been greatly used by him, are also found, on close study, to be those who have endured significant (we might appropriately say, abnormal or pathological) swings in the immediacy of their felt awareness of the presence and power of God. In some of these people it is possible for us, with the benefit of hindsight and informed by the advances in psychiatry at the end of the twentieth century, to be fairly sure that some of their experiences were pathological in the sense that today we could classify them in accepted categories of psychological illness. Some were obsessive compulsives, some were manic depressives, some struggled with specific phobias, and so on. In the context of our discussions in this chapter we are primarily concerned to understand how some of those who suffered from mental illness did so because the nature of their illness almost certainly originated with changes in the neuronal and/or hormonal substrates of their psychological makeup.

As we briefly consider some of them now, we do so to illustrate again the importance of recognizing the psychobiological unity of the human person. To be aware of this unity and of the profound effect that constitutional factors may have on our mental and spiritual life, will, hopefully, sensitize us to the anguish that some of our Christian friends are experiencing, and reassure us at periods of significant mood swings that it is not, as some simplistic views would have it, because we are not walking closely with the Lord or because we are being overtly disobedient to his commands. It may, of course, be for those reasons, but will not necessarily be so, and we need to be wise enough to make the proper distinctions.

In his book *Genius and Grace*, Gaius Davies,[19] on the basis of careful and detailed historical research combined with his experience as a consultant psychiatrist in a large London teaching hospital, gives us a fascinating account of the lives of John Bunyan, Amy Carmichael, William Cowper, C. S. Lewis, Martin Luther, Gerard Manly Hopkins, J. B. Phillips, Christina Rossetti, and Lord Shaftesbury. Drawing on his historical research and clinical insights he offers tentative psychiatric diagnoses of the illnesses from which some of these individuals may, at times, have been suffering. In some cases the diagnoses were such that, on present evidence, it remains unlikely that there were significant constitutional or endogenous factors at work. Our concern here, however, is with those others whose illness probably *did* have a significant biological/biochemical etiology—and these would include Luther, Cowper, Shaftesbury, and Phillips.

Davies notes the stressful path through which Luther came to "joyous faith." He quotes Luther's own record: "After vigils, fasts, prayers, and exercises of the toughest kind, with which as a monk I afflicted myself almost to death, yet the doubt was left in my mind, and I thought who knows whether these things are pleasing to God. . . . the more holy, the more uncertain I became." Davies concludes that "profound anxiety must have formed part of the life of someone who was as much a perfectionist as Luther." And, he continues, "I think Luther learned painfully that he could not, by his own efforts, find what he so much wanted, namely, peace and joy in the presence of a loving and merciful God" (30).

Luther described himself as suffering from what today we would label as an obsessive-compulsive disorder, which became evident at some time or in some degree. Davies comments (32): "It seems to me that during his most obsessional years as a monk, Luther, like all obsessionals I have known, considered that everyone should be like him: perfection was, after all, the goal of any monk with a proper vocation." In his later discussion of Luther's illnesses Davies continues (44): "I believe there was a marked physical and constitutional element to Luther's tendency to depression. I do not see clear evidence that he was ever manic, elated or ill because of an upward mood swing. However, he might now be diagnosed as a cyclothymic personality, with many mood swings which, though significant, were never such as to cause a psychosis."

Another hero of the faith who suffered severe psychological problems throughout his life was William Cowper. Davies describes him as a person "of exceptional interest for Christians and for all who are interested in human suffering. His life," Davies notes, "is also very relevant today. In a special sense he shows what grace can do to a man's personality, and also what it sometimes appears *not* to be able to do. By this I mean that his experience points to a need for an honest explanation of non-healing, and the suffering that can go on and on" (87). Cowper, according to Davies, "suffered six serious depressive breakdowns, several suicide attempts, and endured so much mental pain" (110). With such a history there can be little doubt that Cowper's illness had a significant constitutional or endogenous component. Davies notes in this regard (88) that Cowper "seems to have inherited a marked tendency to depression. Even when he was not ill (in the sense of psychotic or insane) he suffered a melancholy disposition and a delicately anxious temperament."

Lord Shaftesbury, otherwise known as Anthony Ashley Cooper, the 7th Earl of Shaftesbury, lived a long, distinguished, and productive life (1801–85). Social historians who have little sympathy for Shaftesbury's Christian beliefs nevertheless agree that he changed the tone of his world, as they record the long list of what he did for factories, mines, and agriculture, and how greatly he improved their lot. He also fought vigorously to improve the so-called lunacy laws and other aspects of public health provision. And all of this was achieved against the background of a manic depressive illness. The signs appeared early, as Gaius Davies notes (120): "At 29 he (Shaftesbury) writes that he felt 'a peculiar vivacity of heart.' There was no special reason for this, and he knew he would pay for it by a 'corresponding dejection.'" He (Shaftesbury) wrote: "How curious and uncertain is my character . . . sometimes for a while in the wildest and most jovial of spirits; at others for a longer period in cruel despondency." After noting that "for the next 50 years Shaftesbury was to use his diaries and journals to describe these mixed feelings," Davies concludes that "it seems as certain as it can be that he suffered from what would now be called bipolar affective disorder, and what used to be called manic depressive illness" (120).

Our final example of a well-known Christian who contributed greatly to the lives of many fellow Christians, despite his own spiritual awareness at times being sorely disturbed by mental illness that almost certainly possessed a strong biological component, is the translator and author J. B. Phillips. He, said Davies, possessed "a special genius for translating and communicating" (112). This was exercised despite his own clear record of what it was like to suffer from recurrent depression. Phillips himself painted a picture of his father as an extremely meticulous, ambitious, and hard-driven, obsessional man. Davies comments that "the picture that emerges from Phillips' account is of poor parenting, dominated by his rigid and anxious father, whose obsessional personality traits he inherited in full measure" (213).

Having studied all the evidence, including J. B. Phillips's own detailed and revealing autobiography *The Price of Success*, Davies comments that "in the last 40 years or so we have learned a great deal about obsessive compulsive personality and about those who suffer from affective disorders" (213). And he goes on to ask, "What light can such knowledge shed on people such as J. B. Phillips?" (220). Davies's answer may be summarized in the following quotes. First, he notes that "we have already seen how he inherited his personality from his obsessional father, and quite possibly from his unmotherly mother too" (220). Second, he asks, "Might his personality problems have been helped more effectively?" and his answer is "I certainly think so" (220). Third, he later comments (222), "I find it sad that he was not helped by medication (note the help he did receive was by psychoanalytic psychotherapy). Nowadays such non-psychiatric forms of treatment as the use of beta-blockers may alleviate their anxiety by stopping the excessive effects of adrenalin on the body," and, he continues, "by the same token, there are nowadays many forms of anti-depressants which might have helped someone who suffered as much as Phillips." And, "above all, the modern emphasis on cognitive therapy and on behavior therapy might have helped him . . . there is however no evidence that he had any of these modern benefits" (212). And finally, commenting more generally on the plight of Phillips and others like him, Davies states (223), "I believe that the man who (because of some biochemical problems in his brain and constitution) feels ill with depression has as little to blame himself for as a diabetic who feels ill."

SPIRITUAL DEPRESSION?

We have written about the sufferings of these particular four heroes of the faith because, with varying degrees of confidence, we can agree with Davies's diagnoses of the likely nature of their psychological illnesses. We chose them because, in each case, it is likely that, at times, their spiritual depression was a consequence of their mental state, which in turn was attributable in varying degrees to inherited, constitutional factors, manifest in biological and/or biochemical abnormalities of their brains and endocrine systems. Clearly, the outworkings of their psychobiological unity was exhibited in both their mental conditions and their spiritual distress. With these exemplars in mind, and remembering the impressive evidence reviewed elsewhere in this book of the tightness of the mind–brain link, some recent provocative views by Dr. Stephen Judge, a lecturer in neurophysiology at Oxford University, are potentially important as signposts to the way our thinking about the relation between spiritual states and psychobiological processes may be moving.

Judge, a committed Christian, makes a sustained attempt to relate the knowledge that God gives us through the scientific method with what he teaches us through his Word. It is evident from Judge's writings that he shares the view of our psychobiological unity expressed elsewhere in this book. Judge[20] has written, "Let us suppose, therefore, that every aspect of what it is to be a human person, even a redeemed person with Christ's spirit in us, is embodied in the particular brain that is in our body, and the brain, mind and spirit are not separate entities but different aspects of our identity." One implication of Judge's views, which is directly relevant to our present discussion, is that his insistence on the unity of the person challenges the notion that our spirit, independently of our mind and brain, has a state of well-being of its own. I would suggest that the experiences of Luther, Cowper, Shaftesbury, and Phillips all support Judge's views.

In seeking to trace out some of the implications of his views, he has specifically discussed what is often referred to as spiritual depression. He asks what we mean by spiritual depression. His answer is that "if one tries to imagine an independent spirit that is itself depressed, and which therefore fails to provide necessary guidance to mind and body, this appears to make sense, but we get into difficulties when we start to ask more detailed questions. For example, if it is *only* the spirit that is depressed, and the mind is in good shape, can we not remind ourselves that 'at his hand are pleasures forever-more' and that 'the difficulties of the present situation are as nothing compared with the hope of glory'? If this does not achieve anything for us, then surely it isn't only our spirit that is depressed, we are also in a depressed mental state. Therefore we have to say that at least spiritual depression necessarily entails mental depression as a consequence. But the difficulty I see," he continues, "is then that if depression of the spirit always causes mental depression, can we not more economically define spiritual depression as a flavor of mental depression in which we have become unable to savour spiritual realities, understood in terms of belief in the appropriate theological propositions? Isn't the concept of an independent spirit one that does not work in this context? My proposal is that we regard spiritual depression as a state of being in which the ultimate goals of life (e.g., to enjoy him forever) have ceased to connect with our everyday life and practice. . . . I submit that to speak of spiritual depression makes little sense unless being in this state had clearcut consequences in our mental and bodily state, and that we can adequately define spiritual depression in terms of these so-called consequences without appealing to an independent spiritual entity at all."

I suspect that some of my readers will have found Judge's views extremely provocative. I would ask, however, that they reserve judgment until we have considered the biblical account of the composition of human personality given in chapter 6. For the moment, we are content to reiterate the basic point that the understanding of human personality, growing out of late-twentieth-century neuropsychology, psychiatry, and neuroscience, enables us better to understand the well-documented experiences of some of the great heroes of the faith of the past, as well as our own day-to-day joys, trials, and tribulations as Christian disciples.

A BALANCED VIEW AND THE WAY AHEAD

On the one hand, we recognize that there are changes in our brains that occur through no choices of our own. Alzheimer's disease is a classic case. On the other hand, what we do to ourselves may, in some circumstances, affect the workings of the neural substrate of our minds (e.g., alcoholism and other forms of drug abuse); some recent work indicates brain changes due to stress. The cumulative effect of such increasing self-knowledge has the potential to make us more responsible for our own actions and more compassionate and attentive to the plight of those who, through no fault of their own, suffer diseases of the mind. Unfortunately, we readily blame the environment for our failures while being all too ready to take credit for our successes. When thinking of attitudes toward others there is surely wisdom in taking seriously some of the research outlined earlier that shows how people are significantly influenced by their biology and their social, environmental, and cultural contexts. On this view we should regard ourselves as agents responsible for our actions but always be ready to entertain the possibility that others have been unduly influenced by their biology and/or their social and physical environment and to make allowances accordingly.

In this chapter we have presented evidence that should alert us to the possibility that changes in our spiritual awareness, our consciousness of the presence and power of God, are not immune to changes in our bodies in general and in our brains in particular. If we bear in mind the Bible's teaching about our psychobiological unity, such results will come to us as no surprise. Moreover, they do not, as some have falsely claimed, show that spiritual experience is "nothing but" the outcome of changes in our neural substrate. They are as unsurprising as the presumably encouraging discovery that we are still physically alive; they are, moreover, what we should expect if we hold a holistic biblical view of human persons. The content of any theological assertions we make, whatever the state of our biological substrate, must be judged, not on our understanding of the likely mediating neural processes, but by examining the relevant historic and other evidence.

Thus, in taking a balanced view of this new knowledge we need to be vigilant. The reductionist trap is all too often set in our path. To fall into it would be akin to claiming that, for example, by analyzing the compo-sition and distribution of the paints of an artist's masterpiece we have thereby shown that it is after all "nothing but" paint on canvas. If only we stand back, look at the whole, and get the picture in perspective, we shall be able to appreciate the masterpiece for what it is. To study man's mind and brain scientifically is not necessarily to threaten the dignity of man. Properly used, such knowledge can enable us to treat one another with greater dignity and understanding. In the realm of psychiatry this theme was taken up in the lecture by Lipowski from which we quoted earlier. He said that "neither brainless nor mindless psychiatry could do justice to the complexity of mental illness and to the treatment of patients. A comprehensive, biopsychosocial approach to our field is needed."

As Christians, while applauding Lipowski's call for a comprehensive biopsychosocial awareness of our humanity, we would also wish to emphasize the need to take account of the spiritual dimension of our existence. In this context we may note the remarks of the immediate past president of the Royal College of Psychiatrists in Britain. Professor Andrew Sims[21] commented: "Rather belatedly, the Royal College of Psy-chiatrists has recognized the need to consider spiritual issues, with the College Trainees Committee leading the way by recognizing 'the need to emphasize the physical, mental and spiritual aspects of healing in the training of doctors in general and psychiatrists in particular. Religious and spiritual factors influence the experience and presentation of illness' (Kehoe et al, 1992)." He also reminds his readers that "Gellner (1987) has argued cogently that the psychiatrist cannot escape society thrusting a priestly role upon her. If these expectations do exist, we should quite clearly state that we will not fulfil them. We need to balance the impor-tance of the spiritual in the life of our patients with denying absolutely any sort of priestly role for ourselves as psychiatrists (Sims, 1988b)." We take up this issue in chapters 8 and 9.

TAKING STOCK

1. There is a steadily accumulating body of evidence indicating a link between mind–brain states and spiritual awareness. It indicates that it would be wrong to believe that spirituality in some way stands apart and separate from our human embodiment.

2. Evidence for a link between mind–brain states and spiritual awareness is exemplified in Alzheimer's patients at the end of their life span. In midlife, the link is seen in the full flow of our everyday lives. It is dra-

matically illustrated in the experiences of some of the heroes of the faith who overcame great difficulties in the midst of doubt, depression, obsessional states, and the like. It is also evidenced as we begin to discern the beginnings of plausible neuropsychological accounts of what may be happening in our brains at the time of some sudden religious conversions.

3. For a Christian who has a biblically based, holistic view of human nature (see chapter 6) this tight link comes as no surprise. Indeed, it is knowledge that can potentially help us, at times, to relieve unnecessary anguish and distress as we, our friends, and our colleagues pass through periods of what in earlier generations would have been called "the dark night of the soul."

CHAPTER 5

LINKING THE BRAIN
AND BEHAVIOR

It remains difficult, on scientific grounds, to avoid the conclusion that
the uniquely human phenomenon of sexual orientation is a
consequence of multifactorial developmental processes in which
biological factors play a part, but in which psychosocial factors remain
crucially important. If so, the moral and political issues
must be resolved on other grounds.
—John Bancroft, "Homosexual Orientation," *British Journal of
Psychiatry,* 1994

The solution to the problem of social violence will not come from
addressing only social factors and ignoring neurochemical correlates, nor
will it come from blaming one neurochemical correlate alone. Consideration of both social and neurochemical factors is required,
in appropriate measure.
—Antonio Damasio, *Descartes' Error,* 1994

As a father has compassion on his children, So the Lord has
compassion on those who fear Him for He knows how we are
formed, He remembers that we are dust.
—Psalm 103:13–14

THE TIGHTENING OF THE MIND–BRAIN LINK outlined in chapter 3 has
given rise, in some quarters today, to speculative extrapolations about
what it implies for human responsibility in some facets of life currently

widely debated. Homosexuality and aggressive behavior are two such areas. Some view complex social phenomena from personal happiness to racial discrimination as reducible in principle to basic brain chemistry and/or disordered genes. The neuroscientist Professor Steven Rose has noted that for them, personal unhappiness can be handled by the prescription of the widely publicized drug Prozac, and racial discrimination can be handled by selective breeding programs. Such views have arisen when some have linked the dramatic advances in neuroscience with our understanding of the genetic basis of some behavior. From such a link it then becomes all too easy to smuggle their personal ideologies into explaining away those aspects of behavior they wish to condone or encourage. It would certainly be extremely sad if a totally unjustified air of triumphalism were to develop in some areas of psychobiological neuroscience, which, properly used, have so much to offer humankind. It would be all too easy for it to give rise to a widespread willingness on the part of individuals and communities to slip unthinkingly into attitudes that seek to ascribe all their behavior to environmental constraints and changes in neural chemistry rather than facing up to their personal and social responsibilities.

By way of illustration of how such matters are presented today we shall take a specific example of an issue currently widely debated. Posing the question provocatively we may ask, "Does the accumulating evidence that there may be a biological substrate to some aspects of homosexual behavior justify unbridled homosexuality?" One view is that a man is homosexual because he has a "gay" brain, which itself is believed to be the product of "gay genes." Going down that road, it is easy to argue that for similar reasons the violence sadly seen on the streets of many cities arises because certain people have reduced serotonin levels in their brains resulting from violent or criminal genes or that people get drunk because they have genes for alcoholism. Such a distortion of the meaning of the biological evidence occurs when some of the excellent studies of aspects of the neural bases of behavior, as well as of the effects of genetic factors, carried out using experimental animals such as rats and cats, are, unthinkingly and without justification, extrapolated lock, stock, and barrel to human behavior. The results of such animal studies are given simplistic labels and their neatly quantifiable findings are extrapolated without critical thought into the human domain. The next move is to conclude that our behavior is determined by forces beyond our control.

It is interesting that this question was raised at the end of Robyn Dawes's lengthy discussion of psychotherapy in his widely acclaimed book, *House of Cards.*[1] He presents a lengthy critical review of the vast literature addressing the question of whether psychotherapy is effective, a topic we deal with in detail in chapter 9, and if it is, to what extent its success is attributable to the professional credentials of the therapist. In that context, he considers the question we are considering here. He writes (284), "Is our behavior really determined by forces beyond our control? If it is, they are not the 'psychological forces' that we have been led in our culture to believe are responsible." And later he unambiguously gives his own answer to the question when he states: "There is nothing in current psychological knowledge that should lead us—in one way or another—to modify our view of the importance of our own strivings and attempts to change our lives. Even current support for the importance of genetic factors in influencing what we do demonstrates only influence; for example, children of alcoholics or schizophrenics are more likely to suffer from the same problems than children without such parents, but they are still more likely *not* to become alcoholic or schizophrenic respectively than to suffer from these conditions." Do we agree with his conclusions and if so why? We give some examples now for readers to consider in making their own judgment.

THE SEARCH FOR A BIOLOGICAL BASIS FOR SEXUAL ORIENTATION

Scientific interest in the possible biological bases of sexual orientation waxes and wanes. It is often the emergence and application of new techniques that seem to provide fresh ways of tackling enduring questions that spark off a new wave of interest in the topic. Today we are witnessing such a renewed wave of interest. This has been given extra momentum as it coincides with intense public interest fueled by the gay lobby. In such circumstances, scientific objectivity is in serious danger of being put in jeopardy. Most research on sexual orientation assumes that homosexuality represents a relative failure of sexual differentiation and that heterosexuality is the norm. Even in tribal cultures[2] in which homosexuality is expected of all boys before marriage, heterosexuality ultimately prevails. (This, incidentally, indicates that homosexual behavior does *not* always or necessarily indicate a homosexual orientation.)

In considering the possible biological basis of homosexuality we may, with profit, follow the lead given by John Bancroft,[3] a distinguished reproductive biologist and author of *Human Sexuality and Its Problems*. In a recent review paper he organizes evidence under four headings: hormonal mechanisms, brain structures, neuropsychological function, and genetic factors.[4]

As regards hormonal mechanisms he notes that "the early idea that homosexuals are hormonally different was abandoned some time ago" (437). While noting that attention in research switched from the organizational to activational effects of hormones, Bancroft points out that since much of the research used rodents as an animal model, the assumption was made that "the rodents provided a model that was without qualification or justification relevant to the human." However, the overtly sexual manifestations of gender-specific behavior in rodents such as lordosis are, says Bancroft, "clearly unhelpful in studying the human—lordosis has no primate counterpart, and our sexual motor activity cannot be classified in such discreet categories as 'mounting.'" David Myers,[5] in reviewing some of the same evidence as that examined by Bancroft, notes that "female sheep will show homosexual behavior if their pregnant mothers are injected with testosterone during a critical gestation period." He comments that "it seems that exposure to the hormone levels typically experienced by female fetuses during this time (i.e., the critical period for the brain's neural hormonal control system) may predispose the person (whether male or female) to be attracted to males in later life" (230). Again, the question remains of whether the sheep is an adequate animal model and whether the results obtained may be extrapolated without qualification to the human condition. At present, further research seems required to justify such an extrapolation.

In discussing brain structures Bancroft notes the evidence showing sexual dimorphism in the nucleus of the preoptic area of the rat (SDN-POA). Subsequently Swaab and Fliers[6] described a SDN-POA in the human but found no relationship with sexual orientation. Others have focused on the first interstitial nucleus of the anterior hypothalamus (INAH1). Yet others have found another area (INAH3) to be sexually dimorphic, with LeVay[7] reporting it to be smaller in homosexual men than in heterosexual men. Yet other investigators have focused on possible sexual dimorphisms in the corpus callosum and the anterior commissure. Bancroft concludes that the findings are confused and that "there is a lack of either consistency or replication." I would agree, certainly as regards sexual dimorphism in the size and shape of the corpus callosum and the anterior commissure, whose structure and functions I have personally studied for more than thirty years. Thus, the most recent evidence indicates a sevenfold variation in the size of the anterior commissure in a normal population.[8] Bancroft further points out that "there are methodological problems. Numbers are inevitably small, and in most studies homosexual subjects have died of AIDS; the possibility that structural changes could be a consequence of disease, such as AIDS, remains. But even if these findings are substantiated, and specific areas of the hypothalamus or elsewhere are found to be linked to sexual orientation, it is difficult to imagine what the nature of such a link would be. It is certainly unlikely that there is any direct relationship between structure of a specific area of the brain and sexual orientation per se" (438).

As regards neuropsychological functions, Bancroft comments on the increased incidence of left-handedness in both female and male homosexuals: "The proposed hormonal mechanism (i.e., increased exposure to androgen during early development) might explain the findings in lesbians; it is difficult to account for this tendency in gay men with a hormonal explanation. Once again, we have a finding which, if substantiated does not help to explain biological determination of sexual orientation except perhaps indirectly, either as a marker of other relevant processes or via the effects of gender-related behavior on 'sexual development'" (438).

EXPOSING A COMMON FALLACY—
AN ASIDE FOR THE NONBIOLOGIST

There is a common fallacy, which is widely believed, that all of our characteristics are determined by the genes we inherit from our parents. Perhaps the popularity of books such as Aldous Huxley's *Brave New World* must bear some blame for this. It may also have arisen because such a view seemed, at first sight, to be confirmed by the discovery that simply inherited chemical defects could cause gross mental retardation (phenylketonuria was the first to be recognized); that Down's Syndrome was caused most commonly by the presence of an extra chromosome; and that men with two Y chromosomes (instead of the normal one) were aggressive criminals. However, this assumption of genetic determinism has become overstressed in the popular mind; genes only *predispose* us to certain characteristics or behaviors, and their expression can often be modified by changing the environmental conditions.

The primary gene products *are* the direct consequence of a rather simple chemical process that has been worked out in the revolution of molecular biology initiated by Watson and Crick in 1953 with their elucidation of the structure of DNA. At this level, inherited characters can be said to be determined by the genes carried by the individual. However, once we leave the primary gene product level, the occurrence, speed, and direction of the chemical processes in the body are affected to varying extents by environmental influences. This is of considerable importance in clinical medicine, because inherited defects in metabolism can often be corrected once they have been identified. For example, diabetes can be treated by insulin, hemophilia with anti-hemophilic globulin, phenylketonuria and galactosemia by withholding from the diet phenylalanine and galactose, respectively. Thus, it is not true that genetic disease cannot be treated.

The interaction of genes and environment applies throughout normal development. Prenatal growth is slowed by the mother's smoking;

maternal drinking may reduce the intelligence and size of a baby at birth (the fetal alcohol syndrome). Childhood growth can be affected by nutrition and so on. It is often difficult to work out the details of gene–environment interactions in humans where experimental breeding and environmental control cannot be carried out. Animal studies can help here enormously but, as we shall see, their extrapolation without qualification to the human condition is full of hazards. Criminality and sexual deviation have often been attributed to family or inherited influences, but the grounds for distinguishing between these are usually equivocal. There is no doubt that we are affected as radically by our environment as by our genes.

GENETIC FACTORS IN SEXUAL ORIENTATION

As far back as 1952, Kallman[9] reported 100 percent concordance for a sample of homosexuality in monozygotic (MZ, i.e., identical) twins compared with only 12 percent concordance in dyzygotic (DZ, i.e., fraternal) pairs. Since then a series of studies have reported more or less consistent differences in concordance rates between monozygotic and dyzygotic twins. Two recent studies (Bailey and Pillard[10] and Bailey et al.[11]) report 52 percent MZ and 22 percent DZ concordance in males and 48 percent MZ and 16 percent DZ concordance in females. Such evidence, while strongly suggestive of a genetic factor, also indicates that with half of the identical twin pairings differing, genes are *not* the whole story.

A study by Hamer[12] et al. has added further weight to the likelihood of a genetic influence. Bancroft has written, "Hamer et al 1993 first carried out a family pedigree study which indicates the observed increase in homosexual orientation among male relatives involved, apart from brothers, mainly relatives on the mother's side; that is, maternal uncles or sons and maternal aunts. This suggested a sex linkage and justified a linkage study using DNA markers on the X-chromosome. They found a convincing correlation between homosexual orientation and the inheritance of polymorphous markers at the Xq28 sub-telomeric region of the long arm of the X-chromosome."[13]

In discussing the significance of Hamer's findings, Bancroft comments: "This was not, as the media chose to call it, a 'gay gene,' but persuasive evidence of a genetic factor or factors, which in this section of the gay community at least, are sex linked. . . . it is unlikely to be a gene which determines sexual orientation per se" (439).

It is noteworthy that John Bancroft, from the viewpoint of a reproductive biologist, and David Myers, from the viewpoint of a psychologist, reach largely similar conclusions following their respective reviews of the evidence to date concerning the biological bases of sexual orientation. Thus, Bancroft writes: "It remains difficult, on scientific grounds to avoid the conclusion that the uniquely human phenomenon of sexual orientation is a consequence of multi-factorial developmental processes in which biological factors play a part, but in which psychosocial factors remain crucially important. If so, the moral and political issues must be resolved on other grounds." Myers concludes: "Rather than specifying sexual orientation, perhaps biological factors predispose the temperament that influences sexuality in the context of individual learning and experience."[14] Nevertheless, "the consistency of the genetic, prenatal, and brain findings has swung the pendulum toward physiological explanation" (320). David Myers helpfully posed this question: "If our sexual orientation is indeed something we do not choose and cannot change, then how does the person move towards either a heterosexual or a homosexual orientation?" In answering his question, he notes that "some consensus has emerged from hundreds of research studies on sexual orientation (Storms, 1983):

1. Homosexuality is not linked with problems in a child's relationship with parents, such as with a domineering mother or/and an ineffectual father, or a possessive mother and a hostile father.

2. Homosexuality does not involve a fear or hatred of people of the opposite gender.

3. Sexual orientation is not linked with levels of sex hormones currently in the blood.

4. Sexual victimization of children by an adult homosexual or others is not a factor in homosexual orientation."

This very brief review of the lines of evidence to be considered when trying to understand the factors and their interaction, which may influence and predispose an individual toward a specific sexual orientation, should make it clear that there is as yet no evidence for a gay gene that determines that a person must become a homosexual, nor is there clear evidence of an unambiguous effect due to levels of sex hormones. The search for a contribution by specific localized brain circuits continues, but as yet even where evidence for a structural dimorphism is suggested we have no idea how it could work out to predispose someone to a particular sexual orientation. As regards environmental factors, as the above quote from David Myers makes clear, earlier theories of a child's relationships with parents finds no support in empirical studies.

Aggressive Behavior—A Case Study

If you place a mouse in a cage occupied by a rat, in most instances the rat will eventually kill the mouse. You can measure the amount of time it takes for the rat to do this and the time is taken as a surrogate quantifiable measure of the rat's "aggression." Some rats kill quickly, others slowly, and some kill not at all. The rat that kills the mouse in thirty seconds is construed as twice as "aggressive" as the rat that takes a minute. The measure then becomes dignified with the label of "muricidal behavior" and is considered a computable index for the study of aggression. The simple time measure, as just described, of course, ignores many other aspects of the rat—mouse interaction, such as the size of the cage, the length of the time each has been in it previously, features of rearing and handling conditions, and so on. The unjustified extrapolation occurs when "time to kill" as a surrogate for measure of aggression when studying the behavior of rats toward mice is transferred unthinkingly into the human domain and becomes a surrogate for studying human behavior. Criticizing such a view, Steven Rose[15] wrote, "At the recent discussion of violence at the AAAS (American Association for the Advancement of Science) meeting in San Francisco the distinguished psychologist, Jerome Kagan, described his studies on 'temperament' in toddlers, which, he claimed, could be divided between genetic propensities to being either 'inhibited' or 'disinhibited.' Whether a toddler was inhibited or disinhibited could, he suggested, serve as a predictor for whether they would show violent behavior when they grew up. He went on to support this claim by describing an analogous inhibited or disinhibited behavior in kittens which could be correlated with their later muricidal behavior."

Another unjustified tendency, evident in some attempts to interpret and apply the results of neurogenetic research, is to turn a process into a thing. Once the process has become a thing, you can seek to localize it somewhere in an individual's biology. On this way of thinking, there must be a site in the brain for "aggression" or for "sexual orientation." The next step is to look for such a localized site for the tendency in the brain and, depending on the neuroanatomist you consult, you will find that "gayness" is the result of an abnormal size in the INH3 region in the hypothalamus or, alternatively, a differently shaped corpus callosum. Likewise, aggression becomes located in the limbic system, probably the amygdala. To think like this is like locating the impressive power output of your car's engine in its fuel injection system—one essential ingredient of the whole, but still only a part of a complex electromechanical system.

Psychopharmacology and Social Engineering

With the exciting and rapid advances in psychopharmacology and the development of target drugs, the possibility of intervention to change behavior becomes even more tempting. Usually the argument is that such targeted drugs do not have the side effects of earlier generations of drugs. In most instances, however, this is simply not the case. All psychotropic drugs to a greater or lesser extent are spanners inserted into the biochemical machinery, and the consequences are never simple. Prozac, until very recently regarded as the modern wonder drug for depressive illness, is a case in point. A recent meta-analysis reveals it as no more effective than other antidepressant drugs. Rather, its major benefit is that it has fewer side effects. Technically it is classed as a selective serotonin reuptake inhibitor on the grounds that it doesn't interact with other neural transmitter systems. But serotonin receptors are found in many places in the body, from blood platelets to neurons, so the argument for specificity has to make the unlikely assumptions that (1) the primary biochemical deficit in depression is in the serotonin reuptake system; and (2) upregulating the system by means of the drug affects *only* the functioning of the neurotransmitter in respect of its role in depression, leaving its multiple other involvements in biochemical and physiological processes unimpaired. Hence the claims of those who see Prozac as a drug that may be taken and used for "cosmetic" psychopharmacology, by seemingly normal people, is an argument on very dangerous ground. The neuroscientist Steven Rose has reminded us that "the functioning of the nervous system is an exquisitely self-regulated symphony of neurotransmitters and neuromodulators; to argue that boosting one of these can improve on nature is like claiming that the 1812 symphony would be improved if the simulated gunfire was replaced by the sounds of nuclear explosions." This view is echoed and amplified by Antonio Damasio:[16]

> When it comes to explaining behavior and mind, it is not enough to mention neurochemistry. We must know whereabouts the chemistry is, in the system presumed to cause a given behavior. Without knowing the cortical regions of nuclei where the chemical acts within the system, we have no chance of ever understanding how it modifies the system's performance (and keep in mind that such understanding is only the first step, prior to the eventual elucidation of how more fine-grained circuits operate). Moreover, the neural explanation only begins to be useful when it addresses the *results* of the operation of a given system on yet another system. The important finding described

above should not be demeaned by superficial statements to the effect that serotonin alone "causes" adaptive social behavior and its lack "causes" aggression. The presence or absence of serotonin in specific brain systems having specific serotonin receptors does change their operation; and such change, in turn, modifies the operation of yet other systems, the result of which will ultimately be expressed in behavioral and cognitive terms.

These comments about serotonin are especially pertinent, given the recent high visibility of this neurotransmitter. The popular antidepressant Prozac, which acts by blocking the reuptake of serotonin and probably increasing its availability, has received wide attention; the notion that low serotonin levels might be correlated with a tendency toward violence has surfaced in the popular press. The problem is that it is not the absence or low amount of serotonin per se that "causes" a certain manifestation. Serotonin is part of an exceedingly complicated mechanism which operates at the level of molecules, synapses, local circuits, and systems, and in which sociocultural factors, past and present, also intervene powerfully. A satisfactory explanation can arise only from a more comprehensive view of the entire process, in which the relevant variables of a specific problem, such as depression or social adaptability, are analyzed in detail.

On a practical note: The solution to the problem of social violence will not come from addressing only social factors and ignoring neurochemical correlates, nor will it come from blaming one neurochemical correlate alone. Consideration of *both* social and neurochemical factors is required, in appropriate measure.

CORRELATION IS NOT CAUSALITY

Regrettably, insufficient thought has been given to the way in which a simpleminded neurogenetic determinism uses the notion of causality. It is entirely likely that in the course of aggressive encounters between individuals there are dramatic changes in hormone and neurotransmitter levels in those individuals, and, indeed, in specific regions within their brains. It is possible that people whose life history includes repeated such encounters may show lasting differences in a number of brain and body markers. However, to describe such changes as if they were the causes of particular behaviors is to mistake correlation or even consequence for cause. Unfortunately, these are the kinds of argument that extreme neurogenetic determinism routinely offers. They have been caricatured by Rose, who has written, "If you have flu, your nose runs, but the nasal mucus is a consequence, not a cause, of the flu. And if you have toothache, you can alleviate the pain by aspirin, but this does not mean that the cause of the ache is too little aspirin in the brain."[17] We see, then, that some neurogeneticists overstate their case, moving seamlessly from single to many genes, from genes with predictable consequences in virtually all known environments to genes with small or highly variable effects, whose norm of action extends so far as to prevent any claims to predictability.

PERSONALITY TRAITS AND BRAIN PROCESSES

Sexual orientation and excessive aggression are one thing, but what about more subtle psychobehavioral tendencies manifest to varying degrees in different people? Do they have an identifiable biological substrate and, if so, how much control do we have over their emergence? To answer these sorts of questions behavior geneticists have depended heavily on twin studies. In identical twins nature affords ready-made subjects for experimenters seeking to investigate the relative influences of heredity and environment.

Twins developing from a single fertilized egg that has split in two are genetically identical; fraternal twins, developing from separate eggs, are generally no more alike than ordinary siblings. Studies involving thousands of pairs of identical and fraternal twins carried out in widely different countries, such as Sweden, Australia, and Finland, have come up with consistent findings. In each study they administered widely used tests of extraversion (outgoingness) and neuroticism (emotional instability) and found that on both traits identical twins were more alike than fraternal twins. The researchers concluded that there was a substantial genetic influence on both traits.

If a trait such as emotional instability has a measurable genetic component, could it be the case that the outworking of that trait in social relations also has measurable effects in large-scale studies? It seems the answer is yes. A study of 1,500 same-sex, middle-aged twin pairs found that the odds of you divorcing if you have a fraternal twin who has divorced is 1.6 times the normal (the same rate as for those whose parents have divorced). If you are an identical twin and your sibling has divorced, the odds of your divorcing goes up 5.5 times. These and other studies have shifted scientific opinion toward a greater appreciation of genetic influences on behavior. But they do not go unchallenged. Critics point out that at times personality assessments have been carried out only some time after reunions of the separated twins and that adoption agencies try to place separated twins in similar homes. Even so a consensus is emerging that suggests that genetic influences account for almost 50 percent of person-to-person differences in traits such as extraversion and neuroticism.

A CHRISTIAN PERSPECTIVE

Extreme unscientific, uncritical, ideological neurogenetic determinism is totally unacceptable from a Christian point of view. On the one hand, it may lead to assigning unjustified blame for supposed moral culpability rather than seeking to alleviate problems. On the other hand, it could carry an element of fatalism, implying that nothing that we do is our own fault but that our problems lie exclusively in our biology. Such fatalism could certainly bring ready relief to those who wish to evade personal responsibility. There is much less stigma attached to being the carrier or transmitter of deficient genes than having been morally irresponsible. It is perhaps not surprising that in both Britain and the United States leading gay activists readily embrace and publicize the gay brain/gay genes explanation for their condition on the explicit grounds that now they can no longer be held morally culpable for a natural state, nor can they be held responsible for behavior that supposedly flows inevitably from their biological predisposition.

For any who take seriously the biblical teaching on homosexuality and related topics, it is necessary to remember, as John Stott[18] has reminded us, that the first chapter of the apostle Paul's letter to the Romans contains crucial teaching (vv. 26—27) relevant to the debate on homosexuality. As regards what is and is not "natural," Stott expounds Paul's views of what is meant by "nature" as follows:

> Some homosexual people are urging that their relationships cannot be described as "unnatural," since they are perfectly natural to them. John Boswell has written, for example, that "the persons Paul condemns are manifestly not homosexual: what he derogates are homosexual acts committed by apparently heterosexual people." Hence Paul's statement that they "abandoned" natural relations, and "exchanged" them for unnatural (26–27). Richard Hays has written a thorough exegetical rebuttal of this interpretation of Romans I, however. He provides ample contemporary evidence that the opposition of "natural" *(kata physin)* and "unnatural" *(para physin)* was "very frequently used . . . as a way of distinguishing between heterosexual and homosexual behavior." Besides differentiating between sexual orientation and sexual practice is a modern concept; to suggest that Paul intends to condemn homosexual acts only when they are committed by persons who are constitutionally heterosexual is to introduce a distinction entirely foreign to Paul's thought world, in fact a complete anachronism (77–78).

John Stott later adds: "The only context which He (God) intends for the 'one flesh' experience is heterosexual monogamy, and that a homosexual partnership (however loving and committed it may claim to be) is 'against nature' and can never be regarded as a legitimate alternative to marriage" (78).

Recapitulating, we conclude that there is no doubt that the dramatic developments in neuroscience are already changing and enriching our understanding of brain and behavior. There is equally no doubt that if these developments are wisely and compassionately employed, this new knowledge offers enormous potential to reduce human suffering and certainly, to a degree, to increase the overall extent of human happiness. However, if they become trapped and presented in a reductionist mold or hijacked by a libertarian ideology, they are unlikely to benefit individuals or society as much as they might. They must be seen within a wider, integrated understanding of how the relationships among the biological, personal, and social aspects of living act, so that there is a clear abandonment of a simplistic, unidirectional view of the causes of human action. Unless and until that happens, the great potential for good of these developments in science may remain limited and all too easily misapplied by unscrupulous people.

Accepting that on balance the evidence for a genetic influence on personality traits such as extraversion (outgoingness) and neuroticism (emotional instability) is broadly correct, it is interesting to pause and reflect on any implications this may have for Christian behavior. Before doing so it is interesting to note that since writing the previous sentence, and just as this book is going to press, two studies have appeared in the scientific journal *Nature Genetics* that lend further support to a genetic basis for some personality traits. Richard Ebstein and his colleagues in Jerusalem and Dean Hamer in Bethesda in the United States found that a personality trait they characterize as "novelty seeking" was linked with the gene responsible for making the receptor for the brain chemical dopamine. It is known to be involved in brain processes associated with the emotions. In their report in *Nature Genetics,* Richard Ebstein and his group reported that in a sample of 124 unrelated Israeli volunteers, those who scored higher in tests measuring novelty seeking were also more likely to possess the particular sequence of DNA base pairs (the letters that spell out the genetic code) next to the gene responsible for making the dopamine receptor. Although Dean Hamer and his team used a different personality test, their results were similar. They measured the length of the DNA repeated sequences in 315 people and found that about two-thirds of their sample had between two and five of the repeated regions, while a third had six to eight. These differences, they reported, correlated with differences in personality scores. Hamer is quite properly cautious in interpreting his results. He points out that the genetic differences identified account for only perhaps a tenth of the inheritability of the trait—in other words, there must be other genes involved. As so often happens, the caution of the scientists is lost in the headlines given to the report in the popular press where we were told *"Bad tempered and extravagant? Blame it on the genes."* Taken together, the findings from such research raise the question, Could it be that those of our Christian brethren who prefer more boisterous expressions of their faith in congregational worship are, up to a point, manifesting an out-working of their biologically inherited extraversion, while those of our brethren who prefer quieter, more private, sedate, and perhaps seemingly withdrawn expressions of their deep personal faith are, at least in part, manifesting their biological tendency to neuroticism? If these suppositions contain any truth, the implications seem clear. We should respect such differences of expression of religiosity, whether in private devotions or public worship, and avoid any suggestion that only *our* preferred way of behaving in worship is the biblical way. Those sharing the same credal beliefs may at the same time, for genetic reasons among others, express them differently.

Taking Stock

1. Some of the current debates in which science, medicine, and ideology become uncritically intermixed lie in the domain of studies of the behavior–brain links. Sexual orientation and aggressive behavior are two such topics currently given wide publicity.

2. There have been sustained attempts to relate hormonal mechanisms, brain structures, neuropsychological functions, and genetic factors to sexual orientation. There is, for example, clear evidence for sexual dimorphism in some brain structures but it is not clear whether, and if so how, this may be causally related to the expression of sexual orientation.

3. Part of the problem in correctly interpreting some of this data is the prior need to clear up public misunderstanding of what the proper implications of genetic links are. They are certainly not what is frequently assumed. Thus, we constantly need to remember that genes only predispose us to certain characteristics or behavior; their expression can very often be modified by changing environmental conditions. It is clear that once we leave the primary gene product level, the occurrence, speed, and direction of the chemical processes in the body are affected, to varying extents, by environmental influences, a point of considerable importance in clinical medicine. It is not true that genetic disease cannot be treated as was once believed. The interaction of genes and environment applies throughout normal development.

4. Some of the previously unanswered questions about the determining effects of environmental factors on homosexual behavior have begun to be addressed and some consensus has now emerged from the hundreds of reported studies on sexual orientation. It turns out that some of the earlier ideas that gained wide currency turn out not to be true. For example, homosexuality is *not* linked with problems in a child's relationship with parents; homosexuality does *not* involve fear or hatred of people of the other gender; sexual victimization of children by adult homosexuals or others is *not* a factor in homosexual orientation.

5. Another widely discussed topic linked with genetic factors is uncontrolled aggression. Again we saw that there were considerable difficulties in unambiguously interpreting the research data. It is certainly not clear that any effects are all in one direction. In this regard special caution is required in extrapolating from carefully controlled animal studies to understanding human behavior.

6. One often taught lesson in beginning psychology courses is especially important in the context of the topic of this chapter. Correlation does *not* necessarily imply causality. Twin studies have made this clear and they point to a lack of any simple causal link between, for example, genetic factors and the adoption of homosexual behavior.

7. The general pattern of evidence from studies in the field of neurogenetics and behavior is to alert us to the pressures that tend to shape our behavior. Above all, it should sensitize us to the power of such influences and, in so doing, should induce a greater compassion toward those who may be struggling.

CHAPTER 6

HUMAN NATURE

Biblical and Psychological Portraits

The religious vocabulary seems dignified but archaic,
our scientific vocabulary persuasive but barbaric.
—Gordon Allport, *The Individual and His Religion*, 1951

The human person is a "soul," by virtue of being a "body"
made alive by the breath (or spirit) of God. . . . As in the case
of the biblical words traditionally translated "soul" *(nephesh, psyche)*
the Hebrew and Greek words to express physical, emotional and
psychological being are an interpreter's minefield.
—J. E. Colwell, *New Dictionary of Theology*, 1988

The idea that man has a disembodied soul is as unnecessary
as the old idea that there was a Life Force. This is in head-
on contradiction to the religious beliefs of billions of human
beings alive today. How will such a radical change be received?
—Francis Crick, *The Astonishing Hypothesis*, 1994

THE EVIDENCE REVIEWED in earlier chapters points, almost uniformly, to the ever-tightening link between mind and brain, and behavior and brain, to the unity of the human person. In later chapters, as we recount the renaissance of scientific interest in consciousness, we discover that a similar pervasive trend is present. That does not mean that the opinions of scientists and philosophers are all alike on this topic. Some, such as Sir John Eccles and Sir Karl Popper, continue to argue for a "dualism of substance" model of human nature. Others like Francis Crick adhere to their presupposition that you, your joys and your sorrows are no more than the behavior of a vast assembly of nerve cells and their associated molecules. Yet others, such as the neuropsychologist Jean Delacour, while noting that the scientific study of consciousness is already well advanced, detect an emerging consensus among scholars that rejects both dualism and what he calls eliminative monism. The latter, he believes, seeks to mask with scientific arguments an a priori philosophical commitment to reductionism.

The topicality of these issues are well exemplified by the July 1995 issue of *Time* magazine, which entitled its central feature "In Search of the Mind." It reviewed some of the material we consider later in the two chapters on consciousness, as well as that already examined in previous chapters. Three weeks later *Time* published a sample of readers' letters in response to the article. No one would pretend that they were in any way representative, but it was nonetheless interesting to note their flavor. In general, their tone was one of concern at the possible challenge to human dignity posed by mere scientists researching something so personal and intimate as consciousness. Some, seeming to come from religious people, were of the "You will never be able to . . ." variety. Thus, Peter W. Watson wrote, "Analysis of the brain will never reveal the soul, which is 'other' than material though contained within the brain. I hope that scientists may one day realize that we humans are indeed souls made in the image of God." Monica Eichmann wrote, "The best part of your report on the mind and consciousness is the thought that scientists may have to acknowledge the existence of the soul." George H. Pigneron looked to parapsychological events to argue that "the mind at times transcends the brain." Kerry Marshall wrote, "As a trained physicist, I was disappointed by the wholly mechanistic view of the mind portrayed in your report. Consciousness precedes body and mind, and exists beyond them both; this truth can be directly verified by personal experience through the practice of meditation." Clearly the article touched some tender spots on the deeply held personal beliefs, religious and otherwise, of these correspondents. We all have, albeit often not very clearly formulated, models of ourselves and other persons. The quote from Peter Watson would, I suspect, gain the approval of some Christians—but should it? To answer that question we must pause and ask what the salient features of a biblical view of human nature, of soul, mind, body, heart, spirit, and so on, are.

Partnership in Understanding

The Bible has many things to say about humankind and human nature. Classic passages such as Psalm 8 beginning, as it does, with the question, "What is man *that thou art mindful of him?*" remind us of the theocentric context of scriptural statements that primarily deal with humankind in relation to God their Creator, Sustainer, and Redeemer. The kinds of questions posed by twentieth-century scientists were not even framed by the biblical authors, let alone answered by them. Our concern here is, therefore, strictly circumscribed. We are not addressing the question of the fallenness of humankind, nor are we discussing the biblical teaching about the nature of unregenerate man as compared with that of regenerate man, nor are we discussing the natural man and the spiritual man. We recognize that these are all crucial issues in Christian doctrine concerning the human person, but they are not within our present focus. Rather, our concern is narrowly focused on questions such as whether at birth an immortal soul is implanted in each of us, a soul which, at our physical death, will be released from its temporary physical embodiment; questions as to whether there is within each of us some nonphysical part that remains immune from the "changes and chances of this fleeting world"; whether there is within each of us a separate "soul" which, like a pilot flying an aircraft, steers our physical, bodily aircraft through life's varied calm and turbulent conditions; and questions about whether, if there is such a thing as a "soul," where it exerts its controlling influence over our brains, and hence our minds and bodies. Simply raising questions in this way may bring to mind for Christian readers various alternative models held today or championed in the past. They will probably recall debates between Christians about, for example, the bipartite or tripartite nature of the human person and of the biblical proof texts on which these are usually based.

Before we consider some key features of the biblical portraits of human persons, we may avoid gross errors if we remind ourselves of the helpful and timely advice given by John Stott[1] in his commentary on Romans where, as he begins to write about the seventh chapter, he states, "It is never wise to bring to a passage of scripture our own ready made agenda, insisting that it answers *our* questions and addresses *our* concerns. For that is to dictate to scripture instead of listening to it. We have to lay aside our presuppositions, so that we can consciously think ourselves back into the historical and cultural settings of the text. Then we shall be in a better position to let the author say what he does say and not force him to say what we want him to say" (189).

HUMAN NATURE— A PARTNERSHIP OF COMPLEMENTARY ACCOUNTS

Stating the Obvious Recognizing Self-evident Differences

Insights into human nature—at times profound, at times trivial—are recorded in literature, portrayed in art, proclaimed by religions, and, in the majority of cases, long predate recent insights offered by scientists. Meeting such insights in the writings of philosophers or in the literature of great writers, or observing them in the paintings of great artists, at once indicates that what is offered from these sources is not, in any sense, from the same domain as other accounts offered by twentieth-century scientists. In the very limited context of our discussion in this book, namely, exploring the partnership in understanding human nature offered by, on the one hand, Christian faith and, on the other, by modern psychology and neuroscience, we can learn important lessons from earlier attempts to relate knowledge from the scientific enterprise to doctrines of the Christian faith. We have outlined some of these past interactions in chapter 2.

As we look for lessons from other sciences, we recognize, for example, that few people today would regard statements in the Bible about the sun, the moon, and the stars as being in competition, for our acceptance and allegiance, with statements by late-twentieth-century astronomers and astrophysicists. Likewise, leaving aside the champions of so-called creation science, few who read what the Bible has to say about the creation of the universe would see it as competing with what geologists, geophysicists, and astronomers can tell us about the origins and ages of the earth, the sun, the planets, and galaxies. Likewise, though there are those who believe that selected passages of the Bible say things that conflict with evolutionary theory, the majority of Bible-believing Christians now recognize that Scripture is not claiming to tell us, in a scientific sense, how God went about creating the universe, nor to tell us how he sustains it moment by moment.

It is, of course, all too easy for us today to be smug. With the benefit of hindsight, we are overly and unfairly critical of our Christian forebears who in their generation, and for good reasons, had no doubt that it was proper to interpret certain Scriptures literally. For example, they believed that the earth rests on pillars (1 Sam. 2:8, in the AV, but compare the NIV reading, "for the foundations of the earth are the LORD's, upon them he has set the world"); that the earth does not move but stands still (1 Chron. 16:30, in the AV, but again note in the NIV we read, "the world is firmly established, it cannot be moved"); that the earth has ends and edges (Job 37:3, in the AV, but again compare the NIV, where we read, "sends it to the ends of the earth"); and the earth has four corners (Isa: 11:12, in the AV, but again compare the NIV's "from the four corners of the earth"; Rev. 7:1, in the AV, or in the NIV, "I saw four angels standing at the four corners of the earth").

What pertains in the interpretation of Scripture passages in the light of geological and astronomical knowledge applies also as we view some passages of Scripture in the light of modern biology. Consider a few examples. Bats are not birds (Lev. 11:13–14; Deut. 14:11, 18); camels do not have cloven hooves (Lev. 11:4); turtles do not have voices (Song of Solomon 2:12); no four-legged animals fly (Lev. 11:21).

In each of the above instances the contrast is clear between how scientific books and papers in astronomy, astrophysics, geology, zoology, and botany write about the earth, the stars, the plants, and the animals, and how Scripture refers to them. We are no longer tempted to see the scientific accounts as competitors with the biblical accounts. Nor do we seek to intermix them or to incorporate the one into the other; that way lies confusion and an unwitting abuse of Scripture.

There may, however, be other opportunities for misinterpretation. What about familiar passages of Scripture that teach us about human nature? Given our common faith that the Scriptures are indeed the Word of God and will not mislead us as to our salvation, we may yet need to rethink our interpretations of some passages of Scripture in the light of the other knowledge that God gives to us through our involvement in the scientific enterprise, specifically in the realms of psychology and neuroscience. To put it more bluntly, if somewhat provocatively, are we in danger at the end of the late twentieth century of doing to some of our fellow neuropsychologists what others did to Galileo when convicting him of heresy on the basis of their interpretation of Holy Writ? After all was it not clear, "obvious" in Galileo's day, that the earth is indeed fixed, immovable, and nonrotating (Josh. 10:12; 1 Chron. 16:13; Pss. 93:1; 96:10; 104:5). And in this sense, is it not equally clear that humans possess immortal souls? are made up of two parts? or three parts? And is it not clear that man is distinguished from the animals by virtue of possessing a soul?

For several reasons, the problem we face in relating statements in the Bible about human nature with those by psychologists is much less clearcut than it is in the physical and earth sciences. The language used in the two contexts at times looks much alike, especially in the domain of personality theories. The pronouncements of some psychotherapists sound remarkably like some of the statements that we find about human motivation and human nature in the Bible. For that reason alone it is not always immediately evident that Scripture statements differ radically from what we read about human nature in the writings of some psychologists.

Professor Gordon Allport,[2] a leading figure in personality theory nearly fifty years ago, made the point cogently. He wrote of descriptions of personality that "the religious vocabulary seems dignified but archaic, our scientific vocabulary, persuasive but barbaric." "His id and superego have not learned to cooperate," writes the modern mental hygienist; "the flesh lusteth against the spirit, and spirit against the flesh," writes

Paul. "Feelings of guilt suggest poor personality team work," suggests the twentieth-century specialist; "purify your hearts, ye double minded," exhorts James. "The capacity of the ego to ward off anxiety is enlarged if the ego has considerable affection for his fellows and positive goals to help them." Correspondingly, John writes, "Perfect love casteth out fear." "It will be difficult, I suspect," goes on Allport, "to find any proposition in modern mental hygiene that has not been expressed with venerable symbols in some portion of the world's religious literature."

Elsewhere in this book, in chapters 8 and 9, we consider an example of this apparent overlap in detail, taking the specific example of how we should properly relate religious and psychological accounts of human needs. For now we should note how easy it would be, because of surface similarities between the statements of religion and psychology in the domain of mental life, to fail to keep alert to the differences between the two. If all we need to know about mental health is hidden in Scripture, if only we can find it, then we can offer early retirement to both Christian and non-Christian researchers in psychology, psychiatry, pharmacology, and neuroscience! But, in fact, we know that it is from just these disciplines that great benefits have already flowed to those suffering mental distress of many kinds.

The psychologist researching human behavior can only take us as he finds us. Any questions of what we might have been like, had there never been a fall, sit firmly in the domain of the theologian. He writes about our fallen nature, our sinful nature, our unregenerate nature, our regenerate nature, and so on. None of these terms enters into discussions of human nature by scientific psychologists nor in their professional writings, though they are readily used by Christian psychologists in other and appropriate contexts. There is thus a stark contrast between the ways in which theologians write about human nature and the vocabulary, concepts, and theories of scientific psychologists. As an example, typical of how theologians write about human nature, consider the following passage from a recent commentary on Paul's letter to the Romans by the well-known theologian John Stott.[3] The opening paragraph of his chapter giving an exegesis and exposition of Romans 3:21–4:25 reads: "All human beings, of every race and rank, of every creed and culture, Jews and Gentiles, the immoral and moralizing, the religious and the irreligious, are without any exception sinful, guilty, inexcusable and speechless before God. That was the terrible human predicament described in Romans 1, verse 18 to Romans 3, verse 20. There was no ray of light, no flicker of hope, no prospect of rescue." How different all this reads from anything in psychological literature, as it offers us its profound and all-embracing assertions about the plight of "all human beings."

Typical Theological Language

We may reinforce this point by reminding ourselves that in the eighth chapter of the same letter of Paul to the Christians at Rome he speaks repeatedly of our "sinful nature." You could quite rightly say that Stott's commentary on this chapter is full of profound teaching about human nature. And yet anyone who reads it is at once aware that he is reading theology, not psychology, as understood today, though in a more general sense it is very profound psychology. By way of example, the following short passages illustrate how, though explicitly writing about and referring to human nature, it is not in the context of twentieth-century psychology.

Thus, Stott writes, commenting on what Paul has to say about living "according to the flesh" as compared with "according to the spirit" (222), "By *sarx* (flesh) Paul means neither the soft muscular tissue which covers our bony skeletons, nor our bodily instincts and appetites, but rather the whole of our humanness viewed as corrupt and unredeemed, our fallen, egocentric human nature, or more briefly the sin-dominated self" (222).

He then goes on to use a word familiar in contemporary cognitive psychology, the *mind*. But it is at once evident that it has little or nothing to do with mind as written about, for example, by Jerome Bruner, in his book *In Search of Mind*. Stott writes (223), "Here Paul concentrates on the 'mind,' or (as we would say) mindset, of those who are characterized by either *sarx* or *pneuma*." He continues: "Mindset expresses our basic nature as Christians or non-Christians. . . . The meaning surely is not that people are like this because they think like this, although that is partly true, but that they think like this because they are like this. The expressions are descriptive. In both cases their nature determines their mindset. Moreover, since the flesh is our twisted human nature, its desires are those things which pander to our ungodly self-centeredness." And he later sums up this section of his commentary when he writes, "To sum up, here are two categories of people (the unregenerate who are 'in the flesh' and the regenerate who are 'in the spirit'), who have two perspectives or mindsets ('the mind of the flesh' and 'the mind of the spirit'), which lead to two patterns of conduct (living according to the flesh or the Spirit), and result in two spiritual states (death or life, enmity or peace). Thus our mind, where we set it and how we occupy it, plays a key role in both our present conduct and our final destiny."

The reader will have noted repeated references in the above to human nature, to mind, to mindset (akin to what psychologists might call attitudes), to the unregenerate and the regenerate. This all makes good sense to the Christian and is, I believe, self-evidently *not* the language of scientific psychology, but is powerfully and penetratingly true nonetheless.

The Bible, of course, also makes frequent reference to specific psychological functions such as remembering, thinking, and perceiving. But here again the treatment given in Scripture contrasts starkly with the ways in which psychology textbooks consider these same functions. The reason is clear: Their purposes are quite different. For example, Scripture has much to say about remembering. From the very early chapters of the Bible it is clear that remembering is something that God himself does to the benefit of humankind. Thus, in Genesis 8:1 we read that "God *remembered* Noah and all the wild animals and the livestock that were with him in the Ark." Or again, in the following chapter, we read in verse 15 that God says, "I will *remember* my covenant between me and you and all living creatures of every kind." Remembering is also something that the creatures made by God must be diligent to observe. For example, right in the center of the Ten Commandments, in Exodus 20:8, we read, "*Remember* the Sabbath day by keeping it holy; six days shall you labor. . . ." We are also exorted to *remember* God's great works. Thus, for example, in 1 Chronicles 16:12, we read, "*Remember* the wonders he has done, his miracles and the judgments he pronounced." We are exorted to *remember* his mercies; for example, in 2 Chronicles 6:42, we read, "o Lord God do not reject your anointed one. *Remember* the great love promised to David your servant." The psalms are full of exhortations for us to *remember* the greatness of God's works. And so we could go on but the point is a simple one. The function or the faculty of remembering is certainly referred to in Scripture, but the way in which it is referred to is totally and completely different from the way it is referred to in psychological writings.

TYPICAL PSYCHOLOGICAL ACCOUNTS

One of the architects of the so-called cognitive revolution in psychology, Sir Frederic Bartlett,[4] entitled his major work *Remembering*. Today, remembering, or as it is more often described in the psychological literature simply as memory, is written about at great length. For the benefit of any nonpsychologists reading this book and who, therefore, for good reason, are not familiar with psychological writings, we give two brief extracts from one of the most widely used university and college textbooks of psychology in the United States, by Dr. David Myers.[5] In his chapter on memory, he writes, "Although the ordinary human memory stores more information and is more complex than any computer, both systems can be viewed as processing information in three steps. First, information must be *encoded* or translated, into some form that enables the system to process it. Keystrokes are encoded into the computer's electronic language, much as sensory messages are encoded into the brain's neural language. Next, information must be *stored*, or retained, by the system over time. A computer might store information magnetically on a disk; a person stores information in the brain. Finally, there must be a method by which information can be *retrieved*, or located and gotten out, when needed." And later in the same chapter, still discussing memory, but now writing about its neural substrate, Myers writes, "Other neuroscientists are analyzing memory on a finer scale, by exploring changes in and between single neurons. Memory begins as messages whizzing through brain circuits but are then somehow consolidated into a permanent neural change. If by passing an electric current through the brain you disrupt its electrical activity, recent memories will be wiped out but earlier memories will still be intact. A blow on the head can do the same" (268).

What I am suggesting is that it is self-evident that when the Bible talks about remembering, its statements are written with a totally different aim in mind than those that concern the late twentieth-century scientific psychologist.

A Shared Concern?

Granted that in general it is clear that the concerns of biblical writers with human nature are self-evidently different from those of psychologists, it nevertheless remains the case that there is a shared area of interest concerning human nature, namely, the composite makeup of human personality. It is here that theological models and psychological models appear, at times, to be making competing claims. Are each of us some sort of a package composed of several parts, referred to in the Bible as soul, mind, heart, spirit, body, or are we a single entity, a mind–brain unity as described in psychology and neuroscience? In the two contexts, how are the parts making up the composite whole seen to be interrelated? As we saw in chapter 3, such questions have fascinated humankind down through the centuries. How we talk about them in any generation is not confined to the academy, but finds expression in everyday language.

This is well exemplified in Shakespeare's generation. As his plays indicate there were at that time three different theories in circulation. It is fascinating to see the way in which they are found in his writings. We noted earlier that today we smuggle our views of the mind into our everyday expressions. We talk about somebody being "switched on" or "switched off," hinting at the computer analogy of mind. We talk about somebody being "conditioned" to do something, hinting at Pavlov's physiological model of the mind. The same was true in Shakespeare's day. For example, Portia in *The Merchant of Venice* (act 3, scene 2) sits very delicately on the fence, settling for neither the encephalic nor cardiovascular theory as she sings:

> Tell me where is fancy bred,
> Or in the heart or in the head?

Or again, Sir John Falstaff *(Henry IV*, part 2, act 4, scene 2), having just informed the chief justice that King Henry has returned in poor health from Wales, enters into a discussion in which he takes a mixed cardiovascular and encephalic view:

Chief Justice: I talk not of his majesty,
You would not come when I sent for you.

Falstaff: And I hear, moreover, that his highness
is fallen into this same whoreson
apoplexy.

Chief Justice: Well, God mend him. I pray you,
let me speak with you.

Falstaff: This apoplexy is, as I take it, a kind
of lethargy, an't please your lordship;
a kind of sleeping in the blood,
a whoreson tripling.

Chief Justice: What tell me of it? be it as it is.

Falstaff: It hath it original from much grief,
from study and *perturbation of the brain.*
I have read the causes of its effects in Galen:
it is a kind of deafness.

Holofernes, in *Love's Labour's Lost* (act 4, scene 2), holds the ventricular theory:

Holofernes: This is a gift that I have, simple,
simple; a foolish extravagant spirit,

full of forms, figures, shapes, objects, ideas,
apprehensions, emotions, revolutions.
These are begot in the ventricle of memory,
nourished in the womb of the pia mater,
and delivered from the mellowing of
the occasion. But the gift is good
in those in whom it is acute,
and I am thankful for it.

All these lines were written in the 1590s and Shakespeare could select a theory of mind to fit his dramatic purpose.

It is perhaps worth noting that all three plays reflect the various views in common circulation at that time. During the two centuries after Shakespeare, the ventricular and cardiovascular theories finally vanished, despite how well they seemed to match one's immediate experience. They vanished because what seemed "obvious" began to be tested against empirical observations and results of rudimentary experiments. Man had become a part of nature and could, as such, be subjected to increasing scientific scrutiny.

THE BIBLICAL PORTRAITS OF HUMAN NATURE

A Contemporary Issue

The need to set out the main features of the composite picture of human nature derivable from a study of the whole of Scripture is urgent today. In part, this is because, within Christian circles, "the traditions of men" unthinkingly continue to shape the interpretations imposed on Scripture; in part, it is urgent when it becomes evident that some of the leading scientists of this century set up straw men which they suggest capture the essence of the Christian view of humankind and then solemnly attack them and, to their satisfaction, decisively dispose of them as untenable. Consider, for example, the recent book *The Astonishing Hypothesis* by Nobel Laureate Francis Crick.[6] His introductory chapter starts with a quotation from a Roman Catholic catechism in which the question "What is the soul?" is asked and where the answer is given: "A soul is a living being without a body having reason and free will." This, he says, means that Christians assert that "people have souls, in the literal and not merely the metaphorical sense." He then goes on to review much of the evidence we also have briefly described in previous chapters and shows how they seriously question any such view.

In fairness to Crick, one should note that his failure to ask what the biblical view of human nature in general, and of the soul in particular, is, is not confined to non-Christian writers but is not uncommon in some Christian circles also. How many Christians, for example, remember that the great Reformer Martin Luther listed as the last of his "five cardinal errors of the papal church" the doctrine of the natural immortality of the soul? Luther's view concerning this cardinal error was shared by William Tyndale. Those who have read Crick's book will know that his own "cardinal error" is his presupposition and deep commitment to "nothing buttery." Thus, on page 3, he writes, "You . . . are *no more than* the behavior of a vast assembly of nerve cells and their associated molecules"; "You are *nothing but* a pack of neurones." This theme pervades the book and, despite a slight softening in its closing pages where he writes (261), "The words *nothing but* in our hypothesis can be misleading if understood in too naive a way," he does nothing to dispel the inference that, using his own arguments, his "astonishing hypothesis" is *"nothing but* black lines on a white background." As fellow Nobel Laureate, Roger Sperry, has written, "The meaning of the message will not be found in the chemistry of the ink."

What are the main lines of Scripture teaching on the composite makeup of human nature? How are some of the most frequently used words, such as soul, spirit, body, and heart, used in Scripture, and what composite pictures do they offer us to give new insights into our own nature? The need to go to basic sources in Scripture to arrive at a view of human nature is important because, on the one hand, failure to do this can generate unreal conflicts between science and faith, and, on the other hand, it can lead to Christians finding themselves defending "accepted views" that turn out not to be required from biblical teaching.

In seeking to answer our question we follow what we believe to be widely accepted general principles of biblical exegesis and seek to identify consistent themes. At the same time, we note problematic passages with their oft-quoted verses some would argue require us to believe, for example, in the natural immortality of the soul—a view regarded, as we have noted, by Martin Luther and William Tyndale, as erroneous.

Having focused on our particular concerns in this book we must now examine the biblical evidence to find out whether there is one dominant model of the makeup of human nature and, if there is, what its defining characteristics are. As we attempt this we are greatly helped by biblical scholars who enable us to understand how certain key words are used in Scripture. It is, of course, possible to oversimplify by writing about *a* or *the* biblical view of human nature. We hasten to point out that we recognize, as theologians and biblical scholars have pointed out, that word studies alone are insufficient to answer our questions because of our readiness to read modern conceptions back into ancient vocabulary. We recognize that the distinctions made between Hebraic thought and

Greek dualism have, at times, been overstated. We accept that the Jewish Scriptures before Christ had undergone several centuries of Hellenization, that there were several shades of Greek views, and that therefore the right question to ask is: What is the *range* of acceptable diversity in biblical views of the person? However, we must start somewhere and we believe that, notwithstanding all the hazards, the best place to take a look is at the shades of meanings generally agreed by biblical scholars to be attached to key words repeatedly used in Scripture to refer to human nature.

The *New Bible Dictionary*[7] comments on the word *body* that, "contrary to Greek philosophy and much modern thought, the emphasis in Hebrew is not on the body as distinct from the soul or the spirit" (145). Or, concerning the word *heart*, we read, "it was essentially the whole man, with all his attributes, physical, intellectual and psychological, of which the Hebrew thought and spoke, and the heart was conceived of as the governing center of all of these . . . character, personality, will, mind are modern terms which all reflect something of the meaning of 'heart' in the biblical usage . . . mind is perhaps the closest modern term to the biblical usage of heart and many passages in RSV are so translated" (468). Of the "soul" (or *nephesh*) we read, "usually the *nephesh* is regarded as departing at death (e.g., Genesis 35, verse 18) but the word is never used for the spirit of the dead" (1135). Or, compare what the entry under "Anthropology" has to say in the *New Dictionary of Theology*.[8] There we are told

Genesis 2, verse 7 refers to God forming Adam from the dust of the ground and breathing into his nostrils the breath of life, so that man becomes 'a living being. . . . The word 'being' *(nephesh)* . . . should be understood in its own context within the Old Testament as indicative of men and women as living beings or persons in relationship to God and other people. . . . According to Genesis 2 any conception of the soul as a separate (and separable) part or division of our being would seem to be invalid. Similarly, the popular debate concerning whether human nature is a bipartite or tripartite being has the appearance of a rather ill-founded and unhelpful irrelevancy. The human person is a 'soul,' by virtue of being 'body' made alive by the 'breath' (or Spirit) of God. . . . Moreover, that Adam was made alive by the breath of God implies that his life as this soul was never independent of the will of God and the Spirit of God (Genesis 6, verse 3; Ecclesiastes 12, verse 7; Matthew 10, verse 28). The question of whether Adam was created mortal or immortal prior to the fall may miss the point by following Plato in presupposing some form of immortality that is independent of the will of God.

Human life is never to be conceived of in terms of an independent immortality since that life is never independent of the will and Spirit of God. . . . In consequence of his fall, death was pronounced as God's judgment upon Adam since the relationship which was the basis of his 'effective immortality' had been broken. It is this breach of spiritual relationship which constitutes 'the spiritual death' that characterizes the totality of human existence without Christ (Romans 7, verse 9; Ephesians 2, verse 1 following).

The author later comments: "As in the case of the biblical words traditionally translated 'soul' (nephesh; psyche) the Hebrew and Greek words to express physical, emotional and psychological being are an interpreter's minefield" (28–29). We turn now to a detailed consideration of each of these terms, as we tiptoe through this minefield.

The Human Person as a Living Soul (nephesh and psyche)

The logical place to start is in the Book of Genesis, where the creation of humankind is presented. Thus Genesis 2:7 tells us that "The LORD God formed man from the dust of the ground and breathed into his nostrils the breath of life, and the man became a living being." It is not uncommon for us to be told that here we have a description of one aspect of how man was made in the image of God, namely, by being given an immortal soul, and it is then further boldly asserted that this is what distinguishes humankind from animals. Regarded in this way, this verse is seen as a further comment on Genesis 1:27, where we read, "So God created man in his own image, in the image of God he created him; male and female he created them." Such an interpretation, however, fails to recognize and do justice to the fact that the reference to man becoming "a living being" in Genesis 2:7 is a translation of the Hebrew word *nephesh,* which has already appeared on four occasions in Genesis 1 to refer to the nonhuman animals (vv. 20, 21, 24, 30). The straightforward interpretation, therefore, of these verses is that both humankind and animals are living beings or souls. They are not to be regarded as bipartite creatures made up of two kinds of "stuff," a soul and a body, which can be separated and can each go on subsisting on its own. According to these passages the soul describes the *whole* of the living organism, whether animal or human, and comprises their bodies as well as their mental powers. We note that they are spoken of as *having* soul, that is, conscious being, in order to distinguish them from inanimate objects that have no life. There are a further nineteen passages in the Old Testament and one in the New Testament that also use the word *nephesh,* or its Greek equivalent, in connection with animals. In this context it is also worth noting especially the passage in Leviticus 17:11, where we read, "For the life *(nephesh)* of the flesh is in the blood." Here the word translated *life is* again the word *nephesh* in the Hebrew. In these and other passages in Leviticus "all flesh" points to references to the *blood* as comprising *both* man and animals. Thus, in this sense what is translated *soul* elsewhere is identical with what is translated *blood* in these passages.

On occasion, *nephesh* refers to a dead body; for example, in Leviticus 21:11, we read, "He [the high priest] must not enter a place where there is a dead body." A similar use is found in Leviticus 22:6, where *nephesh* is translated as *corpse.* The Bible also speaks of human death as the death of the soul; there are at least thirteen such instances in the Old Testament. It is thus evident from Scripture that a human being is a soul, in the same sense that an animal, for example, a bird or a fish is a soul. The difference between man and animal is one of degree, not of kind, in respect of its soulishness.

We have already noted that the human person is described in the Bible as a soul or living being by the Hebrew word *nephesh.* The corresponding word in the Greek translation of the Old Testament, the Septuagint, is *psyche.* Lest we think that a very simple analysis of the use of this word and its translations is possible, we should be warned that it is translated in forty-five different ways in the Old Testament alone!

More detailed study of the different shades of meaning of the word *nephesh* in the Old Testament and of the Greek word *psyche* in the New Testament enables us to identify a number of shades of meaning, depending on the context in which the words are used. The following are some of the more important ones. However, before dealing with them, we should note that the word *psyche* as used in the Old Testament was used in classical Greek in the Homeric poems of the eighth and seventh centuries B.C. There it had the meaning of life, of the whole man and of the seat of the desires and of thought. In the Homeric poems the *psyche* was consistently represented as surviving after death as a ghost in a shadowy world. In the fifth and fourth centuries B.C., culminating in Plato, we begin to find the idea of the immortality of the soul being elaborated. Moreover, the association of *psyche* with *nephesh* in heathenism gave opportunity for its introduction, by semiconverted heathens, into Christian thought about the turn of the second and third centuries A.D. and then subsequently for reading back this meaning into the word *psyche* as it occurred in the New Testament. Thus we find the Septuagint follows the Hebrew, and the New Testament follows the Septuagint. This background is important, since it helps us understand how particular meanings of *soul* were introduced and firmly implanted in the Christian church. We now briefly list and indicate key references giving rise to the main usages and meanings attaching to the word *soul* in Scripture.

Soul (nephesh) *as meaning me or myself*

There are many uses of *nephesh* in the Old Testament and *psyche* in the New Testament where "my *nephesh*" equals "me" and "his *nephesh*" equals "him." Thus the word may be used with a proper noun so that, for example, "David's *nephesh*" would be equivalent to "David" or "David himself." In this sense the word is used more than 280 times in the Old Testament. For example, consider Genesis 27:19, where the AV reads, "Sit and eat of my venison, that thy *soul* may bless me." The NW reads, "Sit up and eat some of my game so that *you* may give me your blessing." Or again, note Leviticus 16:29, where the AV reads, "You shall afflict your *souls*"; the NIV reads, "You must deny *yourselves*"; in Numbers 16:38 the AV reads, "These sinners against their own *souls*," while the NIV reads, "Men who sin at the cost of their *lives*"; in Deuteronomy 14:26 the AV reads, "Whatsoever thy *soul* lusteth after"; the NIV, "Whatever *you* like." Or, for a final example, consider Isaiah 38:17, where the AV reads, "Thou hast in love of my *soul* delivered it from the pit of corruption," and the NIV renders it, "In your love you kept *me* from the pit of destruction." Note, incidentally, that the death from disease that Hezekiah was expecting in this passage was the death of his *soul*. In the New Testament there are twenty-four examples of the use of *psyche*, equivalent to the Hebrew *nephesh*, in this same sense, seven of which are quotations from the Old Testament.

The soul (nephesh) *associated with the emotions*

There are more than 120 Old Testament passages where the soul, the translation of *nephesh*, is connected with the desires or emotions. It is worth noting that in one instance the same is also said of an animal (Jer. 2:24). In addition there are twenty-one instances in the Old Testament where the word *soul* is added to the word *heart*. Close scrutiny of these passages points to the consensus that the common meaning is "with all my might and main." In the New Testament the word *psyche* appears on twelve occasions used in this same sense. As with *nephesh* in the Old Testament, here *psyche* indicates an inner aspect of a person but gives no hint that the *psyche* alone carries personality nor that it survives the body, nor that it is immortal.

Under this heading we may also consider those Old Testament references where mind and feelings are closely related. Such instances where mind and feelings are emphasized, rather than the whole person, amount to more than fifty occasions. Examples would be in Genesis 23:8, where the *nephesh* is the organ of resolve; Exodus 23:9, where feelings in general are mentioned; Leviticus 26:16, where the soul is the seat of sorrow; Deuteronomy 23:24, where it is the seat of desire; Judges

18:25, where it is the seat of anger; Proverbs 27:9, where it is seen as the origin of good counsel. In none of these instances, however, is there any justification for making such origins of specific feelings into separate things; rather, they focus on selected aspects of the unified person as required by the context of what is being discussed or described.

The use of the word nephesh *to mean what is commonly translated by the English word* life

There are more than 150 examples of this in the Old Testament, for example, in Exodus 21:30, where the AV reads, "He shall give for the ransom of his *life* whatsoever is laid upon him" and which the NIV renders, "If payment is demanded of *him*, he may redeem his life by paying whatever is demanded"; or, again, consider Isaiah 53:12, where the AV reads, "Because he hath poured out his *soul* unto death"; it is rendered in the NIV, "Because he hath poured out his *life* unto death." Notice, incidentally, that it is Christ's *soul* that dies on the cross. The equivalent of *psyche,* in the sense of life, is the most frequent use of the word in the New Testament, there being some forty-six instances. Here *psyche is* sometimes translated life, sometimes soul, and the basic meaning is of the person or the self. For example, consider Matthew 10:39, where we read in the NIV, "Whoever finds his life will lose it, and whoever loses his life for my sake will find it."

PROBLEM PASSAGES

1. Some problem passages are those associated with occurrences of the use of the word *psyche* in the New Testament meaning human being exactly in the same sense as the Hebrew *nephesh* in the Old Testament. One passage in particular is often problematic. In Matthew 10:28 we read, "Fear not them which kill the *body* but are not able to kill the *soul*: but rather fear him which is able to destroy both *soul* and *body* in hell." At face value this could certainly provide a proof text to argue for the survival of the separate soul at death. However, it is important to note that here to kill the body means to take the present life on earth. But this does not annihilate the person himself. It puts him to sleep in death. He is finally destroyed, according to other Scriptures, in the second death, when his person or self is killed forever.

In this regard, we may compare our Lord's declaration that Jairus's daughter was "not dead but asleep" (Matt. 9:24). She was actually dead (equivalent to kill the body) but as she was going to wake up she could rightly be said to be asleep (the word frequently used in Scripture to describe physical death). In this context, there is another seemingly problematic passage, Revelation 6:9, where souls are spoken of in a way that is often thought of as the disembodied spirits of the martyrs. However, in keeping with the whole of the Apocalypse these verses are most naturally interpreted as symbolic. The key to their meaning lies in Leviticus 17:14, where the soul is identified with the blood. The souls are the dead persons of the martyrs.

2. Another passage adduced to argue for the separate existence and natural immortality of the soul is Micah 6:7, where the prophet is rehearsing different views about what worshipers might render to God as they come before him. Having listed various alternatives in verse 6, he continues in verse 7: "Will the LORD be pleased with thousands of rams, or with ten thousands of rivers of oil? Shall I give my first-born for my transgression, the fruit of my *body* for the sin of my *soul?*" This contrast between body and soul is retained in the New International Version, which likewise reads, "Shall I offer my first-born for my transgression, the fruit of my *body* for the sin of my *soul?*" To understand this verse one first needs to note that the Hebrew language had no word for body and no conception of the body as a whole, only separate parts of the body. The nearest, to the body as a whole for the ancient Hebrew, was indeed *nephesh* and thus in Micah 6:7, the word translated *body* in fact means *belly* and thus the sin of my soul simply means my sin. In this sense, it would read, "Shall I offer my first-born for my transgression, the fruit of my *belly* for my sin?" This then becomes the familiar parallelism so often found in Scripture.

3. Another passage that may be problematic is 1 Kings 17:21–22. Here we have the account of the raising to life of the widow's son at Zarephath by Elijah the prophet. The AV renders this, "let this child's soul come into him again . . . and the soul of the child came into him again." It is informative to compare with this the NW, which reads, "let this boy's life return to him . . . and the boy's life returned to him." This is a clear example of where the word formerly translated *soul* should, in line with the other passages we have quoted, be rendered *life*; it is referring, not to a separate part of the child going away and coming back again, but rather that the boy dies and the boy comes to life again.

4. Another passage that for some has become the basis of a whole model of humankind, usually called a tripartite model, is 1 Thessalonians 5:23, which is rendered in the NIV, "May your whole spirit, soul and body be kept blameless at the coming of our Lord Jesus Christ." First, one should note the context. At the end of this letter the apostle is exhorting his readers to a sanctified life and thus he says, in the beginning of this verse, "May God himself, the God of peace, *sanctify you through and through.*" He wants his readers to be sanctified in *every* part. He then reinforces this

and emphasizes it yet again when he goes on, "May your whole spirit, soul and body be kept blameless at the coming of our Lord Jesus Christ." In understanding the meaning of this text we should first note that it would be dangerous to build a whole doctrine on this one verse, particularly a doctrine that is inconsistent with the whole thrust of the remainder of Scripture. Second, noting that it is Christians who are being addressed, the apostle has taught elsewhere that in this life, in the flesh, they are aware of two aspects of their nature, at times portrayed as two natures—the Adamic nature of their birth and the new spiritual nature of their rebirth. The former is called *soul*, and this is the *nephesh* of the Old Testament and the *psyche* of the New Testament, the *body* in the outward visible form of this Adamic nature. In this passage, as in Hebrews 4:12, the *psyche* stands in contrast to the *spirit*, a translation of the word *pneuma* that as yet we have not dealt with in detail. The same contrast is found. Thus we read, "The word of God . . . penetrates to the dividing of *soul* and *spirit*, joints and marrow." Set in their proper context these words mean that the study of the Scriptures will indeed show us which desires, aspirations, emotions, and thoughts lie on the old and sinful Adamic side of our nature and which on the regenerate side resulting from the new birth. In this regard it is instructive also to remember that in 1 Corinthians 2:14–15, we find the "natural man" and the "spiritual man" contrasted. Here the natural man is a translation of the word *psychikos* (the adjective from *psyche)* and means a man who only possesses *soul* and not *spirit* in the sense of a regenerate principle of life.

Our review thus far allows, we believe, three generalizations that are warranted by an examination of the uses of the word *nephesh* in the Old Testament and *psyche* in the New Testament, where it is normally translated *soul* in our English bibles. The first is that normally it is a way of referring to the whole person; the second is that on occasions it is used to accentuate or point to particular aspects of the functioning of the individual characterized by being linked with, for example, emotions or feelings. The third is that its most frequent use in the Old Testament is where *psyche* carries the meaning of life. There are more than forty instances of this in the New Testament; at times the word is translated *life*, and at times, *soul*, but the basic meaning is that of the person or the self, as, for example, in Matthew 10:39.

THE SPIRITUAL DIMENSION OF HUMANKIND

Just as we have seen that *psyche* in the New Testament corresponds normally to *nephesh* in the Hebrew of the Old Testament, similarly we find that *pneuma* in the New Testament corresponds to *ruagh* in the Hebrew of the Old Testament, and in both instances it is frequently translated by the word *spirit*. But what does this imply? Does it mean that there is another part of human nature and that spirit is distinguishable from the rest of the human person and is indeed a separate part?

Any discussion of the word *spirit* well illustrates the need to observe the approach to exegesis recommended earlier by John Stott. In his entry on spirit in the *New Bible Dictionary*, Dr. Dunn[9] begins by pointing out the basic range of meanings of the Hebrew *ruagh* and the Greek *pneuma*, which are translated *spirit* and which he says are more or less equally present. These include "1. Wind, an invisible, mysterious, powerful force 2. Breath or spirit, the same mysterious force seen as the life and vitality of man (and beasts) 3. Divine power, where *ruagh* is used to describe occasions when men seemed to be carried out of themselves, not just the surge of vitality, but a supernatural force taking possession." Each of these, he stresses, represents a point on a spectrum of meanings that develop and change from pre-Christian usage into Christian usage in the Gospels and Epistles. For our present limited purposes here we stress once again that our concern is with those passages and meanings most directly relevant to helping us understand the biblical account of the composite nature of human personality.

The basic elementary meaning of *ruagh* is *wind*. As in the case of *nephesh*, so in the case of *ruagh*, we find it possessed by both humans and animals (Gen. 6:17; 7:15, 22; Eccles. 3:21). It also appears in a very familiar passage in the Psalms. In Psalm 31:5, we read, "Into thine hand I commit my spirit." These words spoken by our Lord on the cross say that he entrusted to God his human spirit, the principle of life that he possessed as a man, so that it could be restored to him in resurrection. Or, in similar vein, in Psalm 104:29–30, we read, "Thou takest away their breath (*ruagh*), they die, and return to the dust. Thou sendest forth thy spirit (*ruagh*), they are created." Or again in Psalm 146:4, "His [i.e. man's] breath (*ruagh*) goeth forth, he returneth to his earth"—man's spirit, the principle that makes him a living being and keeps him alive, is taken from him at death.

It is this same life principle that is referred to in Genesis 2:7. There we have been told that man is made of the dust of the ground and then that "the breath of life" is given; it is a life principle issuing from the Lord God. It is used in this way at least twenty times in the Old Testament to refer to the life principle inbreathed by God; it is also noteworthy that in two passages animals are included as well as man (Gen. 7:22; Ps. 150:6). Breath and spirit in many of these passages are essentially parallels, as in Job 34:14 ("He withdrew his spirit and breath").

There is another theme in the meaning and usage of the word *ruagh* also evident in Scripture. We find that the Hebrew Scriptures attach great importance and significance to an intangible quality that is captured in the *ruagh* or *spirit* of a person.

The Hebrew writers note that a man's quality is, in a sense, more than the sum total of his actions and that he sometimes acts other than in the manner the circumstances surrounding him would lead one to expect. This intangible quality is labeled the *ruagh* or spirit in the Old Testament. While the word often denotes God's quality (the "spirit" of God), it can be applied also to heathen man (Deut. 2:30; 2 Chron. 21:16 RV). It can also be equated with character, in our sense of the word, that is, the quality we associate with a person, his wisdom or his folly, his humility or his pride. It is this spirit that shows what man is truly like and so, by implication, what the source of inspiration for his living must be (see, e.g., Prov. 20:27).

It should be noted that the Old Testament seems to know nothing of a purely intellectual response to life. The Word of God speaks to and is written on the heart; it is never given simply as academic information. From this it might follow that the scientific quality of objectivity, which we prize so highly, finds little place in Old Testament thought. Moreover, the response that a man makes to events and circumstances of any kind, whether he is considering kindness or persecution shown by others, or viewing the creation in which he lives and of which he is a part, is never regarded in the Old Testament as a dispassionate activity, but is seen as a total involvement, a total reaction, whether of anger or of worship.

We noted that corresponding to *ruagh* in the Old Testament is *pneuma* in the New Testament. As well as referring to the life principle, the word *pneuma* is also often used simply to describe a person. There are, for example, more than two hundred instances where it refers to the Holy Spirit and fifty-six instances where it denotes a person. Most of these, interestingly enough, are references to evil spirits and occur in the Synoptic Gospels and the Acts of the Apostles. All three persons of the Trinity are at times referred to as Spirit. Thus, in John 4:24, God the Father is referred to as spirit ("God is a spirit"); in 1 Corinthians 15:45, Christ is referred to as spirit ("The first man Adam became a living being [*psyche*]; the last Adam a life-giving spirit [*pneuma*]"). And in yet other instances the references are clearly to God, the Holy Spirit.

There are several instances in the New Testament where the word *pneuma* carries the meaning of life principle in the same way that *ruagh* does in the Old Testament—for example, in Matthew 27:50 and in James 2:26, where we read, "As the body without the spirit is dead, so faith without deeds is dead."

There is yet another meaning of *pneuma* in the New Testament and this is when it refers to the regenerate nature. There are twenty-nine such occurrences. Here it combines the sense of *pneuma* as a life principle with that of its disposition or character. The new nature is certainly a new life principle; it is an essentially moral life principle. It is in itself a holy disposition or character.

As in the case of *nephesh* and *psyche*, so in the case of *pneuma* there are seemingly problematic proof texts. One often quoted is 2 Corinthians 7:1. Here we read, "Let us purify ourselves from everything that contaminates *body* and *spirit*, perfecting holiness out of reverence for God." Here, the apostle is exhorting believers to holiness and to the avoidance of all defilement in things of the flesh, by which he means immorality, and in the things of the spirit, by which he means false religion. There is certainly no need to reify the spirit on the basis of this text.

We thus find that of all the instances where *ruagh* and *pneuma* occur, only a handful could be construed as supporting the idea of the spirit surviving the body. These would include Ecclesiastes 12:7, where the spirit is said, at death, to go back to God who gave it. Others are Luke 23:46 and Act 7:59, where the spirit at death is commended into the hands of God. When these texts are set alongside all the others that show that the spirit is a life principle breathed into man to make him alive and conscious and that it was certainly not conscious when it was given to man, we can see that there is no warrant whatever for supposing it to be conscious when it returns to God. Its return simply means that God takes a man's life away.

In conclusion, we must note a further word that appears in reference to the nature of humankind, namely, the heart. The Hebrew and Greek words translated *heart* are not used in Scripture in connection with the creation of man, as are *nephesh* and *ruagh*. There are, however, some passages that seem to imply, certainly in the AV, a possible separate existence for the heart. So, for example, in Psalm 22:26, the AV has "Your heart shall live forever." This same verse is rendered in the NIV "May your hearts live forever." While some may wish to argue that these are grounds for some sort of proof of natural immortality for all individuals, however, before drawing such a conclusion one should note first that the passage in question is concerned with the "meek" and with "they that seek the Lord"; second, the expression *your heart* is in fact frequently used in the Psalms to mean simply "you." It seems clear that the heart is the deepest aspect of the human function—what in the past might have been described as the seat of the will and conscience. Certainly, as in the above case, at times the heart means simply the person himself or herself. Thus in 1 Thessalonians 3:13 we read, "May he strengthen your hearts so that you will be blameless and holy in the presence of our God." The meaning and sense here is simply may he strengthen *you* so that you will be blameless, and so on.

CONCLUDING COMMENTS

Our reason for offering these brief biblical cameos of human nature is the renewed interest in human nature currently stimulated by scientific advances in psychology, neuroscience, ethology, genetics, and cognate disciplines. Each of them, with their specialized tools and approaching a common problem at different levels of analysis, continues to shed new light on the mystery of what it means to be human.

We do not claim, nor do we pretend, to have decisively resolved an ongoing discussion and debate among fellow Christians about the issues raised in this chapter. We recognize that the differing views represented, for example, by Bruce Reichenbach[10] and John Cooper[11] will continue to be debated. Our concern has been to help the typical psychology student, faced with courses that imply and demonstrate the ever-tightening link among mind, brain, and behavior. We believe the way in which recent translations of the Scriptures have changed the use of the word *soul* and how biblical scholars have been at pains to warn us away from some earlier translations that tended to reify the soul, the spirit, and other aspects of personhood talked about in Scripture is noteworthy. The seeds of a conflict between the emerging scientific picture of humankind and some traditional Christian ones are already sown. If they take root and flourish, they may generate unreal and unnecessary conflicts for the average pew dweller who hears the sound bite on science and current affairs programs and who reads popular science reports in newspapers and magazines. We hope that our discussion here will also help them be prepared to reconsider the biblical evidence and, if we are correct, see that reinterpreted, comparing Scripture with Scripture, it produces a portrait of human nature complementary to and not in necessary conflict with the emerging scientific picture.

When we turn to consider the Christian view of human nature, we are warned immediately by biblical scholars that as we examine statements in the Bible that seem to be relevant to this issue we are entering an exegetical minefield. Biblical scholars point out that the precise meaning of the words used by different authors in the canon of Scripture vary, as do the cultural contexts within which they were writing. They also remind us that today, in the Western world, we are richly indebted to the brilliance of Greek thinkers who had strong views on human nature. These Hellenistic influences have, down through the centuries, had a powerful impact on the development of Christian theology. It calls for constant vigilance, therefore, to remain aware of and sensitive to such influences. As we saw earlier, this is particularly the case as one begins to consider the meaning of, for example, the soul. We are also warned by theologians and biblical scholars that at any particular epoch in the history of the Christian church the prevailing theological climate may have an explicit or implicit influence on new translations of the Scriptures made at that time. The AV of the Bible in English is no exception to that kind of influence.

One of the principal aims of our brief survey was to highlight the fact that the word commonly translated *soul* in the older English versions such as the AV has now, in recent translations, disappeared and, with that, the implication that the soul is some separate entity that is somehow built into, tagged on to, or constitutes a separate part of, the human person, is no longer tenable. Quite often it simply means "I myself' or "he himself," the kind of usage we encounter frequently, for example, in the Psalms. Again we noticed that a careful examination of *all* the relevant Scriptures soon makes it clear that nonhuman animals are souls just as much as are human beings. We saw that in the early Genesis narratives the *soul* refers to living beings and this applied equally to fish, foul, and four-footed creatures as well as to human beings. We also noted a fascinating parallel in the way that "the coming into existence" of living beings, referred to in the Bible as being "God-breathed," or the conferring of "a life principle," is taken up again in the pictures given about what happens at death. Thus we find that in the case of persons, at death, "the life principle," "the spirit" returns to God. It is taken from the organism and again this applies equally to animals and to humans in the accounts given in Scripture.

One central and dominant view found in Scripture is of the unity of humankind. The human person is a unified being who manifests several different aspects of his nature as he lives and acts. In this regard, we find different words used, words such as *heart.* Several different and important functional aspects of humankind are thus identified by different writers in Scripture, depending on the context. What distinguishes humankind from other living creatures is first the clear teaching that in some profound sense humankind is made in the image of God. Again, we must watch out that we do not immediately seize on this and assume that, for example, it means that man is immortal or has an immortal soul. There is no more warrant for doing this than there is for assuming that we share with God his omniscience or omnipotence. As we saw, the clear teaching of Scripture is against any doctrine of the natural immortality of the soul of humankind. One of the aspects of man that is distinctive is related to the specific teaching of Genesis, reiterated elsewhere in Scripture, that man is called on to be a responsible steward of

God's creation. He is to subdue it, to rule over the fish of the sea and the birds of the air and over every living creature that moves on the ground, but this is to be seen as balanced by the delegated authority of a responsible steward. We are indeed accountable to God.

This same theme is reiterated in, for example, Psalm 8, in the form of the question, What is man? And elsewhere in the Old Testament the question is repeated in various forms, but it is ultimately answered only in the New Testament with reference to Christ. It is Christ who is "made a little lower than the angels" and it is he who is "now crowned with glory and honour because he suffered death" (Heb. 2:6–9). Ultimately the answer to the question of what man is can be discerned only in Christ. There can be no truly authentic knowledge of human nature independent of what is disclosed to us in Christ, the perfect man. In this century aspects of this theme have been reiterated most strongly by Karl Barth, who speaks of Jesus as the revelation both of the real man which we are and of the true man which we are not. He would argue that the person of Jesus Christ alone is the determinative source of any valid theological anthropology. The true goal and nature of human life can be discerned primarily by studying him and only secondarily in ourselves.

The precise identity of the *image* in describing humankind as made in the image of God continues to be an issue of lively debate in Christian thought and doctrine. Perhaps the whole idea of the image of God should not be thought of in static or individualistic terms but rather in functional terms, in terms of relatedness. Thus, men and women are called in Christ *to be* the image of the eternal in the relatedness of the Trinity (John 17:21–23).

One feature of our brief examination of the relevant Scriptures has emphasized repeatedly that the Christian's hope for the future is not bound up with any idea of possessing a natural immortal soul but that our hope is fully embedded in the doctrine of the resurrection. As one author wrote, "The Gospels' testimony to the resurrection appearances of Jesus implies that the future resurrection body will exist as a physical phenomenon with physical continuity." Paul, however, refers to this resurrection body in 1 Corinthians 15:44 and following as a "spiritual body" in contrast to a "natural body." In this he suggests a degree of physical discontinuity as well as continuity. In this sense the final resurrection will be a divine creative act just as much as our originally coming into existence is ultimately seen as due to God's gracious creative act. In this regard we remember again that the great creeds of the Christian church all emphasize the doctrine of the resurrection and say nothing of any doctrine of natural immortality.

Bringing together the Old and New Testament emphases, we may summarize the main features of the Hebrew-Christian view of man as follows. It enshrines a message for individuals in all generations. It tells man what his calling is, what his nature is, and what his destiny is. He is called to worship and honor his Creator, to exercise stewardship over the creation as a loving, obedient son to a father, to enjoy fellowship with his Father Creator, while standing in awe of him as a creature to his Creator. He is encouraged to recognize the manysidedness of his mysterious nature. He must hold in a delicate balance three aspects of his nature highlighted by Old and New Testament writers alike: his physical makeup; his capacity for mental life; and his capacity for making moral decisions, including an appreciation for the importance of a spiritual dimension to life. Working harmoniously together these are involved in maintaining a right relationship with God and with men.

A man's destiny depends on how he responds to his Creator's invitation to enter into his spiritual inheritance. To do so he must recognize and accept his Creator's diagnosis of his true condition: that he is by nature and inclination a sinner—an unpalatable truth. He must accept that his Creator is also his Redeemer and that there is a remedy to match his diagnosis—a remedy, moreover, which is yet another expression of the love of his Creator, the one who "loved the world so much that he gave his only Son, that everyone who has faith in him may not die but have eternal life." In short, a man's true destiny is union with Christ. And that means fullness of life now and continuing life after physical death.

TAKING STOCK

1. The biblical account is, in a very profound sense, a timeless view. It made sense to our forebears long before science appeared; it said important things about them relevant to their daily living. That alone should warn us against misconstruing it today by trying to impose on its vocabulary a precision, familiar to us today within science, which it was never intended to have. We discover that its main concern is with what God thinks about man. It has little interest in one man's analysis of another man's nature. It is a God-centered view and is preoccupied with relationships—first and foremost the relationship of God to man but also of person to person and of humankind to the created order, of which he is both a part and a steward. It thus provides advice and enduring truths on how to live our lives day by day.

2. It is abundantly clear that the various terms used to talk about man in the Bible, and there are many, are not those we find in contemporary sci-

ence. It does not talk about species, it talks about people; it is not biological, it is biographical. It is not concerned with the properties of human beings, whether physiological, biochemical, or psychological (in the scientific sense), but with how individuals act in history. It is also evident that a variety of accounts, pictures, models, whatever we choose to call them, are given to us in the library of books that make up the Bible. Each enriches the other and sheds new light on the common themes and as such each amplifies what is given elsewhere.

3. From the variety of pictures given, certain common features are detectable. From the opening pages of Scripture there is a contrast between man as very firmly a part of creation and as distinguished from all other living things since he alone has the capacity to have fellowship with his Creator, who walks with them in the cool of the day (Gen. 3:8–9). Man is made from the dust of the ground (Gen. 2:7) and, like other living creatures, he becomes a living creature (Gen. 2:8). His creatureliness is highlighted over and over again: "you are from dust and you will return to dust," or, as the psalmist put it, "He knows how we were made, He knows full well that we are dust" (Ps. 103:14). We are reminded never to forget our intrinsic mortality. "God alone is immortal," says the apostle Paul to the Corinthian Christians (1 Cor. 15:53). And he reminds Timothy that "God only hath immortality" (1 Tim. 6:16).

4. In trying to fill out something of the mystery of what it is to be a human being, the Old Testament writers identify several aspects of personhood. They emphasize that man is physically alive, a living creature, a tangible material being. In this context the word *soul* is frequently used. Even so, the many different ways in which it is used seem to defy any attempt to give it a precise definition and consistent usage. The biblical writers are primarily concerned with the way in which human beings act and react to one another; what happens when men become weary, when they become covetous, when riches are denied. There is a key aspect of man that may be loosely defined as the spiritual aspect. This very important intangible quality gives man his special significance. It seems that if you can say something about this aspect of a man, you reveal something of what he is really like; you say what it is that inspires him for his daily living. Know what people set their hearts on and you know a good deal about their essential character, their spiritual dimension.

5. The New Testament presents a more extensive treatment of man and his nature. But that does not mean that a more precise model can be constructed. The words used there carry different meanings in different con-

texts and in the hands of different authors. Like the Old Testament, the New Testament emphasizes the unity of man. Man is a psychophysical or somatopsychic unity. Moreover, he is a unity, in this present earthly life and in some new form in the new heavens and the new earth to which he looks forward.

In the New Testament, as in the Old, the spiritual aspect of man receives extensive treatment. But, again, spirituality is not an abstract quality. True, it is in part revealed in what a person says he believes about God and about his fellow humans, what he claims are his goals in life. Equally it shows in what he endows with greatest worth, and what he shows are his moral priorities. It is embodied in what he does, how he treats other people, how he treats the created universe. In a sense, just as we saw that mental activity or the mind is embodied in the physical workings of the brain, so the spiritual aspect of a person is embodied in his activities as a mind–brain unity.

Commenting on past debates about the spiritual aspect of a person in the Christian tradition, the authors[12] of *What Then Is Man?* wrote (319), helpfully, "The word spirit is used over and over in the sense of what might be termed the operational content and direction of man's thoughts, words and actions. . . . Spirit, then, is a fruit, an outcome of the individual's life and experience." They went on: "If spirit is regarded as a functional outcome rather than a separate structural entity, the difficult and troublesome trichotomy theory becomes entirely unnecessary."

In similar vein a more recent book by Dallas Willard[13] contains the following paragraph: "Spirituality in human beings is not an extra or 'superior' mode of existence. It's not a hidden stream of separate reality, a separate life running parallel to our bodily existence. It does not consist in special 'inward' acts even though it has an inner aspect. It is, rather, a relationship of our embodied selves to God that has the natural and irrepressible effect of making us alive to the Kingdom of God—here and now in the material world" (31).

6. Humankind is not as God created it. An event described as the fall occurred in which humankind's filial obedience to God turned to disobedience. Seen in this way the fall is interpreted primarily as a break in the relationships of God, man, and nature. We remember the Bible's account of Adam and Eve being excluded from God's presence and death being introduced into the world—death that "reigned from Adam" (Rom. 5:12–14). It is important to note, however, that physically Adam and Eve lived on outside Eden and produced a family. The fall is conventionally described as having "marred" or "obscured" God's image, which can be restored in Christ. But our physical existence has continued without interruption despite the fact that unredeemed humankind has been

"dead in trespasses and sins" since then. Thus, while biological and spiritual life can be distinguished from each other, we must be careful not to overemphasize this possibility, since they are part of a whole.

The rich fabric of the total picture given to us in Scripture brings to mind the similarly rich complexity of the total picture of human nature given to us through the scientific endeavor today. Both emphasize the complexity of human nature, the need to understand and study it from many diverse aspects or perspectives, and the need to recognize that essentially human nature is a unity—a unity now in this present life and, by the grace of God, a unity in the life to come.

CHAPTER 7

HUMAN NATURE
AND ANIMAL NATURE

Are They Different?

It is dangerous to show man too clearly how much he
resembles the beast, without at the same time showing
him his greatness. It is also dangerous to allow too clear
a vision of his greatness without his baseness. It is even
more dangerous to leave him in ignorance of both.
—Blaise Pascal, *Pensées*, 1659

IN CHAPTER 3 we examined the evidence pointing to an ever-tightening
link between mind and brain, noting the trends from research in neuropsychology. In that regard, it is worth remembering that while a substantial amount of neuropsychological research is carried out on
brain-damaged patients and normal people, an equally important seg-
ment of research continues to be carried out on animals, most often rats,
cats, and monkeys. In humans, for obvious ethical reasons, our understanding of the effects of changes in the structure of the brain on mental
life and behavior depends on studying the consequences of brain damage
due to genetic factors or through brain damage occurring before, at, or
after birth. While the techniques available for locating brain damage in
patients have made enormous leaps and bounds in the past three decades, there remains a measure of uncertainty about the precise location
and extent of any damage. That uncertainty can only be resolved if and
when there is a post-mortem examination. This is one reason why work
on nonhuman primates has proved so important. With careful surgery it
is possible to produce circumscribed localized changes in the brains of

nonhuman primates and then study differences between preoperative and post-operative performance on a variety of experimental tasks given to the animals. Carrying out such studies helps reduce the uncertainties that remain if we only study accidentally brain-injured people.

Underlying the use of animals is a tacit assumption that the results of such studies, while interesting in themselves, throw further light on the understanding of human mind–brain links. That assumption makes further tacit assumptions about similarities between the brains of humans and the brains of animals. This is not new in psychology. For decades the understanding of human conditioning and learning has been driven to a considerable extent by carefully controlled studies on animals. Classic examples are Kohler's work during the First World War with nonhuman primates and Skinner's studies of classical and operant conditioning using rats. Both of these, of course, were preceded by Pavlov's work on classical conditioning using dogs. The question naturally arises, What, if any, wider implications does this have for our understanding of human nature as compared with animal nature?

As one begins to interpret these findings, undisclosed presuppositions and metaphysical beliefs built into the design of the studies emerge. One such area of research that has received wide publicity in recent years is sociobiology, now recast as "evolutionary psychology." There are, however, other important areas like neurogenetics, the results of which have at times been widely misinterpreted, often in ways so as to justify preconceptions about, for example, the biological bases of behaviors such as homosexuality and extreme aggression in humans. Our task now is to review the evidence pertaining to the similarities and differences between animal and human nature and to ask what such similarities might imply for our understanding of human nature. In doing so we shall have in mind also those beliefs we may hold as Christians about animal and human nature, their shared properties and their differences.

HUMAN AND ANIMAL NATURE

As we noted in our general review of the landscape of contemporary psychology, the study of animals continues to loom large in several of its most active subdisciplines. The traditional interests that comparative psychologists have in animal behavior have been extended by ethologists, primatologists, and evolutionary psychologists. Animals make possible, under more controlled conditions than is possible with humans, the investigation of processes such as conditioning, learning, perceiving, and remembering. Scientists are also intrinsically interested in how, for example, animals from different phyla possessing nervous systems of increasing complexity reflect this in changes in behavior, both instinctive and learned. The brilliant work of ethologists like Konrad Lorenz, Karl von Frisch, and William Thorpe helped psychologists break free from the straitjacket imposed by some earlier generations, who tended to focus rather narrowly on conditioning, maze learning, escape from puzzle boxes, and the like. It is encouraging to see that most recently some psychologists and primatologists, such as Richard Byrne and Andrew Whiten, have set the pace in studying the development of social intelligence in animals and of what they claim is evidence of "mind reading" in nonhuman primates.

At the same time, other psychologists with a primary interest in how brain processes mediate cognition and behavior continue to use animals widely in their neuropsychological research. One important reason why such research has proved so revealing about human brain functioning is the strong similarities between features of the human brain and features of the nonhuman primate's brain. Even so, we need to recognize that those who conduct research in these areas, while often sharing common research objectives, scientific training, and skills, are as diverse in their personal metaphysical beliefs, ideologies, and hidden agendas, whatever one chooses to call them, as any other group of scientists or nonscientists. When it comes to interpreting the results of their research, they sometimes differ widely; if they start as materialist reductionists they will present humankind as "nothing but" exceptionally complex primates; others, while not adopting a Christian position, will still write readily about the "uniqueness" of humankind, though each may attribute such uniqueness to a different aspect of human cognition and behavior. Yet others, starting from Christian presuppositions, will recognize the many similarities of humans with nonhuman primates while noting the significant differences.

Whatever the metaphysics of the investigators, they share the belief that the study of the similarities and differences of brain and behavior between humans and other animals is an important scientific issue in its own right. Much of the value of research in neuroscience and in the specialized field of neuropsychology depends on making legitimate deductions from experiments on animals in tackling problems of human disease, cognition, and behavior. We already make extensive use of animal models in studies aimed at a better understanding of Parkinson's disease, an understanding which, it is hoped, will help in devising ways of alleviating the suffering of Parkinson's patients. For example, recent work on neural tissue transplants, developed on animals, has been extended, with limited success, to humans. It is crucial, therefore, to have as securely based an assessment as possible of the similarities and differences between humans and animals.

Similarities and Differences between Animals and Humans—What Do They Signify?

In his 1974 Gifford lectures, the late professor W. H. Thorpe[1] listed a number of abilities which, so it had been confidently asserted forty years earlier, animals would never be able to show. His list included the following: Animals could not learn, they could not plan ahead, they could not conceptualize, they could not use tools, they have no language, they cannot count, they lack artistic sense, and they lack all ethical sense. Today, in light of the evidence gathered by ethologists and psychologists, it would be very difficult to defend any item on this list. That was the view that Thorpe himself took in his Gifford lectures.

On the question of whether language is the crucial feature separating humans from animals, Thorpe wrote, "Personally I believe it is safe to conclude that if chimpanzees had the necessary equipment in the larynx and pharynx, they could learn to talk, at least as well as children of three years of age and perhaps older." Today, that view would be contested by some but it gives the flavor of the strength of his conviction at that time. He went on to make other strong claims, and, while noting that when used by humans language is propositional, syntactic, and expressive of intention, he pointed out that all these features can be found separately, and at least to some degree, in the animal kingdom. Even so he concludes that "there comes a point where more creates a difference, *quantity* produces *a qualitative* difference," thus foreshadowing the point made later by Hinde.

More recently, writing in *The Oxford Companion to the Mind*, Robert Hinde[2] (also at Cambridge) expressed a similar view. He concluded that the main difference between animals and humans lies in the complexity of human language. He believed that animal communication falls so far short of human language that the difference is best seen as one of *quality* rather than *quantity*. He also takes the view that animal models can provide data relevant to human behavior and experience and that the similarities and differences between animals and humans can be usefully exploited. No doubt he had in mind some of the collaborative work he had carried out with his wife Joan Stevenson-Hinde. The results of their careful studies on animals and humans have led to a better understanding of the effects of the social and interpersonal environment on behavior and the functions of the brain.

Working on both rhesus monkeys and humans, Hinde conducted a series of studies to assess the effects of early relationships. Some years before Hans Kosterlitz had demonstrated the importance of naturally occurring opiates in the human body, the so-called endogenous opiates, and Hinde and his co-workers investigated the possible importance of these substances for the development of mother–infant relationships. Their working hypothesis was that one of those endogenous opiates, the brain's beta-endorphin-containing system, provided a reward for social behavior. They proposed that either underactivation or overactivation of this system, due to social and environmental circumstances, may have effects on the infant's bond with its mother and may also have long-term consequences for the development of the infant's relationship with its peers. They showed that social interactions of monkeys had significant consequences for beta-endorphin in the cerebrospinal fluid (CSF) of the animals studied and that the levels in CSF could be related to the behavior of individual animals. They showed that although a multiplicity of functions can be attributed to the brain's beta-endorphin system, nevertheless they all have in common behavioral reward. They showed that social interaction not only acquires the status of rewarding behavior, but in so doing carries with it the risk of disruption of this system in the event of social breakdown, and with that a series of malfunctions may occur to primary motivated behavior, such things as sexual behavior, feeding, and maternal behavior.

With children the influence of close relationships on individual development has been the subject of intensive study for many years. Stevenson-Hinde's own studies had already demonstrated links between shyness and the interactions going on in a family. The essential point of these kinds of studies is that they point to an intimate relationship between the behavior of the organism (in this case, the mother–infant link) and the infant's link with other infants, and the naturally occurring chemicals in the brain. Where, for example, there has been stress resulting from the infant being separated from the mother, it has been shown, in guinea pigs and puppies, that the administration of opiates can alleviate this stress. Conversely, other studies using rodents and dogs have reported that blocking of opiate receptors in the brain interferes with normal maternal behavior and disrupts pup retrieval behavior, characteristic of rodents and dogs. In addition, it has been shown in monkeys that the beta-endorphin system is actually activated by social grooming.

For the purposes of our present discussion, the take-home message from the studies of Robert Hinde, his wife Joan Stevenson-Hinde, and others like them is that something so seemingly unphysiological as social interaction between mother and infant, and between infant and infant, can produce changes in the biochemical substrates of brain function that have both short-term and possibly long-lasting consequences. Moreover, these longer-lasting consequences can, it seems, in some situations, be reversed by the administration of the depleted beta-endorphins. The animal studies, for example, make it clear that when an infant is separated from its mother and emits distress calls, these can be reduced by administering opiate agonists or made more intense by administering opiate antagonists.

Brain Structure and Specialized Functions

An area of contemporary psychology where inferences about human behavior and cognition depends on the validity of comparisons between animals and humans is neuropsychology. In 1984, Professor George Ettlinger[3] wrote a paper entitled "Humans, Apes and Monkeys: The Changing Neuropsychological Viewpoint." He argued that "the majority (of neuropsychologists) would . . . agree . . . that, within the primates brain size (relative to body weight) increased suddenly with the emergence of modern man; that a large mass of brain tissue endowed man with a stepwise superior intelligence; and that language followed from man's superior intelligence." One implication from Ettlinger's presentation is that intellectual capacity increased only slowly within the primates until, at some stage related to the emergence of the modern human, a totally new skill—for human language—evolved. That language, in turn, allowed man to gain intellectual preeminence and to devise technologies and cultures. Ettlinger further argues that "in man, language has more than a communicative role—it also organizes the representation of information *within* one individual's mind. It has yet to be shown that language-competent apes can solve any of the kind of cognitive problems more proficiently than can non-trained apes. By contrast, aphasic patients can be shown to be impaired on a variety of cognitive tasks." His conclusion about language-competent apes, while a fair representation of research in 1984, may need revision today in the light of some of David Premack's findings.

Ettlinger's review showed how, within a twenty-year period, there emerged a fresh recognition and wide acceptance of the relevance of neuropsychological research using monkeys to address issues in human neuropsychology. As such, it is an object lesson that illustrates well the mistakes that occurred in the past when, for whatever reason, people tried to either think up differences between animals and humans they believed would remain unchallenged for all time, or claimed, without evidence, that similarities in brain structure seemed so close that they could assert that ultimately no clear distinction was possible between animals and humans. More recently, as we shall see in a moment, others such as Richard Byrne, also noting the sudden increase in brain size in man related to body weight, links it with the emergence of social intelligence.

Brain Anatomy, Intelligence, and Language

It is salutary to recall how, in 1858, Richard Owen, in his exchanges with Huxley and seeking from the highest motives to defend human dignity, argued for humanity's uniqueness on the grounds that "the great ape does not possess a hippocampus minor." His attempt we now see as misplaced. But the questions posed then remain relevant today. The best reference work for those wishing to pursue this topic in detail is Richard Passingham's 1986 book *The Human Primate*.[4] He begins by saying that "anatomically we differ from the apes much more extensively than would have been supposed from the similarity of the DNA and many proteins. The difference in size between the human and the chimpanzee brain is greater than the difference between the brains of the chimpanzee and the shrew." Thus, if you are looking for a way of asserting the uniqueness of man, you might grasp at this quotation. But be warned: As you read on in Passingham, the story changes. He raises the question, "What is the distinctiveness of the brain of humans?" and suggests that there are three different ways we can consider this: first, in terms of size; second, in terms of the relative proportions assigned to particular functions in the brain; and third, whether there are specialized areas in human brains not found in other brains.

We shall examine each of these briefly. As far as size, at once certain facts become obvious. Elephants and whales have much bigger brains than we have. So sheer size isn't very good grounds from which to argue the uniqueness of *Homo sapiens*.

Consider for a moment the typical primate. Passingham plots brain weight against body weight and comes up with a regression line for the nonhuman primates. Against this line the human brain is 3.1 times as big as we might expect for a nonhuman primate of identical weight. On the basis of this, you may therefore say that we are indeed special creatures. The human brain is unique in terms of overall size in relation to body weight. If size alone is important, there are grounds for asserting difference. But there are other ways of thinking about a typical primate brain.

You may ask, "Is there anything special about the *proportions* of the brain assigned to different functions, such as areas that receive sensory information or control motor output? Regarded in this way, is there anything special about our brains as compared to the typical primate brain?" Looked at this way, Passingham concludes, "The human brain seems to fit very nicely the typical primate brain." However, he makes a further important point. To say that differences are predictable—that is, predictable from the model of a typical primate brain—is *not* to say that they are unimportant. The question then becomes, Is our brain just an expanded brain of another primate, such as a chimpanzee? This returns us to the question of the distinctiveness of the human brain. Is there one and, if so, what is its nature?

Passingham points out that there are two specializations that are often said to be unique to the human brain: cerebral asymmetries and the existence of "speech areas" in the neocortex. Two areas of the brain, the cerebellum and the neocortex, are largely responsible for associating information that comes from other parts of the brain as a system. These areas in the human brain are roughly three times the size they should be for a typical primate of our size. The cerebellum is about two and a half times as big as it should be for a brain of human size. On these grounds, Passingham concludes that the gap between man and chimpanzee is probably much greater than we had earlier supposed. Thus, specialization does provide some clue to a difference between humans and animals.

To sum up Passingham's contribution: There are four conclusions to be drawn when you study brain structure having in mind the question, How does the nonhuman primate differ from the human primate? First, many of the distinctively human features can be derived simply by following the rules governing the anatomy of other primates. If you ask, "What is a typical primate brain like?" and you follow these rules, you get the human primate. Second, Passingham thinks that the case for man's uniqueness rests on language, invention, conscience, and free will. For some of these it is difficult to know what sort of evidence you would appeal to in order to establish that a nonhuman primate did not have them. It is not clear to me what constitutes evidence that a monkey does not have free will. Passingham further points out that the account he gives lacks mystery. It attributes the peculiarly human form of mental life to relatively simple changes in the human brain. Finally, he says that in his view it is without doubt language that has led to the transformation of society. Rules can be issued by means of it, strategies can be discussed, roles can be laid down, traditions can be passed on.

Clearly for Passingham, the crucial difference is language. For that reason I think we have to reflect a little more on just what we mean when we talk about language. As far as Passingham is concerned, he doesn't simply mean communication, because right across the animal phyla animals communicate subtly and elegantly with one another. It is not simply communication that Passingham has in mind; rather, it is that aspect of language that enables us to handle not just symbols—chimps and apes can do that—but to represent words to ourselves, to manipulate *internal* symbols. It is this aspect of symbolic behavior conferred by language that he believes is the crucial difference between humankind and nonhuman primates and in this regard he reaches a very similar conclusion to that of Ettlinger.

The wisdom of the conclusions drawn by Passingham and Ettlinger is underlined by the more recent results of studies on animals designed to investigate the hypothesis that one aspect of language, auditory temporal processing, regarded as a precursor to speech processing, may be in evidence in species other than man. Moreover, in the species studied it is also found as a left hemisphere specialization.

Some researchers have identified left hemisphere specialization for the discrimination of species-typical calls in monkeys and mice, results that have been interpreted as evidence of left hemisphere specialization for communicative information processing. Other researchers, however, have called this interpretation into question, pointing out that monkeys exhibit left hemisphere specialization for performing complex auditory discriminations of stimuli that have no communicative relevance. They have found that the key information used by monkeys in discriminating species-typical calls is peak frequency position, a specifically temporal cue. Putting these findings together they point to left hemisphere specialization for auditory temporal processing in species other than man and that it is this mechanism that is critical to the discrimination of both coo calls in monkeys and ultrasonic noise bursts in mice. Further details of this research are not appropriate to cover here, but they are relevant for two reasons. First, they support the critical importance of a basic, nonlingual process—auditory temporal processing—to the existence of left hemisphere specialization for language processing in humans, and suggest that critical precursors to this function can be found in other species. Second, the identification of neural mechanisms for this critical function in an animal model provides the opportunity for asking questions that cannot easily be addressed in human subjects. If this way of approaching the problem turns out to be correct, then the evolutionary hypothesis that auditory temporal processing represents a precursor of speech processing adds further understanding to the way in which human cognitive processes may have developed. They do not, of themselves, deny the points made by Passingham and Ettlinger concerning the aspect of symbolic behavior conferred by language as being crucial to the differences we now observe between humankind and nonhuman primates. It may well be that with increased complexity of the neural networks in humans there has been a phase change that makes possible this property of symbolic behavior.

More recently, Richard Byrne,[5] examining evidence similar to Passingham's, and acknowledging his indebtedness to Passingham's book, presents the same data in a slightly different way. His focus is whether there are any precursors to ethical behavior that are found in extant nonhuman primates. He is careful to point out, however, that "this is not to claim any ethical appreciation in the primate species" (108). Like Passingham, Byrne points out that since larger animals have larger brains, simple comparisons of sheer brain size are not very informative. In most mammals much of the brain is taken up with sensory and motor processes. Moreover, as the absolute size of living things changes, so the relative proportions of their parts are liable to change. Thus, absolutely larger animals have relatively smaller brains than one would expect from linear extrapolations from smaller animals. Byrne notes that one technique that tries to take account of these difficulties is allometric scaling. Thus, to quote Byrne, "In allometric scaling, a double logarithmic plot of something, in this case brain size, is made against body size for the given group of animals. This forces the species points onto a straight line. Then we can see whether any particular animal in the group lies above the line (has a relatively larger brain than one might expect), on the line (has average brain size), or below the line (has a relatively small brain). This technique has many limitations (including doubt as to whether a straight line is the best fit to the log–log transformed data; see Deacon, 1990), but it is the one now used most often to compare animals' brain sizes. With this approach, we find that humans have brains three times as large as we would expect from even a monkey of human size (Passingham, 1982), which of course tends to give us confidence in the relationship between relative brain volume and intelligence!" (111). In this he follows Passingham.

The other main strand of Byrne's approach is to note and document fully those widespread instances among some nonhuman primates in which "it is very hard to doubt these animals understood each other's minds rather well." For example, Richard Byrne and his colleague Andrew Whiten[6] catalogued the potential evolutionary importance of what they call Machiavellian intelligence. This refers to the ability to prevail in a complex society through the judicious application of cleverness, deceit, and political acumen. They point out that deception is widespread in the natural world. Much of this, however, does not justify the attribution of deception of the kind Byrne and Whiten discuss. Their concern is with tactical deception, involving situations that suggest that animals have the mental flexibility to use "honest" behavior in such a way that they deceive and mislead another member of their own social group. The evidence is, on the face of it, compelling. It remains, however, a topic of lively debate among ethologists and psychologists. Humphrey, for example, has said, "In my opinion the word [Machiavellian] gives too much weight to the hostile use of intelligence. One of the functions of intellect in higher primates and humans is to keep the social unit together and make it able successfully to exploit the environment. A lot of intelligence could better be seen as driven by the need for cooperation and compensation." To which Byrne and Whiten reply that cooperation is itself an excellent Machiavellian strategy—sometimes. The purpose of mentioning this new development here is to illustrate how, yet again, some of the most seemingly cunningly intellectual capacities of humankind seem to be represented in the natural behavior of the higher nonhuman primates. Again this causes neither surprise nor concern to the Christian scientist with an openly peaceable mind. It only becomes contentious if, for whatever reason, a position has been taken (in the absence of empirical evidence either way) that such deviously cunning behavior calls for intellectual capacities confined to humankind.

It is interesting to note in passing that Byrne is not, unlike some, desperate to show that modern apes possess language in the human sense. He has written, "Modern apes may completely lack the formalizing systems of language, but they do not lack the understanding of what this kind of communication is all about. From this perspective, we can predict that when the heated arguments over 'ape signing' experiments have finally died down, the apes will be acknowledged to understand and use true communication, even if they never double-embed a relative clause."

Cerebral Asymmetries—
A Distinguishing Human Characteristic?

The classic studies of Nobel Laureate Roger Sperry and his co-workers on the so-called split brain are now well known. The term *split brain* refers to a surgical procedure used as a last resort on patients with intractable epilepsy for whom every other kind of medication had been tried and found ineffective. The forebrain commissures, pathways containing variously estimated at between 5 and 8 hundred million fibers connecting the two cerebral hemispheres, are surgically severed, effectively disconnecting the hemispheres. In individuals subjected to this procedure a state of affairs was produced that offered a unique opportunity to study the functions of each cerebral hemisphere without interference from the other. It soon became clear that the two cerebral hemispheres do indeed have distinct abilities. As a result, there was a great resurgence of interest in the whole question of hemispheric specialization of function and the unity of consciousness. Clear functional differences between the two hemispheres in human beings earlier documented by neurologists became well established. It was not long before there were those who asserted that here is all obvious instance where humans differ from animals. Animals, they said, do not show such asymmetries. In humans the most obvious hemispheric asymmetry is associated with the fact that the majority of people are right-handed. In such people it is clear that normally their left cerebral hemisphere deals with language whereas the right side of the brain deals with visuospatial ability.

By 1983, however, the late Norman Geschwind, at the time professor of neurology at Harvard, could write, "It is now likely that no animal species, no matter how humble, lacks cerebral dominance." The lesson again is clear. If in 1963 you were desperate to maintain the uniqueness of man on the grounds that humankind alone possessed the kind of cerebral dominance most dramatically portrayed in language lateralities, then twenty years later you would be confronted with a situation where functional brain asymmetries had been demonstrated in a wide variety of species, birds, rodents, and nonhuman primates to name but a few.

The Emerging Picture

From the evidence from comparative psychology, two things stand out. The first concerns language. In their different ways, Hinde and Thorpe both identified this as one of the crucial distinguishing features—a view endorsed by Richard Byrne. Hinde regards the difference as one of quality rather than quantity. It is not that the nonhuman primate does not have some form of language. We know from the work of David Premack and others that they are able to use forms of language. It is, rather, that in man the capacity is so much greater than in animals that it is most meaningfully thought of as qualitatively different. Not all take this view, however. Fooks, for example, has argued that the possibility of chimpanzee language challenges the notion of a sharp break between human and animal cognition. Depending on what aspect of cognition is under consideration, it is clear that Byrne also would endorse a similar view, at least as regards "reading the minds of others." Thorpe nevertheless argues that there is a point where "more" creates a difference. We also note here that coming at the same issue from the questions studied by neuropsychologists and comparative anatomists, both Ettlinger and Passingham conclude that aspects of language such as "the ability to represent information *within* an individual's mind" (Ettlinger) and "our ability to represent words to ourselves; to manipulate internal systems" (Passingham) are the basis of the crucial difference between humans and nonhuman primates.

Thorpe, in his Gifford lectures, having reviewed a vast amount of empirical evidence, makes the very strong claim that we are left with a tremendous chasm—intellectual, artistic, technical, linguistic, moral, ethical, scientific, and spiritual—between ape and man. He adds that we have no clear idea how this gap is bridged. Man is unique in all these aspects and we may never know how this happened. In the light of the more recent work by Byrne and others, I would wish to qualify this slightly and argue for the possibility (depending on interpretation) for some evidence of what we would label ethical behavior in the way that chimpanzees look after their young and conduct their family life. As regards scientific, literary, artistic, cultural, and technological achievements, there is clearly a vast chasm between humankind and all other animals. As regards the spiritual dimension, it is true that animals can be made to exhibit superstitious behavior, as B. F. Skinner did with his pigeons, but that is hardly what we mean by spiritual! While we have no scientific grounds for denying this possibility, equally there are no grounds for asserting it.

In some of this there is perhaps a lesson for those of us who, as Christians, wish to emphasize, assert, and defend the uniqueness of humankind. We should be wise to start from the biblical teaching (which we shall review later) rather than following a late-twentieth-century version of Richard Owen's 1858 claim that "the great ape does not possess a hippocampus minor." Owen had also said that there were three structures that were unique to the human brain. He was very anxious to have something that would uniquely define the human brain and thus set man apart from the rest of creation. But Huxley was scornful of those, who, as he put it, sought to base man's dignity on his great toe or to assert that we are lost if an ape has a hippocampus minor. An ape does have such a structure, so presumably on Owen's argument we are lost. Equally, it would certainly not be open-minded to assert that there are no structures unique to the human brain and it would be in accord with the evidence, as of now, to note that the neural substrate of *Homo sapiens* appears to confer a language capacity for internal representation and symbol manipulation of an order of achievement far beyond anything observed in nonhuman primates. What the final story is on this issue remains to be seen. We have no religious stakes in the outcome any more than we should have had any religious stakes in 1963 of claiming the uniqueness of cerebral asymmetries in humans (which, by 1983, had been revealed in monkeys).

A Christian Perspective

It is salutary to remember that some of the issues raised ninety years ago by Professor A. M. Fairbairn[7] in his *The Philosophy of the Christian Religion* remain as pressing today as they were then. He wrote concerning the position of man and his nature, "Do the eloquently minimized differences which we find in the structure of man as distinguished from the man-like ape, explain the differences in their histories?" (45). And the burden of his argument remains today, namely, that we still, from a purely scientific perspective, are puzzled to understand how such seemingly small differences between man and the nonhuman primates have given rise to such vastly different outcomes in terms of the achievements of men in art, literature, science, music, religion, technology, and so on—the "vast gap" described by Thorpe. This same point is strongly emphasized by Professor Steven Rose,[8] although in a different context, when he writes, "Great disservice has been done to biology by the contingencies of the historical development of our subject which meant that in the early years of this century two separate sub-disciplines emerged; genetics, which essentially asks questions about the origins of *differences* between organisms, and developmental biology, which asks questions about the processes which ensure *similarity*. The careless language of DNA and molecular genetics serves to widen this gap rather than help bridge it so as to open the route towards the synthetic biology that we so badly need. Let me state the biological problem in its bluntest possible terms," he goes on. "Chimpanzees and humans share upwards of 98% of their DNA, yet no-one would mistake a chimpanzee phenotype for a human phenotype. We have no idea at present about the developmental rules which lead in one case to the chimp, in the other to the human, yet this, surely one of the great unsolved riddles of biology, seems a matter of sublime indifference to most molecularly orientated geneticists."

Nothing is to be gained scientifically or theologically by glossing over real differences between man and animals. Fudging the issue of the implications of the far-reaching differences conferred by, for example, some aspects of human language with high-sounding sentimental slogans, serves the best interests of neither animals nor men. We simply "deceive ourselves and the truth is not in us." At the same time there are no scientific or theological issues at stake in fully recognizing the many and equally important similarities between men and animals. Scientific and medical research has so much to gain by recognizing and building on these similarities. And Scripture suggests that a careful study of animal behavior offers much to challenge and instruct aspects of our own ways of living and behaving. We can find no biblical reason for denying that animals have conscious experience and limited mental abilities. Indeed, as we saw in the previous chapter, the term *nephesh* or "living being" applies in Scripture equally to animals and humans. The logic of the argument about what similarities and differences imply needs watching carefully here, however. As has been pointed out,[9] "a weak mixture of gas and air may contain the same kinds of molecules and lie on the same continuum as a richer mixture that burns, but that does nothing to prove that some kind of flame must be possible in the weaker mixture. Below a certain minimum concentration the mixture is simply inflammable.

By the same token, the fact that a human brain organized in a specific way can embody conscious mental and spiritual life does nothing to prove that similar mental and spiritual capacities must be present in the brains of animals." And "if the biblical claim were that man is distinguished from lower animals . . . by having a brain sensitive to non-physical influences, and that these non-physical influences are what make his behavior essentially human, then of course the question of the capacities of animals . . . would become crucial. Once this claim is recognized as without biblical foundation, however, the polemical pressure disappears, and the whole issue becomes of marginal interest to the biblical apologist, whose primary duty regarding it is to keep an open mind."

TAKING STOCK

1. In the study of differences between animals and humans, important scientific issues are involved. For example, when someone suffers brain damage it is usually difficult to know precisely what structures have been damaged. It is, therefore, unwise to draw strong conclusions about the functions of brain structures from human clinical material alone. It is important when studying the function(s) of a particular part of the brain to augment the clinical evidence by studying the effects of surgical ablations on the brains of animals. Such methods minimize unwanted damage and therefore make it safer to draw conclusions about specialized function.

2. There is little encouragement in the Bible for trying to establish the distinctiveness of humankind on the basis of certain physical or behavioral traits. That being so, the question remains, What is distinctive about humankind? The key to what it means to be distinctively human is not to be found in looking for every possible physical and mental difference between ourselves and the animal kingdom. Rather, the crucial clues for the Christian are to be found in the biblical witness to humankind's capacity for a personal relationship with our Creator.

Biblical scholars remind us that the Hebrew-Christian doctrine of creation is not, as too often assumed, *anthropocentic*, with humankind seen as the "crown" of creation, but rather it is *theocentric*. There is, they tell us, no biblical basis for the arrogant claim that humankind is the ultimate purpose of creation. That view is now seen to be of Greek origin, adopted from Greek philosophy by the early Church Fathers. The theocentric view asserts, rather, that the creation is God's, and the ultimate purpose of creation is not humanity, but the embodiment and expression of God's greatness and majesty in the universe. Thus, for example, Cas Labuschagne[10] has written, "The purpose of both Psalm 8 and 104, the two psalms of creation, is primarily to praise the majesty and splendor of the Creator, who is said to rejoice in his works." And he continues: "The context, in which the psalmist speaks about the high status of humanity, is the universe. The extraordinary position of the human being in comparison with other living creatures, is set against the backdrop of the author's amazement about God's vast creation, and about his care for humankind as an infinitively small object in the universe."

He notes:

> The high status of the human being is defined as "being little short of divine": God has made him "little less than a god, crowning him with glory and honor" (vs. 5). The human being owes this privileged position not to himself, but to God who endows him with the capability and the competence to rule and have dominion over other living creatures:

> "You make him master over all that you have made, putting everything in subjection under his feet: all sheep and oxen, all the wild beasts, the birds in the air, the fish in the sea, and everything that moves along ocean paths" (vss. 6–8).

> The human being is given his high status not for his own sake, but in view of his divine commission to be master over other living creatures. There is no room here for human haughtiness, for arrogance or for a feeling of superiority above other living beings. Humans owe their high status not to themselves, but to God, whom they are called to serve by ruling over God's other creatures on earth (125).

It is thus clear that, in this regard, exercising our stewardship requires the minimum use of animals and, as far as possible, the exclusion of suffering. While Labuschagne points out in Genesis 1—2 that "the human being is fundamentally a breathing, living creature like other creatures," he believes that humankind has the unique potential for a personal relationship with his Creator, Father, God. He may "walk with Him in the cool of the evening." This relationship, however marred by disobedience, is gloriously restored in Christ.

In addition, we should note and underline that for us as Christians what is very special about humankind is to be found in the mystery of the incarnation. As one biblical scholar has written,[11] "The most remarkable fact about the human race, as we learn from the Bible, is that a genuinely human life, the fully perfect human personality of the historic existence of Jesus, served as a mode of existence of God Himself without ceasing in the least to be fully God. . . . If human life is a vehicle equal to that task," he wrote, "it is glorious indeed." These it seems to me are firmer grounds for recognizing our special status than looking for psychological differences and differences in brain structures.

3. This leads on naturally to our third general comment. We may helpfully take note of the writings of philosophers of religion such as Keith Ward[12] who, when discussing the question, Is God a Person? highlights the logical fallacy that "because two objects possess the same kinds of property, they are therefore objects of the same kind." Rather, he continues, "It all depends on what other properties they possess," having earlier written, "Suppose I suggest that possessing weight, position and velocity are properties that molecules have; that I possess weight, position and velocity; and that therefore I am molecule. The fallacy is clear" (260). In the context of our present discussion we see that because animals and humans possess many common properties, it does not follow that humans are therefore "nothing but" animals. Some would argue that they are different on the basis of certain unique properties such as language. As Christians we would argue, additionally, on the basis of revelation, that humankind is distinctively different primarily on the grounds that humankind has the potential for a personal relationship with the Creator and that, wonder of wonders, human life was once indeed "a vehicle equal to the task of the incarnation."

There will always be a delicate balance to be maintained. Pascal, we believe, had it right when he wrote, "It is dangerous to show man too clearly how much he resembles the beast, without at the same time showing him his greatness. It is also dangerous to allow him too clear a vision of his greatness without his baseness. It is even more dangerous to leave him in ignorance of both."

CHAPTER 8

PERSONOLOGY AND PSYCHOTHERAPY

Confronting the Challenges

Without adherence to the scientific standard of "show me,"
professional psychology and psychotherapy become a matter
of "views" and "schools," with the result that they are highly
influenced by cultural beliefs and fads: currently, the obsession
is with "me."
—Robyn Dawes, *House of Cards*, 1994

Reality is the overseer at one's shoulder, ready to rap one's
knuckles or to spring the trap into which one has been led
by overconfidence, or by a too-complacent reliance on mere
surmise. Science succeeds precisely because it has accepted
a bargain in which even the boldest imagination stands
hostage to reality. Reality is the unrelenting angel with
whom scientists have agreed to wrestle."
—Paul R. Gross and Norman Levitt, *Higher Superstition*, 1994

Unthinking sentimentality, be it remembered, is the great
enemy of genuine compassion.
—Paul R. Gross and Norman Levitt, *Higher Superstition*, 1994

IN CHAPTER 1 we saw that contemporary psychology encompasses an
extensive and diverse scientific landscape, from neuroscience through
neuropsychology, behavioral pharmacology, psychopharmacology,
physiological psychology, genetic psychology, comparative psychology,
cognitive psychology covering studies of perceiving, remembering,
learning, and thinking, cross-cultural psychology, social psychology, and

personality psychology. Aware of such diversity of both subject matter and investigating techniques, it came as no surprise to find that attempts to relate knowledge from such disparate areas to Scripture's views of human nature have resulted in more than one solution being proposed by Christians who nevertheless share the same basic theological beliefs.

As regards those areas of contemporary psychology which, in terms of subject matter, methodology, and techniques, have the clearest links with the biological and physical sciences, we can benefit from the substantial amount of earlier thinking and writing about how properly to relate the knowledge derived from them to biblical revelation. These are represented in the writings of, for example, historians and philosophers of science such as Hooykaas, Barbour, Russell, and Brooke. The general consensus seems to be that the two sets of knowledge should be viewed as complementary, originating from distinct perspectives. Such views have been labeled by philosopher Steven Evans[1] and others as "perspectivalist." There are, however, other areas of contemporary psychology, small in terms of their share of the total landscape of academic psychology but large in terms of their applications to clinical problems and counseling, which generate problems of their own as we seek properly to relate them to biblical revelation. Prominent among this group of subdisciplines is what Mary Van Leeuwen[2] has called personology. By this she refers to those parts of psychology that deal with theories of personality and the theory and practice of psychotherapy.

The difficulties we face in conceptualizing how to relate theories of personality, and their applied aspects in the theories and practice of psychotherapy, to Christian beliefs, arise from a number of special factors. First, in considering, say, a cognitive theory of short-term memory, or a neuropsychological theory of perceptual or thinking disorders, or a psychophysiological theory of eating disorders, or a psychopharmacological theory of depression, there is little temptation to intermix our values or wider beliefs into our scientific models. The reason is that whether the models are cognitive, neuropsychological, psychophysiological, or psychopharmacological, they readily remind us of their cognate disciplines of neuroanatomy, neurophysiology, and neuropharmacology, which are self-evidently not value-laden as regards their science (though they may be as regards their applications). The data on which they are based are relatively objective and hence available for any suitably trained observer to examine and criticize. The same, however, turns out not to be the case as regards some of the central concepts in most personality theories or theories of psychotherapy. Here data are not readily available for public scrutiny and the hypothetical constructs are not so self-evident nor can they be so demonstrably tied to shared observations by outside skilled observers. One result is that it is notoriously difficult to make and test unambiguous predictions from the theories in question. In such circumstances, personal values readily intrude and may play a significant part in theory construction. This leads on to the second point, widely recognized by psychologists themselves and reiterated, for example, many times by Allan Bergin[3] and others, that we confront the ubiquitous influence of values in both the theory and practice of psychotherapy. Bergin has made clear, for example, that many of the dominant values today in psychotherapy stand in sharp contrast to a theistic approach rooted in faith in God. According to secular, clinical-humanistic values, humans stand supreme. What matters is that they be free from all external authority, free to be themselves, to do as they please, to define their own self-worth through the way they relate to others, and to discover purpose and meaning in life from within their own thinking, feeling, and reasoning. By contrast, theistic values begin by acknowledging that God is supreme, that a proper attitude is one of humility and the readiness to accept divine guidance, teaching, and authority; that self-control, not self-expression, self-sacrifice not self-satisfaction, are the highest good and that our true worth is defined through our relationship to God so that meaning and purpose depend heavily on the spiritual dimension to life.

While in other areas of science personal values certainly influence such things as which problems we choose to study, which methods we will use, and if, how, when, and where any results will be applied, nevertheless the values do *not* intrude into the science per se. Ohm's law applies, however much two scientists' values may differ; Kepler's three laws of motion also apply and chemical reactions take their same courses regardless of the values of the scientists doing the research or applying their findings. It is, in this sense, that personality theory and the theory and practice of psychotherapy are so different and present such special problems.

There are, however, other aspects of the theory and practice of psychotherapy which, for whatever reason, have hitherto received less attention from Christians than perhaps they deserve. We shall explore some of these in a moment and as we do so we may benefit from the focus given to our discussions by the recently published, widely discussed, and in general (though not universally) highly acclaimed book by Robyn Dawes,[4] *House of Cards: Psychology and Psychotherapy Built on Myth.*

House of Cards: A Timely Focus for Discussion

In a feature review in the May 1995 issue of *Psychological Science,* the journal of the American Psychological Society, Gregory Miller[5] saw

Dawes's book partly as a response to "the anger with which many psychologists (clinical and nonclinical) view much of the professional practice of diagnosis and psychotherapy" (129). Miller emphasizes a point we take up later when he writes, "This is not a book by a hostile outsider attacking things of which he is ignorant. It will surprise many readers in various camps that Dawes concludes unequivocally, 'Psychotherapy works overall in reducing psychologically painful and often debilitating symptoms' (p. 38)." Later, he states, "Psychotherapy works. The magnitude of its positive effects is greater than the magnitude of many physical treatments, deleterious lifestyles, and changes in those lifestyles" (73). Miller's general conclusion is that "this is a major work—strong in its science, impressive in its scope of issues and examples treated knowledgeably, and bold in its policy statements." But that does not prevent Miller from voicing criticism when it is called for. Thus, he writes, "The book can be faulted for occasionally offering firmer negative conclusions than the data warrant. For example, whereas Dawes takes the confident position that more experienced therapists are not more effective ones, there is considerable controversy about whether the available research is adequate to settle this issue." Later he continues: "Finally, in a few places Dawes seems to substitute his own biases for empirical findings. For example, he apparently doubts the legitimacy of medication for psychological problems." Miller believes that "Dawes' attack on pharmacotherapy detracts from the book. . . . It does not need to win this argument to make its main points."

It is, however, Miller's concluding comment that adds weight to our decision to use Dawes's book as a contemporary focus for some of the issues which, I believe, should concern us as Christians. Thus, he concludes: "This powerful book will become a focal point for the escalating debate on science and practice in and out of psychology. It will feed some biases and challenge others" (213).

It is, we believe, often the case that students choose to study psychology because they see it as a means to an end. They want to do something to help other people. Such a motive is, we suspect, especially salient among Christian students. They see it as a way of following in the steps of their Master who, by example and in his teaching, showed care and compassion to all in distress. It thus became a natural step to view the study of psychology as opening the way to a career as a psychotherapist or counselor. There, surely, they assume, they will be ideally placed to fulfill their Christian calling.

The strong, and some would say at times excessive, claims made for the efficacy of this or that method of psychotherapy continue to receive close critical attention by psychologists. It is for that reason that Dawes's book is particularly timely. Though not written for that reason, it raises some special problems for Christians who are engaged in or are training for a career in psychotherapy. We discuss these now as a lead into the more general questions that Christians face in evaluating theories of personality.

Typically in an undergraduate course in psychology a student will learn certain agreed conclusions about psychotherapy. David Myers[6] summarizes these in his widely used textbook as follows:

1. There are in the psychological marketplace more than 250 types of psychotherapy.

2. Half of all psychotherapists describe themselves as eclectic.

3. There are a limited number of basic theoretical perspectives on which the aims and techniques of particular therapies are built: psychoanalytic, humanistic, behavioral, and cognitive.

4. It is extremely difficult to evaluate the effectiveness of psychotherapy. How should it be done? Should it depend on how the patient feels about her progress? On how the therapist feels about her progress? On how friends and family feel about it? On how another clinician acting independently judges the progress? Or how the patient's actual behavior has changed?

5. There are some generalizations arising from the hundreds of studies designed to evaluate the effectiveness of therapies that receive very wide agreement from professionals in the field:
   (i) People who remain untreated often improve (spontaneous remission).
   (ii) Those who receive psychotherapy are somewhat more likely to improve than those who do not regardless of what kind of therapy they receive and for how long.
   (iii) Mature, articulate people with specific behavior problems often receive the greatest benefits from therapy.
   (iv) Placebo treatments or the sympathy and friendly counsel of paraprofessionals also tend to produce more improvements than occur in untreated people.

While it is one thing to set one's sights on training to be a psychotherapist, it is not always appreciated how many serious issues have to be faced by a Christian before embarking on such a career. For example, some of the personality theories on which the practice of psychotherapy is based are found, on close scrutiny, to be guided, at times, by undisclosed, often non-Christian presuppositions about what life is all about, what one's primary goals in life should be, and what the highest good to which humankind should aspire is. Paul Vitz, Allan Bergin, and Mary Van Leeuwen, among others, have helpfully drawn attention to some of them.

Paul Vitz[7] exposed the antireligious assumptions of some secular psychologies. These, he says, include atheism or agnosticism, naturalism, reductionism, individualism, relativism, subjectivism, and gnosticism (knowledgism). Bergin[8] exposed and criticized some of the assumptions of humanistic psychology—that, for example, people are fundamentally good and not disposed to evil, that to be true to oneself is the highest good, and that self-analysis can reveal more important truths than scientific analysis. Van Leeuwen,[9] while agreeing with Vitz's exposure of some personologists' non-Christian or anti-Christian presuppositions, comments (49) that "it does mean that neither naturalism nor evolutionism will suffice as the foundational anthropology for the Christian Psychologist." Rather, she goes on, "central to the Christian's understanding of human nature is the conviction regarding the person's ongoing relationship with God, a relationship that was intended to be of both a providential and a covenant sort." We should hasten to note that the need to expose hidden assumptions and undeclared metaphysical aims in psychotherapy is not a concern exclusive to Christians.

The intrusion of nonpsychological influences into psychotherapy is, Dawes argues, well illustrated by the contemporary influence of the New Age movement.[10] Noting its great emphasis on self-esteem, Dawes writes that according to the movement's proponents, "we all suffer from deficiencies in self-esteem, and these deficiencies are responsible for our problems, definitely not vice versa" (234). In view of the contemporary importance of these New Age influences, it is worth quoting Dawes at greater length on this issue. He goes on (234): "Poor self-esteem is often cited as the 'root cause' for everything from a failure to learn in elementary schools, to failure in business, to 'over achievement,' to divorce, or even to 'sexual co-dependency.'" He later comments: "Let me state categorically that there is *no* 'scientific evidence' that people who have deep insecurities and self doubts have nothing to contribute to the world." The most casual reading of biographies indicates that many admirable people, like Abraham Lincoln, often suffered from "deep insecurities and self doubts," and that many less than admirable people "suffered no self doubts whatsoever, at least until they were caught or disgraced" (234, 235). And, later he goes on: "The 'scientific evidence' to which Branden (a typical author on this theme) refers is *a correlation* between the level of self-esteem and the degree to which people engage in personally and socially positive activities and avoid negative ones. My great grandmother would not be surprised by the existence of this correlation. Of course, she might say it's because people who do rotten things feel bad about themselves and people who do good things feel good about themselves. She might add, damned good thing too, or society would fall apart" (235). Dawes notes later the consequences of this obsession with self-esteem to the exclusion of almost everything else when he writes (243), "the obsession discourages trying to change one's behavior or life course. Instead, it encourages shoring up self-esteem first by running to a therapist or group."

The reader is encouraged to consult Dawes's careful exposition of the outworking of the pernicious effects of this New Age preoccupation with self-esteem as it is applied in education as well as in other aspects of social life. Dawes concludes (250): "Professionals in psychology and psychotherapy clearly benefit from a New Age Psychology—it brings them clients. Unfortunately, they in turn contribute to and reinforce that psychology. Having lost sight of scientific skepticism and the need for careful research, the 'professional's view' has become highly compatible with the New Age view. In particular, that very egoism Paul Newman decries has to be viewed as a necessary component of 'mental health.'" And later Dawes concludes that "without adherence to the scientific standard of 'show me,' professional psychology and psychotherapy become a matter of 'views' and 'schools,' with the result that they are highly influenced by cultural beliefs and fads: currently, the obsession is with 'me."

There is another aspect of the case argued by Dawes that I believe should be of considerable concern to Christians and may indeed help us recall some aspects of life in the church, the fellowship of believers, which our current preoccupation with individualism may have caused us to neglect. He notes that "emotional suffering is very real, and the vast majority of people in these expanding professions sincerely wish to help those suffering. But," he asks, "are they really the experts they claim to be? . . . Are they better therapists than minimally trained people who may share their knowledge of behavioral techniques, who are empathetic and understanding of others?" (4). Dawes goes on to note that "these questions had been studied quite extensively, often by psychologists themselves. There is now an impressive body of research evidence indicating that the answer to these questions is no." If Dawes is right, there are potentially serious and far-reaching consequences for a Christian psychologist, because while she is indeed committed to fulfilling through psychotherapy her calling to show care and compassion and to relieve suffering, she is equally committed, in following the one who was himself "the Truth," to seeking always to align herself with that which is true. If some of the claims of psychotherapy are not demonstrably true and/or if the theories of personality undergirding the practice of psychotherapy cannot be defended from relevant evidence, then the

Christian psychotherapist must be the first to expose error and call into question any false claims. Here is an issue where Christians will indeed stand out as radical reformers, fulfilling their functions as salt and light and exposing error in a fallen world.

As we have already noted, we can identify distinguished Christian psychologists such as Paul Meehl and Allan Bergin who, over a period of many years, have sought to address just these issues. For more than forty years Meehl,[11] a Lutheran Christian, has compared clinical with statistical predictions of the outcomes of psychotherapy. He has consistently maintained that the predictions of outcomes in psychotherapy by clinicians do not surpass the success rates of similar predictions made on the basis of test results and statistical modeling. Bergin, reviewing much the same evidence as Meehl (with his colleagues Michael Lambert and David Shapiro), however, reached a somewhat different conclusion. They argued in the *Handbook of Psychotherapy and Behavior Change*[12] that "although the failures in this literature generally to show unique therapeutic effectiveness for trained professionals are sobering, these studies are flawed in several respects."

Whether Bergin would maintain that position ten years later and having read Dawes's most recent book, we do not know, and await his verdict with interest. In the meantime we may note that Dawes[13] also recognizes the flaws referred to by Bergin and has written "but all studies are 'flawed in certain respects.' Psychology is a difficult field in which to conduct a good study let alone one without any flaws at all." But, he continues, "are we to ignore what all these admittedly flawed studies indicate in common? Ignoring them would make sense only if they were all generally flawed in the same respect but they are not. Without such common flaws it is extremely improbable that all the separate and unrelated flaws would lead to the same conclusion. No specific common flaw has been found or even proposed that would systematically bias the results against the professional. This absence poses the biggest problem for those attempting to ignore their implications, namely, that there is no *positive* evidence supporting the efficacy of professional psychology. There are anecdotes, there is plausibility, there are common beliefs, yes—but there is no good evidence."

We are obviously not going to resolve these important issues here and now. That is not our present purpose. Rather, it is to remind ourselves that it is vital for us, as Christian psychologists, properly motivated by care, compassion, and concern, to be ever alert to the danger of allowing this to degenerate into a form of sentimentality that ignores or soft-peddles that other clear Christian commitment—the commitment to truth. And it is not mere academic issues that are at stake here.

Dawes has reminded us, when contrasting therapy based on valid scientific principles with that based on subjective clinical impressions, that "when the practitioners ignore valid principles, they can even become outright dangerous to our civil liberties, as when they ignore what they presumably should know about the malleability of human memory or the suggestibility of young children" (no doubt having in mind the widespread damage and distress caused by the myth of repressed memory and of linking false memories with allegations of sexual abuse).

For Christians there is a further issue concerning the stewardship of our resources. If Dawes is right, then "we should not be pouring our resources and money to support high priced people who do not help others better than those with far less training would, and whose judgments and predictions are actually worse than the simply statistical conclusions based on 'obvious' variables. Instead, we should take seriously the findings that the effectiveness of therapy is unrelated to the training and credentials of the therapist." And Dawes goes on: "The conclusion is that in attempting to alleviate psychological suffering, we should rely much more than we do on scientifically sound community based programs and on 'paraprofessionals' who can have extensive contact with those suffering at no greater expense than is currently incurred by paying those claiming to be experts" (6). Applying Dawes's conclusions in the context of the Christian church raises questions such as, Have we lost or underplayed some of the benefits of mutual support and understanding clearly taught in Scripture as intrinsic features of the local Christian church, the community of believers? Have we failed to mobilize the considerable resources of gifted "paraprofessionals" at the expense of focusing too much on a small, select band of so-called professional psychotherapists? It is these professionals of whom Dawes has written, "virtually all the research—and this book will reference more than 300 empirical investigations and summaries of investigations—has found that these professionals' claims to superior intuitive insight, understanding, and skill as therapists are simply invalid" (8).

At this point it is very important to reiterate and to underline several times that Robyn Dawes is *not* anti-psychotherapy. He is very emphatic about what clinical practice in psychotherapy can be at its best as we indicated in the earlier quotes which we repeat here. He has no doubt that "psychotherapy works overall in reducing psychologically painful and debilitating symptoms" (38). He asserts that "psychotherapy works. The magnitude of its positive effects is greater than the magnitude of many physical treatments, deleterious life styles, and changes in those life styles" (73). Dawes is supportive of psychotherapy but only under conditions that he believes much psychotherapy currently does not meet or even aspire to. Dawes should certainly find ready allies among Christians who are firmly committed "to cleaving to that which is true," "to telling the story as it is," and to bending every effort through participation in the scientific enterprise to achieve those aims.

Dawes also claims that in the United States there is another feature that characterizes much professional psychotherapy. He argues repeatedly that the professional community, having cut itself adrift from clinical research, is concerned with self-preservation and self-aggrandizement. That should certainly be something of which Christians should be critical and in which they should have no part. Thus, what I am urging is, first, that Christians be as concerned about evaluating the validity of the claims of successful outcomes from this or that form of psychotherapy as about extending the availability of some particular brand of psychotherapy within the Christian community; second, that if we are convinced about the strength of the case for greater use of paraprofessionals, as argued by Dawes and others, then we should carefully examine the implications of this for the Christian community who, by its nature as taught in Scripture, should contain an above average number of concerned and possibly unusually empathetic individuals, ready to offer their talents without financial rewards to their fellow Christians.

Toward a Constructive Relationship

The widespread intrusion of religious, moral, and metaphysical beliefs into psychotherapeutic practice has recently been given wide publicity by Stanton Jones.[14] He notes, writing of the relation of the science of psychology to religion, that "there is an even more substantial overlap with a moral/religious domain in the applied area of professional therapeutic psychology than there is with the area of scientific psychology." This brings to mind the points made so effectively by Van Leeuwen[15] about the dangers of going down some of the integrationist paths that had been proposed for psychology and Christian belief. She pointed out the danger of selecting one of several personality theories currently in the psychological marketplace and seeking to baptize it with Christian orthodoxy. Van Leeuwen pointed out this tendency as well exemplified by McKeown's exposure of the way in which some Christians have "overtranslated" the Bible into behaviorist language as a means of supposedly integrating the two. She quoted McKeown[16] with approval when he wrote,

> In such an analysis, eschatological doctrine is equated with positive reinforcement, the conscience functions as a negative reinforcer, and the beatitudes are analogues to a system of token rewards. Indeed, it is asserted that Hebrews 11, Verse 6 establishes God as a positive reinforcer. At issue in this translation, more than its being trite and

superficial (comparable to declaring God as my "co-pilot" or "cosmic power") is that it *legitimatizes the fiction of behaviorist metapsychology* and in so doing debases religious language and symbolism and sterilizes, if not destroys, traditional religious images, meanings and significance. The translation is dangerous because it substitutes a new set of symbols for those essential to historic Christian faith.

Jones[17] insists that in the realm of personality theory it is vital that "presuppositions and expectations . . . be explicit and accountable" (195). Certainly, "where taxonomic boundaries are less readily obvious, it would seem that the influence of philosophic and religious presuppositions upon the scientists' preconceptions will be more extensive" (195).

There is we believe one important issue raised by Jones that calls for special scrutiny. It is exemplified by his assertion that "the explicit incorporation of values and world views into the scientific process will not necessarily result in a loss of objectivity or methodological rigor." What does he mean by "incorporation"? What does it look like in a concrete example? It is a pity he did not illustrate how such "incorporation" takes place using a specific instance. Without that his meaning remains ambiguous and, on some interpretations, problematic. Taken in one sense it becomes an assertion with which many Christians who are natural scientists would wish to take issue. We suspect, for example, that Van Till[18] and his colleagues, following their detailed study of how properly to relate worldviews and scientific knowledge concerning the origins of the created order, as given in their book *Portraits of Creation*, might have serious reservations about Jones's view. However, having made an ambiguous statement which on one interpretation is problematic, Jones quickly returns to safe and consensual ground when he continues: "What is new about this proposal . . . is that psychological scientists and practitioners be more explicit about the interaction of religious belief and psychology. . . . If scientists, especially psychologists, are operating out of world view assumptions which include the religious, and the influence of such factors is actually inevitable, then the advancement of the scientific enterprise would seem to be facilitated by making those beliefs explicitly available for public inspection and discussion." But why, we may ask, is "the influence of such factors actually inevitable"? A lot depends here on what he means by "inevitable" and where and how this inevitable influence occurs. If he means what we would regard as an unjustified intermingling of psychological concepts and religious beliefs in theory construction, then that is certainly not inevitable; neither is it acceptable. In such contexts the exclusion of their influence may be difficult, and may require eternal vigilance in order to detect whenever they creep in, but it is certainly not inevitable.

Jones goes on to note three important implications that follow from the recognition of the special problems faced when working out how properly and productively to relate the theory and practice of psychotherapy to extrascientific influences of religion, morals, and metaphysics. First, he argues that in training clinical psychologists more attention and time should be devoted to "the philosophical, ethical, and religious dimensions of human psychology and of professional practice." Within the limits of the time available in such training courses, this is a worthy and commendable aim. It should, however, be balanced with an equal determination to highlight the limitations of current theories of personality and the techniques in the practice of psychotherapy. It is here that Dawes's insistence on carefully examining the effectiveness of psychotherapy should be noted and implemented in any training program. Certainly Jones's appeal for a greater self-awareness by psychotherapists of their own moral and metaphysical theorizing and practice cannot be repeated too often.

His second implication is closely related to the first. He advocates greater "honesty in public relations by practitioners about the value-ladenness of the mental health enterprise." Again, he is to be strongly supported. We believe that there should be an equal openness about the effectiveness of different forms of psychotherapy and about the potential significant contributions that could be made by "paraprofessionals." Unfortunately, if a similar openness about the *effectiveness* of psychotherapy, of whatever variety, were widely publicized, it might undermine the confidence of clients in practitioners to such an extent that any help they could afford would be severely impaired. Be that as it may, his noting that "patient-therapist similarity on religious values may be one of the best predictors we have of successful outcome and thus a variable on which client and therapist ought to be matched" seems obvious, and his advocacy that "we might therefore be acting in the best interest of clients by directing them to therapists of similar religious commitments" is understandable. However, such advice should be given within the wider proviso that the most important requirement is that the psychotherapist should be thoroughly up-to-date with developments in the field, and with critiques of current practice. What the client needs most, and is entitled to, is the best-trained, most knowledgeable psychotherapist—not one who shares the client's religious views while at the same time being out of date, out of touch, and not deeply concerned about the truth value of any theories or the actual effectiveness of any practices.

To Incorporate or Not to Incorporate?

We suggested above that Jones's proposal that we should incorporate religious values and worldviews into scientific theories or models calls for closer scrutiny. While he did not provide detailed examples of how his desire for closer integration involving incorporation might work in practice, he did spell out very effectively how it should *not*. We would agree with Jones that it is wrong for Herbert Simon to infiltrate his personal metaphysical beliefs into his psychology; it is wrong for Skinner to interpret his approach to psychology as if that is an intrinsic part of the discipline rather than metaphysical beliefs he chose to bring to it in the first place; we agree that it was wrong for Maslow to present his theories as if his personal views were an intrinsic part of the theory and flow from the data (the same would apply to Rogers). But if it was wrong for these psychologists to incorporate *their* metaphysical beliefs and worldviews as they did, how can Jones go on to suggest that it is right for Christians to incorporate *their* beliefs? From his other statements we must conclude that when he advocates incorporation into the scientific process he does not mean incorporation into the scientific models or scientific theorizing. Each can certainly inform and enrich the other in appropriate instances, but that does not justify attempts to incorporate, in the sense of "to produce an amalgam" *(Concise Oxford Dictionary* definition of "incorporate") made up of psychological data and models with elements of Christian belief. The *Concise Oxford Dictionary* further tells us that to "incorporate" means to "unite in one body with another thing or combine (ingredients) in one substance." That sort of incorporation we believe is not justified and should not be encouraged.

It is interesting that among those who responded to Jones's paper, several shared the concern expressed here. Thus Herman Aquinis and Marco Aquinis[19] wrote that "although Jones's contention seems to be valid regarding the practice of psychology, we suggest that the fundamental differences between the science of psychology and religion may not be so easily bridged as Jones indicates." They continued by noting that "Barbour (1974), one of Jones's most frequently cited sources regarding similarities between science and religion, also noted important differences between science and religion that we think should be addressed in any attempt to integrate them," and that "we believe that to posit a mutually beneficial relationship between psychological science and religion, one must address the more fundamental and core features pertaining to the essential nature of the scientific method and religion." They conclude: "In summary, fundamental differences between science and religion are widely documented. These differences indicate that science and religion are two distinct modes of knowing and explaining reality. These are the fundamental differences and conflicts that need to be addressed to posit that the science of psychology and religion 'are not radically incompatible' (Jones, 1994, p. 193) and that a constructive and mutually influencing integration between the two is possible."

In view of Jones's provocative reference to incorporation, in the next chapter we explore how it might or might not work by taking a specific example where there appear to be clear overlaps between the concerns of psychologists and the concerns of theologians. We refer to how we understand basic human needs—as we saw earlier, a timely topic in view of the great emphasis given today by New Age advocates of the need to, seemingly at all costs, increase our self-esteem. We believe that this example positively demonstrates how each domain of knowledge can enrich the other, thus providing a fuller account of the whole. It also indicates how *not* to go about the integration or incorporation of science and religious beliefs.

TAKING STOCK

1. As we remind ourselves of the diversity of topics studied by psychologists today, we meet important implications flowing from this diversity. Not only do research methods differ, but the degree to which a particular theory is tied to publicly available data also varies. It turns out, on close scrutiny, that personality theories are especially vulnerable to the intrusion of the personal beliefs and values of the theorists.

2. The special problems of the influence of personal ideologies in personality theory and psychotherapeutic practice have been widely recognized by psychologists, particularly by Christians such as Allan Bergin, Mary Van Leeuwen, and Paul Vitz. But it is not an issue unique to Christians. That it is a general issue of wide concern among psychologists is vividly illustrated by the recent book by Robyn Dawes, *House of Cards*. It has been widely acclaimed and has proved to be a useful focus for our present discussions.

3. Dawes documents carefully a number of serious concerns about the theory and practice of psychotherapy in North America at the present time. He argues that theory and practice in psychotherapy have become separated from soundly based empirical data. It is not worthy of psychology's claims to be a science to depart in this way from the data. Moreover, it is apparent that, at times, theories have been hijacked by influential contemporary movements such as the New Age movement.

4. Dawes has argued that, granted the clear beneficial effects of some forms of psychotherapy, the evidence also argues for the greater involvement of well-trained paraprofessionals whose effectiveness is often indistinguishable from that of professional full-time psychotherapists.

5. Dawes's point about the potential contribution of paraprofessionals prompts the thought that, by its nature, the Christian church, the fellowship of believers, constitutes a natural resource for effective care and counseling.

6. Dawes's exposure of the rampant self-aggrandizement by some psychotherapists in North America highlights a situation where the Christian practitioner should stand clearly separate from non-Christian colleagues, since greed is shunned as part of one's commitment as a Christian disciple.

7. Finally, one aspect of this debate should, we believe, be vigorously emphasized by all Christians involved in personology and psychotherapy. It is the Christian commitment to adhere to the truth. Granted that, for a variety of reasons, it is harder, unambiguously, to arrive at an undisputed, sound, empirically based theory for the practice of psychotherapy, nevertheless Christians should be vocal in their insistence on an answer to the question, Is this theory true? If it is not, they should have no part in it.

8. There remains much more work to be done determining how properly to relate personology to Christian beliefs. However, we doubt the wisdom of incorporation as an appropriate way of describing it. Rather, Christian beliefs should motivate research and practice in psychotherapy, and Christian values should inform the compassionate practice of psychotherapy. But above all, the Christian commitment is to "telling the story as it is" and this must remain paramount in an area of psychology where personal values can so readily intrude.

CHAPTER 9

HUMAN NEEDS

Psychological and Theological Perspectives

We need something "bigger than we are" to be awed by and
to commit ourselves to in a new, naturalistic, empirical,
non-churchly sense.
—Abraham Maslow, *Psychology of Being*, 1968

The "primitive horizontalism" or "anthroegoism" that seeks
to reduce God to a mere fulfiller of human needs is "the unique
heresy of our time."
—Karl Rahner, *Faith in a Wintry Season*, 1990

We cheapen the gospel if we represent it as a deliverance
only from unhappiness, fear, guilt and *other felt needs*.
—John R. W. Stott, *The Message of Romans*, 1994

IN ADDRESSING BASIC HUMAN NEEDS, we are following Mary Van
Leeuwen's[1] encouragement for us to relate convictions "central to the
Christian understanding of human nature" to other accounts of human
nature provided by, for example, personologists. The discussion of basic
human needs is an example of where, at least superficially, the language
used by theologians and personologists suggests an overlap of interests. Undertaking this exercise may help us better understand and identify any distinctive perspectives and presuppositions underlying the
approaches taken by the two groups. A long and detailed study of theological and psychological accounts of human needs covering more psychologists and theologians, and in great detail, is contained in Kenneth
Boa's Oxford thesis.[2]

The Human Predicament:
Some Psychological Accounts

On close scrutiny we discover that psychological, especially psycho-dynamic theories of personality, contain, either explicitly or implicitly, certain basic, nonscientific claims about human nature. Each theory presents a model made up of various hypothetical constructs or entities that are said to interact in specified ways, both within the individual and with the environment, and the outcome of such interactions explains our thoughts, feelings, and behavior. Such models all aim at increased understanding of normal as well as abnormal psychological mental life and behavior. Not surprisingly, since they all confront essentially the same manifestations of psychopathology, they possess certain common features and repeat certain pervasive themes. One such theme, though variously expressed, amounts to identifying common human needs, locating their etiology, and investigating what goes wrong if and when such needs are frustrated, unfulfilled, or conflict with other needs either within the personality (the intrapsyche models) or with the demands of the interpersonal, social, and cultural environment (the psychosocial models).

In order to get a clearer idea of how such psychological accounts of human needs are construed and function, so that we may then compare them with the way such needs have been identified by theologians, we shall succinctly review the views of five of this century's most influential personality theorists, Freud, Erikson, Maslow, Rogers, and Fromm. By so doing we may be able to detect any features common to such models and identify implied or explicitly stated recurring psychological needs. We may thus be in a better position to understand how, if at all, the needs as described by them relate to the accounts of fundamental human needs given by theologians. Our aim will be to examine, with this specific example in mind, the wider question of how the accounts of human nature given by psychologists and theologians should be constructively related.

Sigmund Freud

The influence of Freud has dominated both the theory and practice of psychotherapy this century. Freud, like any good scientist, was prepared to modify his theory in light of new evidence. For him "evidence" was primarily his personal observations gained in clinical practice, which in general he limited to those suffering from neurotic illnesses. Early in his career, having already made distinguished and lasting contributions as a neurologist, he became convinced that the more serious mental illnesses, the psychoses, would ultimately be shown to be linked to biochemical abnormalities in the brain—a view increasingly turning out to be the case. Freud's psychodynamic model, as is well known, proposed a small number of basic psychic processes whose mutual interactions shaped or, as he would say, determined, the mental health status of an individual. Thus the strident demands of the id arising from innate processes had to be reconciled with the demands and threats of the real world and of the external world. Hence there arose a psychosocial conflict for every individual; how that conflict was handled determined the mental life and the interpersonal relationships of that individual.

While, as mentioned above, Freud steadily modified his model, nevertheless, ultimately for him all behavior is motivated by the quest for the optimal gratification of instincts within the bounds set by society. Freud directed a disproportionate amount of attention to the early years of an individual's life during which he believed personality structures became more or less fixed. He hoped that further developments of his ideas would make possible the fulfilment of basic human aspirations. Thus, for example, in claiming to expose religious beliefs as "illusions" he, at the same time, placed great faith in the progress of science, writing that "We believe that it is possible for scientific work to gain some knowledge about the reality of the world, by means of which we can increase our power and in accordance with which we can arrange our life."[3] However, the pertinent point for our present discussion is the centrality in Freud's theorizing of how we handle "the tensions caused by the *needs* of the id."[4] And such "needs" are also variously attributed to "somatic demands." "The forces," he writes, "which we assume to exist behind the tensions caused by the needs of the id are called instincts. They represent the somatic demands upon mental life." For Freud there were two basic instincts: the eros and the destructive instinct.

Erik Erikson

That the so-called evidence gained from clinical experience, especially in the course of psychoanalysis, is capable of a variety of explanatory models is clear from the writings of a disciple of Freud, Erik Erikson. He was, and remains, another very influential figure in the history of the therapeutic theory and practice arising out of psychoanalysis. Erikson, working initially largely within a Freudian framework, offered his own particular account of how development occurs, in the process extending it throughout life and encompassing eight stages. According to him, as an individual moves through the developmental stages, a psychosocial crisis occurs at each stage. How that crisis is handled will lead to either enhanced or impaired development at later stages. Erikson firmly believed that his science "deals directly with the *immediate needs* of man" and that there is "Cultural variability as to the inborn and provoked qualities of a need."[5] Throughout his theorizing, then, Erikson comes back to the important part played by human needs. The eight qualities that correspond to his developmental stages, if frustrated during a psychosocial crisis, can lead to fixation at that particular stage. The details are not relevant here; what is important is the emphasis on human needs and the manner in which they are used in Erikson's theorizing.

Abraham Maslow

We now turn to briefly consider the views of two psychologists whose views were in many respects different from those of Freud and Erikson. Some have described them as the architects of "the humanistic movement" in modern psychology. Others have called them "the third force" in psychology. The first of the two is Abraham Maslow (1908–70). Maddi in his text on personality theories regarded Maslow's views as a variant of the so-called fulfilment model because intrinsic to it is the idea of personal fulfilment. In addition to the maturational tendency that Maslow saw toward "actualization" of inherent potentialities, he also recognized that the core of personality was the tendency to survive in order to satisfy physical and psychological needs. He uses the term "self-actualization" introduced by Kurt Goldstein to describe the fulfilment tendency he identified and to argue that this tendency builds up and grows upon, rather than conflicts with, the survival tendency. Unlike Freud, for Maslow human nature is essentially good or at the very least neutral and therefore should be actualized. He argued that humanity shares certain basic needs that are not necessarily culturally determined. We therefore find that needs and metaneeds figure prominently in Maslow's theorizing.[6] Maslow constructs a hierarchy of needs; the ones at one level must be satisfied before those on the next level begin to dominate the motivation of a person. In addition to deficiencies and growth needs, Maslow also proposed cognitive and conative needs. Again, the details are not relevant here; what is important to note is that when his psychological account of needs spills over into claiming to be a general philosophy of life, it moves from psychology to metaphysics. For example, he portrayed the third force in psychology, the humanistic approach, as "one facet of a general *Weltanschaung*, a new philosophy of life, a new conception of man."[7] It comes as no surprise, therefore, to discover that Maslow considered his third-force psychology as a secular surrogate for religion. Thus he wrote

The human being needs a framework of values, a philosophy of life, a religion or religion-surrogate to live by and understand by, in about the same sense that he needs sunlight, calcium or love.

Without the transcendent and the transpersonal, we get sick, violent, and nihilistic, or else hopeless and apathetic. We need something "bigger than we are" to be awed by and to commit ourselves to in a new, naturalistic, empirical, non-churchly sense.[8]

Carl Rogers

Carl Rogers exerted an enormous influence on both the development and the popularization of humanistic psychology. He believed that the time had come to express his new ideas, a central plank of which was "the gradually formed and tested hypothesis that the individual has within himself vast resources for self understanding, for altering his self concept, his attitudes, and his self directed behavior—and that these resources can be tapped if only a definable climate of facilitative psychological attitudes can be provided."[9] The essence of the therapeutic approach developed by Rogers became the creation of the necessary conditions to enable an individual to utilize and express this inward, growth-directed tendency that, according to his beliefs, is so fundamental to every human organism. He used the term *client-centered therapy* to distinguish his approach from other, and in some ways similar, therapeutic approaches. A client is someone who voluntarily seeks help for a problem, but does not relinquish responsibility for the overall situation. Rogers also used the term *non-directive* to describe his particular method of counseling, although later he seemed to prefer the label *person-centered approach.*

Within the context of the dominant guiding motive for the individual, namely Rogers's "actualization tendency," he also noted a number of needs subservient to that tendency. Thus, he wrote, "To me, it is meaningful to say that the substratum of all motivation is the organismic tendency towards fulfilment. This tendency may express itself in the widest range of behaviors and in response to a wide variety of needs. To be sure, certain basic ones must be, at least partially, met before other needs become urgent."[10] In his theories of therapy and of personality, Rogers focuses his attention on two critical needs: the need for positive regard and the need for self-regard. According to Rogers, a fully functioning person exhibits the freedom to adapt to his environment so as to gain the maximum satisfaction of his deepest needs; such a person is "a fit vanguard of human evolution" (194).

Like Maslow, Rogers progressed from presenting a psychological model to developing a philosophy of life. In *A Way of Being*, he thus writes, "I am no longer talking simply about psycho-therapy, but about a point of view, a philosophy, an approach to life, a way of being, which fits any situation in which *growth*—of a person, a group, or a community—is part of the goal" (ix). Within this perspective Rogers believes that there is no evil and no genuine guilt, nor can valid external judgments be made.

Eric Fromm

The final psychologist we consider was strongly influenced by both Freud and Marx. He took the ideas of Freud dealing with individuals and sought to apply them to a deeper psychological understanding of groups. He believed that man exemplifies the contradiction between the coexistence of an animal nature and a human nature. The human being, unlike animals, is characterized by self-awareness, awareness of others, an awareness of the past, and an awareness that death awaits in the future. Thus he wrote,[11] "Man transcends all other life because he is, for the first time, life aware of itself." According to his formulation, humanity is both a part of nature and not a part of nature—as he put it,[12] "partly divine, partly animal; partly infinite, partly finite." Fromm believed that the deepest human tendency is the attempt to move away from animal limitations toward a fulfilment of human possibilities. Thus, he wrote, "The necessity to find ever new solutions for the contradictions in his existence, to find ever higher forms of unity with nature, his fellow men and himself, is the source of all psychic forces which motivate man, of all his passions, affects and anxieties" (25). He believed that while the animal aspect of human nature manifested physiological needs such as hunger, thirst, and sex, which had to be satisfied, there were in addition other needs that are uniquely bound up with his humanness and had to be satisfied if true happiness was to be gained. These needs, he believed, transcended those of animal origin and required a new harmony to replace the one lost through the lack of harmony with nature. Humanness continued to be shaped by the economic and so-called social structures we say have developed and in which people live, but this adaptability is limited by the nature of the individual's and the group's psychological needs.

Fromm developed a detailed list of psychological needs, those for what he called relatedness, routedness, transcendence, sense of identity, frame of orientation and devotion (religious need), effectiveness, excitation and stimulation, and development of character structures. The details are not relevant here. The important point is that he made the presence of and the fulfilment of human needs a crucial part of his psychological theorizing. It is evident that the particular needs he was able to identify were not limited by anything other than his ingenuity in constructing a theory in the light of his own experience.

ARE THERE ANY COMMON PSYCHOLOGICAL NEEDS?

It is obvious that the lists of psychological needs suggested by these different personality theorists contain both divergencies and convergencies. How one is to decide which, if any, of these lists to believe and accept is a fascinating issue in itself and one that should certainly exercise anyone claiming a "scientific" status for any of these theories. If personologists wish to attach the label *scientific* to their models, they will need to indicate where the relevant evidence is that would enable one to decide which of the models best fits the facts. They will also need to make clear how one is to decide among the various lists of needs present in the psychological marketplace. To what extent, for example, should one continue to take seriously needs that arise primarily from psychic forces within the unconscious? Is the notion of the unconscious meaningful, and how does one decide its relative importance compared with conscious forces? Or, again, is a degree of tension in the personality desirable or undesirable? While Freud could view the increase in the amounts of energy and excitation as being unpleasurable to the id, which would then seek to reduce the tension-producing stimulation in order to return the organism to a state of homeostasis, others, such as Jung, believed that the psyche was a self-regulating system that always attempted to maintain a state of equilibrium. Rogers, on the other hand, believed that psychological help was not a matter of tension-reducing equilibrium but a process of increasing potentiality.

These psychologists also diverge in their assessment of human nature. On the one hand, the theoreticians who stress conflict are more negative about the inherent nature of man than the so-called fulfilment psychologists. Freud was distrustful of people; Maslow and Rogers believed that such a perspective is jaundiced and arises from concentrating on the psychopathology of those who are mentally and emotionally dysfunctional. For them, human nature is essentially positive and tends toward self-actualization and fulfilment.

In addition to the clear areas of divergence there are also a number of areas where the different theoreticians converge in their views of human needs. Freud identified certain survival needs that exert a constant pressure on the individual and have to be handled to maintain the state of equilibrium. Rogers emphasized an inner growth-directed "actualizing tendency" that moves the organism toward the satisfaction of both physiological and psychological needs. Fromm could relate the physiologically conditioned needs such as hunger, thirst, and sex to the animal aspect of human nature while still contending that survival needs extend beyond the merely physical. Or again, each of them in different ways had ideas about what might be called identity needs. For

Freud, identity relates to the object/cathexes of the ego; the ego must replace the pleasure principle with the reality principle so as to harmonize the conflicting forces of the id, the world, and the superego. Erikson emphasized a need for a sense of coherent ego identity to help protect the individual. Maslow had his hierarchy of needs in which the fourth level or the esteem needs as well as the so-called meta-needs were associated with self-actualization as it relates to personal identity. According to Rogers's personality theory, there was an identification need for positive self-regard; for Fromm, humans had a need to transcend the state of passivity they found themselves in and go on to achieve a sense of identity and self-awareness as the subject of their actions.

This very brief look at how some of this century's most influential personality theorists have characterized human needs and incorporated them into their theorizing gives, at least, a flavor of how human needs are thought about by psychotherapists. With that scenario in mind, it is interesting to turn now to the writings of theologians, this time spanning many centuries, and including differing ecclesiastical and theological traditions. What did they say about human needs?

THE HUMAN PREDICAMENT: SOME THEOLOGICAL ACCOUNTS

Augustine

Augustine, widely regarded as the greatest of the Latin Church Fathers, had no doubt that every human being's predicament before a Holy God resulted in universal basic needs. Augustine contrasted the depths to which humanity has fallen through sin with the heights to which it can be raised by the redemptive grace of God. This theme permeating much of Augustine's writings was "the corner stone of Augustinian anthropology."[13] Thus, Augustine's writings in, for example, his *Confessions*, ring many bells that resonate immediately with the human predicament in the late twentieth century. Augustine had no doubt that without the direct intervention of God's grace, the natural man has no hope of redemption.[14] That Augustine's perspective was so different from that of the "actualizers" or "self-fulfilment" psychologists of the second half of the twentieth century is at once evident when one reads his profound analysis of whether and how the possibility of human happiness can ever be satisfied. Thus, he writes,

> The simple truth is that the bond of a common nature makes all human beings one. Nevertheless, each individual in this community is driven by his passions to pursue his private purposes. Unfortunately,

the objects of these purposes are such that no one person, let alone the world community, can ever be wholly satisfied. The reason for this is that nothing but Absolute Being can satisfy human nature *(De civ. Dei* 18.2).

It was not that Augustine was advocating an ascetic mentality toward the things of this world. According to him temporal blessings are indeed profitable so long as they do not lure the heart away from the higher calling of eternal blessings. Thus he wrote, "Use the world: let not the world hold thee captive" *(In Yohan Ioh. Ev. Tract.* 40.10).

Aquinas

Another major figure who exerts an enduring influence on Western Christendom is Thomas Aquinas, who sought to systematize aspects of Aristotelian philosophy with Christian theology. In Aquinas's writing and thinking, the notion of human needs is prominent. Thus, as Gilson[15] has observed, "At the basis of Aquinas' philosophy, as at the basis of all Christian philosophy, there is a deep awareness of wretchedness and need for a comforter who can only be God." Noting how Aquinas had many profound things to say about human needs, Gilson has written, "Natural reason tells man that he is subject to a higher being, on account of the defects which he perceives in himself and in which he needs help and direction from someone above him: and whatever this superior being may be, it is known to all under the name of God."

We may also note in passing that Aquinas expressed views about the unity of personhood that resonate strongly with the trend at the end of the twentieth century evident in the scientific evidence concerning the mind–brain link. Thus Kirk[16] comments that Thomas is "perhaps the first Christian philosopher to take the corporeal character of human existence calmly." Humans are embodied souls and the soul "is not entombed in, but endowed with, a body."

Jonathan Edwards

Moving on to a different era, a different tradition, and a very different theological position, we may briefly consider the views of Jonathan Edwards. His writings were largely shaped by his religious experiences, and thus the themes of God's sovereignty, holiness, and grace stand alongside those of human sinfulness and the need for redemption. Steeped in the older puritan authors, his views illustrate and represent key features of the Reformed tradition.

He certainly recognized and taught the need for a basic change in the condition of the human heart by the power of the Spirit of God. Indeed, the transformation that he saw as necessary was as radical as that which takes place in going from death to life. Thus he writes,

> Truly gracious affections are produced by a supernatural, spiritual, and divine influence on the heart. . . . The influence of the spirit of God, thus communicating himself and making the creature a partaker of the divine nature, is what I mean by truly gracious affections arising from spiritual and divine influence. . . . Natural men are represented in the sacred writings as having no spiritual light, no spiritual life, no spiritual being; and therefore regeneration is often compared to the opening of the eyes of the blind, to the raising of the dead, and to the work of creation. . . . Grace is the seed of glory in the heart, and therefore the earnest of the future inheritance.[17]

The human needs of which Edwards wrote were the fundamental need for the restoration of the broken relationship with God and the need to place all one's affections and hopes in God's promises of a future inheritance in Christ.

Karl Rahner

Finally, moving to the twentieth century and yet another theological tradition, we may briefly consider Karl Rahner (1904–94), who has been called "the father of the Catholic church in the twentieth century." Rahner's approach has been described as transcendental-existential. Thus, Johannes B. Metz in his foreword to Rayner's *Spirit of the World*[18] (xvi) quotes Rayner as saying, in a lecture given in Chicago in 1966, "Anthropocentricity and theocentricity in theology are not contradictories but strictly one and the same thing seen from two different aspects, and each aspect is unintelligible without the other" (89, 90).

For Rahner,[19] man "does not possess within himself what he essentially needs in order to be himself." Man is "always exiled in the world and is always beyond it" (406, 407). The difference between Rahner's concept of human needs and the psychologist's concept should certainly warn us against any attempt to integrate the two within a single theoretical formulation. Rahner stresses that the approach to God must be for his own sake; God cannot be shaped to fit our needs. According to Rahner, the "primitive horizontalism" or "anthroegoism" that seeks to reduce God to a mere fulfiller of human needs is "the unique heresy of our time" (2, 27). John Stott[20] has written in somewhat similar terms that "we cheapen the gospel if we represent it as a deliverance only from unhappiness, fear, guilt and *other felt needs*, instead of a rescue from the coming wrath."

Thus, according to Rahner the universal human need is for a transcendent relationship with "the mystery we call God" and this in turn may be seen to consist of the need for faith, love, and hope.

THE HUMAN PREDICAMENT: RELATING THE PSYCHOLOGICAL AND THE THEOLOGICAL ACCOUNTS

The four theologians mentioned above come from a wide range of historical periods, theological traditions, and philosophical perspectives and differ in significant ways from one another. All, however, in their own ways have profound things to say about the deepest human needs and each underlines and expounds the New Testament accounts of the universal need for forgiveness and grace, for love of God and neighbor, and for that eternal sense of purpose and sure hope that only God can give.

The Christian psychologist knows that telling the whole story about human nature and, in particular, about our deepest needs must go beyond the various psychological accounts of human needs, whether offered by Freud, Maslow, Rogers, or Fromm. These tell only the horizontal, imminent story and must be complemented by the theological, vertical, transcendental story given by revelation. But that does not mean trying cleverly to "incorporate" bits of one with bits of the other. Such an attempt misunderstands the nature of psychological theorizing while unwittingly abusing Scripture.

Thus, to take Aquinas as typical of the other theologians, while he undoubtedly provides many rich and profound insights into human nature, they do not constitute nor are they couched in the categories of twentieth-century personality theories. Led astray perhaps by the use of similar words, by references to desires and needs, it would be all too easy to try to integrate or incorporate Thomistic wisdom into psychological theories or vice versa. The question must be asked, however, what the warrant for attempting this is, since the categories used in Thomistic theology are not those of twentieth-century personology. The outcome is likely to be a muddle that does justice to neither and violence to both, and hence reduces rather than increases our overall understanding of human nature. Rather, we should gratefully and thoughtfully accept the enrichment that insights from the theological, the vertical, or the transcendent perspective gives to those from the psychological, the horizontal, or the imminent perspective. Each has something to offer to the other. There is certainly no compelling reason why our non-Christian psychology colleagues should find fresh understanding from our exposition of the understanding of human nature that we find so helpful in God's revelation in Scripture. They may, but then again they may not. They will certainly, and rightly, look askance at any attempt on our part

to smuggle our metaphysical or religious beliefs or our theological doctrines into our psychological theorizing.

As Mary Van Leeuwen and Paul Vitz have made so abundantly clear,
on close scrutiny we find that the presuppositions of the personologists
are often radically different from those held by Christian theologians,
resulting in a quite disparate meaning behind what appear superficially
to be identical terms. To assume congruence between the accounts of the
theologians and the psychologists because of the surface similarities of
the language used is a prescription for confusion—this quite apart from
the fact that it would be very unwise for theologians, apologists, or anyone else to attempt to build upon a foundation so liable to change or
rejection as, for example, psychoanalytic theory. It is one thing to recognize that analysis in terms of psychological models may enrich our overall understanding of human nature, but it is quite another thing to then
seek to interweave the psychological and theological insights into a composite model that amounts to mixing up the two in a quite uncritical and
unjustified way.

Rahner accurately identified the real issues when he argued that while
psychology may indeed offer many insights on what it is to be human, it
cannot define the human person, nor can the mystery of what it is to be
a person be reduced to psychological concepts, however sophisticated
and refined. For that reason he criticized psychological attempts to
explain away guilt and, while he acknowledged that some forms of psychoanalysis may help relieve a measure of sickness and suffering, it is
only through God that people can be delivered from real guilt. People
cannot liberate themselves by means of their own resources; if guilt is
removed, it must be through divine forgiveness. One cannot reiterate too
often the account given by Paul Vitz,[21] which exposed clearly how some
psychologists shift their categories from the scientific to the philosophical and to the normative and move, without justification, on to theories
of moral obligation. In so doing they blur the conceptual boundaries
between science and the broader views of humankind already richly
found in literature, philosophy, and religion down through the centuries.
That some psychologists are either unaware or unwilling to expose their
own metaphysical and moral presuppositions continues to be a problem,
especially when they seek to invoke what they believe is the authority
of science to authenticate their opinions. Those psychologists working
at the more experimental, biological end of the psychological continuum
view with considerable skepticism the claims to be scientific made by
most of the personality theorists.

With this brief glimpse of how psychologists and theologians talk
about human needs in mind, we may return to our earlier question of
how properly to relate the two so that the benefits of a potentially enrich-

ing partnership may be realized. Should it be by "incorporation," as Stanton Jones suggested? Should there be a closer integration of psychotherapeutic theory and religious beliefs?

Would we find it at odds with Jones's other statements if we were to believe that, in the case of Freud, he would wish to add to Freud's other hypothetical constructs, in his psychodynamic theory, a constant labeled God? Or, in the case of Erikson, would he wish to add a further developmental stage to the eight already identified by Erikson, labeled the religious stage? Or, in the case of Maslow, would he wish to build upon the hierarchy of needs and cap the whole structure with one labeled religious needs? We believe his answer to all these questions is no. In his other publications he warns against that kind of intermixing of languages from different domains and points out that it can lead to nothing but confusion. To seek to invoke God in that way would be to commit the error Austin Farrer[22] pointed out of invoking the Holy Spirit as an explanatory concept to fit into a psychological account we may have constructed of some aspect of religious behavior. It would be to ignore the important truth underlined by Farrer that "the Holy Spirit is God. He is not to be fitted in to any psychological, or for that matter personal, explanation that we choose to give." Equally, the God of the Christian is not a hypothetical construct to be fitted in, at our convenience, to this or that personality theory. The God of the Christian is one who upholds and sustains all things at all times (Heb. 1:3). This must never be forgotten as we think about the relationship between scientific, psychological accounts of behavior and therapy and those held in the religious domain. We believe that in seeking to understand human nature we can thankfully acknowledge how the psychological accounts enrich those from theology as each makes its distinctive contribution, albeit from different perspectives.

TAKING STOCK

1. At times psychologists and theologians sound alike. This is not surprising, since both are interested in human nature. However, the ways they talk about human nature differ as fundamentally as, for example, the ways that cosmologists and theologians talk about the earth and the stars, although, after hard-learned lessons, in that instance, all seem now to appreciate and recognize the different domains so that we are able to gain maximum benefit from both and not generate pseudoconflicts.

2. Personality theories almost invariably seem to include and manifest some of the strongly held personal beliefs of their creators. This was vividly demonstrated by the different theories of Freud, Fromm, Rogers,

and Erikson, who each conceptualize and portray the basic human needs which, according to them, we are all striving to fulfill.

3. Theologians also write about human needs. Their framework is, however, theocentric rather than the anthropocentric framework of the psychologists.

4. It is, as we saw in the previous chapter, notoriously difficult to tie personality theories unambiguously to shared observations and to draw clearcut inferences from the theories.

5. Theological accounts of human needs can, and must, be tested against what God has chosen to tell us about himself, ourselves, and our relationship to him. Our fertile imaginations are ever ready to work overtime to modify his revealed truth to make it more comfortable, more flattering to our self-assessment, and more acceptable to us.

6. Vigilance is called for in always remembering how psychological and theological accounts of human needs differ; their differing frameworks, the anthropocentric and the theocentric; and their differing purposes. By heeding these differences we may gain maximum benefit from and do minimum violence to both.

CHAPTER 10

CONSCIOUSNESS NOW

A Contemporary Issue

I hope that before long every laboratory working
on the visual system of man and the other vertebrates
will have a large sign posted on its walls reading:
CONSCIOUSNESS Now.
—Francis Crick, *The Astonishing Hypothesis*, 1994

FRANCIS CRICK OPENS HIS BOOK, *The Astonishing Hypothesis*, by stating that "this book is about the mystery of consciousness—how to explain it in scientific terms." "The message," he says, is that "now is the time to think scientifically about consciousness (and its relationship, if any, to the hypothetical immortal soul) . . . and that it is the time to start the experimental study of consciousness in a serious and deliberate way" (xii). He believes that what he has to say can make an impact on religion. In his introduction he writes, "Most religions hold that some kind of spirit exists that persists after one's bodily death." Continuing a few lines later, he notes that "there is broad agreement (in religions) on at least one point. People have souls in the literal and not merely the metaphorical sense" (4). There is little doubt that the resurgence of interest in consciousness by scientists, biologists like Crick, mathematician-physicists like Sir Roger Penrose, and psychologists will stir up more widespread interest among religious people as they consider the implications of scientific research on consciousness for some of their cherished beliefs. For that reason, in this chapter we seek to give the reader the flavor of the developing scientific debate and to ask what implications it may have for a biblical view of human persons. We have deliberately let the contributors speak for themselves, often in long quotations, rather than risk misrepresenting their views.

THE CHANGING SCENE

One hundred years ago discussion of "the stream of consciousness" took center stage in William James's[1] *Principles of Psychology*.[2] Fifty years later psychologists had relegated consciousness to the wings. Today, a further fifty years on, once again it is moving to occupy center stage. This change is not due solely, or even primarily, to the efforts of psychologists, but rather to the curiosity and widespread interest shown by physicists, mathematicians, neurologists, and neuroscientists. For psychologists this renewed interest is one aspect of the cognitive revolution in psychology that began four decades ago. Today psychologists take mental events seriously and have no doubts that their careful study, using diverse experimental techniques, can yield new insights into how the human mind works.

This renewed interest in consciousness is not confined to psychologists and physicists. As we saw, biologists generally, like Crick, are showing an active interest in the topic. In emphasizing his conviction about the importance of consciousness as a topic for scientific study, Crick proclaims, "I hope before long every laboratory working on the visual system of man and the other vertebrates will have a large sign posted on its walls reading CONSCIOUSNESS NOW" (253). The whole book addresses the question, What is consciousness and how can we find out?

Interestingly, within psychology, the neuropsychologists as much as the cognitive psychologists are responsible for the renewed interest in the study of consciousness. For example, the 1990 St. Andrews international conference *The Neuropsychology of Consciousness*,[3] subsequently published by Academic Press under the same title, is a good example of this renewed interest. Most recently (1995) the international journal *Neuropsychologia* devoted a special issue to the biology and neuropsychology of consciousness.[4] Most influential of all, perhaps, have been the contributions of the late Roger Sperry. In 1952 he began, somewhat tentatively, to suggest that conscious experience should be taken more seriously and given more weight in constructing models of the whole person as a mind–brain unity. It is clear that the time when a generation of psychologists could, with some success, foist on students of human behavior the doctrinaire refusal to acknowledge human consciousness is mercifully past.

The Background

When Wilhelm Wundt established the first psychological laboratory in Leipzig in 1879, one of the principal methods of investigation he and his small band of highly trained associates employed was to gather and undertake detailed analyses of the introspections of the subjects of their experiments. In the early experiments this meant their own introspections. Conscious introspection formed the primary source of data for the newly emerging science of psychology. Developing from their studies, and within a decade, the so-called imageless thought debate was well under way among experimental psychologists. This demonstrated that when thinking is studied using the method of introspection, it isn't always possible to catch the mental processes that have occurred when even a simple task, said to involve thinking, takes place. As the debate livened and feelings grew high, the net result was to underline the dangers of relying exclusively on the introspective reports of experimental subjects, however highly trained. They did not always agree in what they reported and thus their data became an insecure basis on which to build an infant science of psychology. Within four decades of the pioneering work of Wundt and his collaborators in Leipzig, as well as that of his former doctoral student and great admirer Titchener in America, the tide turned. A heavy reliance on studying a limited number of subjects who had undergone intensive training in the technique of introspection came under increasing criticism from John B. Watson and others.

Watson argued that human psychology could well do without the concept of consciousness and the technique of introspection. It was his view that research on consciousness had led nowhere because those investigators who contemplated consciousness could never really agree about what was "going on" in the mind. On the other hand, Watson argued, behavior was public. Two scientists, working independently, could objectively study and measure behavior, something not possible for consciousness. Behaviorism quickly became a self-declared revolution against consciousness. By the middle of the century, B. F. Skinner, at that time the leading exponent of behaviorism, was reasserting that consciousness is merely an epiphenomenon; feelings, he said, are not the causes of actions but merely their consequences.

Despite the behaviorists' temporary success in almost banishing consciousness as a legitimate and serious topic for psychologists to study, its primacy in individual experience and its ubiquitous and mysterious features in all of us guaranteed its eventual return to center stage. After all, the one thing of which we are all more confident than anything else is that we have experiences. We enjoy sensations, we suffer pains, we entertain ideas, we make plans, and we consciously deliberate about the present and the future. At the same time, the puzzle remains: What on earth can this consciousness be?

Physicists, less inhibited than psychologists and not needing to persuade others that they were "real" scientists, have reopened speculation about the nature of consciousness. They raised, in a more precise way, the question of how it is that we, as physical bodies in a physical world, can experience, contain, and give evidence of such a phenomenon as consciousness: How does the material brain produce an immaterial thought? The question seems different from the other topics typically studied by scientists. It is not like optics or embryology or cell biology which, in principle, are equally accessible to any properly trained observer with the right skills and the appropriate apparatus. Indeed, any particular instance of consciousness seems to have a very favored and private status. Access to this phenomenon is unlike that to any other, no matter how sophisticated the apparatus to study it may be. The moment one starts to think seriously about consciousness, a whole series of related questions arise: Are other animals besides ourselves conscious? Are they conscious in the same way that we are conscious? Could a highly sophisticated computer or robot we have constructed be conscious without us knowing it? At what stage does a baby become conscious—before or at birth?

There seems to be at least one starting point held in common by most philosophers and scientists, though expressed in different ways: namely, that consciousness includes two logically separable sets of considerations and observations. The philosopher might describe them as from the *inside* and from the *outside.* The neuropsychologist would talk of the *subjective* and *objective* aspects of consciousness. For the early philosophers such as John Locke, it seemed that the essential and outstanding feature of the mind was consciousness, in particular, self-consciousness. The mind was transparent to itself; nothing was hidden from its own inner views. Hence for Locke the notion of unconscious thinking or perceiving was either not considered or, if it was, it was dismissed as too incoherent to handle systematically. It is for this reason, among others, that when Freud first suggested the existence of unconscious mental processes he was greeted with some derision and stark denial. It wasn't long, however, before Freud's conceptual impossibility began to become respectable among some theorists, especially since it enabled us to begin to think about some aspects of our mental life and behavior inexplicable in other ways. As we shall see later, one of the important contributions made by recent studies by neuropsychologists has been that the somewhat nebulous notions of conscious and unconscious have begun to be sharpened and given operational definitions in terms of awareness or lack of awareness. Though these terms are clearly not identical or synonymous with conscious and unconscious, there is sufficient similarity to constitute the beginnings and the possibility of a more systematic and scientific approach to the task of understanding consciousness.

Converging Recent Scientific Approaches to the Problem of Consciousness

One recurring message shared by today's varied approaches to the study of consciousness is that mind matters. Mind has recaptured its ontological priority—something either denied or quietly submerged in much psychological writing for the past four decades.

Conscious Mind in the Physical World

The heading to this section is also the title of a book by Euan Squires,[5] a professor of applied mathematics at the University of Durham, England. His own major interests have been the theory of elementary particles and their interactions, as well as the foundations of quantum theory. Squires, reviewing and reflecting on the remarkable progress in our understanding of the physical world, from the smallest constituents of atoms to the remotest distances seen by our telescopes, remains puzzled by the phenomena of mind and consciousness. Noting that it is with our minds that the remarkable discoveries in physics have taken place, Squires asks, Where, within physics, do mind and consciousness appear? Can physical things be conscious, or is consciousness something forever outside the range of physics? Is it meaningful, he asks, to talk about mind interacting with a physical thing such as the brain?

Squires's declared starting point is clear. "It is a fact," he writes, "still not properly appreciated by many scientists and philosophers, that quantum phenomena have revolutionized our view of the physical world." That being so, it is his opinion that "this revolution should not be ignored in any serious discussion of conscious mind" (2). He notes that, enozrmously impressed though we are with the great steps forward in theoretical physics and quantum theory, so that today physicists dare to speak of a "theory of everything," nevertheless this enormous increase in knowledge did not suddenly appear from nowhere. Rather, Squires says, *"Everything we know, we know by means of the conscious mind"* (8). The ontological primacy of the conscious mind is further underlined when Squires writes, "As a theoretical physicist I believe, for example, in the existence of quarks. The evidence on which this belief is based is extremely indirect; it comes to me personally only through having read articles by people who have done the relevant experiments or who have provided the detailed interpretation of these experiments, perhaps even mainly through having heard talks by people who themselves have read these articles. Although I might not myself be able to repeat many of the crucial steps in the argument, I accept that they have been done properly. The information is essentially n'th hand where n is quite large" (9). With such n'th hand information he contrasts the immediacy of our personal conscious awareness. Thus he writes, "The evidence for conscious experience, however, is totally personal; I do not have to trust the skill, or the reliability, or the integrity of any person to *know* the reality of redness, or fear, or love, or happiness, etc. It is impossible to define what we mean by 'being real' or 'existing,' but on any reasonable interpretation of these words, that which I experience cannot be less real, or have less claim to exist, than that which I deduce. Nobody who wishes to be interested in the theory which tries to explain everything, can be wholly unconcerned with the conscious mind."

The interest of the physicist will be different from that of the main-line psychologist. Questions the physicist might ask include, What is the mind made of? What are the key constituents required before an object becomes conscious? The process of trying to understand objects by means of the properties of their constituents is reductionism. Here we note the fear, sometimes expressed, that the attempt to reduce "everything to physics" is tantamount to losing the things we cherish most. But for Squires this fear is unfounded so long as one regards reductionism, as he believes we should, as a method, not a metaphysical belief. The method depends on trying to explain the properties of an object in terms of the known properties of its constituents, which are in some sense smaller and simpler. At the same time Squires notes that "a composite object may have properties that are not in themselves properties of the constituents, *and* may indeed not have any meaning for the constituents, without in any way invalidating the reductionist method" (17). On this same topic Squires takes exception to the views of some philosphers, such as Karl Popper, who has written, "New atomic arrangements may lead to physical and chemical properties which are not describable from a statement describing the arrangement of the atoms, combined with a statement of atomic theory."[6] "This assertion," says Squires, "is surely false." For "if we found that a substance containing a particular arrangement of atoms had a property that was not, in principle, deducible, then first we would be astonished and, secondly, we would conclude that in fact the substance contained *something else.*"[7]

Squires acknowledges that, appropriately applied, the reductionist method works "for studies of sodium chloride, for a sugar crystal, for a bicycle, for an aeroplane etc." (18). He believes that "with almost equal confidence we can expect it to be valid for a plant, for a piece of the human body, e.g., a heart or a kidney; but for an animal or a man," he writes, "our doubts begin to dominate and we are left only with questions. Is *a person* completely explainable in terms of the particles of which he is made or is there *something else?*" And, he goes on: "More particularly, is consciousness a property of some special arrangements of quarks and leptons (and if so what are the key features of these arrangements), or is it not? It seems as though most people who have thought about these questions fall readily," he says, "into one of two groups, those who answer definitely yes, and those who with equal confidence answer no, having in common only the view that the opposite opinion is nonsense and hardly worthy of consideration!" (18, 19). For him, it seems evident that to jump from "machines" to the conscious mind "means that we have ignored the claims of, for example, a piece of music, or a sunset, to possess something, beauty, which is not a consequence of their constituents" (19). In so doing he points out that beauty, for example, "is not an intrinsic property of the object but depends for its existence on conscious mind" (19). In this he seems to share the view of Paul Davies,[8] whom he quotes with approval when he writes, "Such a claim is as ridiculous as asserting that a Beethoven symphony is nothing but a collection of notes (Davies, 1983, p. 62)." It is Squires's claim, therefore, that it is only because of conscious mind that the particular sequences of the sounds that make up the symphony acquire the significance of being music.

A further plank in Squires's argument is shared with other mathematicians and theoretical physicists who have drawn attention to the significance and importance of Godel's theorem, published in 1931. The story here begins with the continuing attempt to give the foundations of mathematics a proper logical structure. Godel's theorem states that "in any finitely describable formal system that is consistent and that is rich enough to contain the rules of arithmetic there are true statements that are not theorems" (147). What this all means, says Squires, is that there cannot exist a complete logical basis even for all the results of arithmetic, let alone for all truth. It is Squires's belief that the result published by Godel helped ensure that mathematics would remain a "creative" intellectual activity that would not be exhausted by the routine application of a set of rules. As he put it,[9] "There would be employment for mathematicians, as well as for computers!" (149). It is at this point that Squires sees the relevance of this to the study of the conscious mind. He asks, "If mathematicians are not just computers then what is it that is distinctive about *their* ability at computation?" It is Squires's view that "conscious minds can learn things about any logical system that a computer, following the rules of the system, can never discover." And he goes on: "If we accept this at face value it seems to say that a computer can never model a conscious mind." He gives as an example of this the view expressed by Lucas (1961): "Godel's theorem seems to me to prove that mechanism is false, that is, that minds cannot be explained as machines" (150). Squires, in fairness, points out that there have been, and continue to be, attempts to rebut this claim, but he appeals not only to the views of Lucas but also to the more recent views of Sir Roger Penrose.[10]

What is the relevance of quantum theory, as Squires sees it, to the problems of consciousness? Classical physics, he points out, is about things that are experienced (indirectly) by the conscious mind. We are aware of particles and of their positions and these are the things that enter, for example, into Newton's laws of motion. Thus, claims Squires, in describing the theory,[11] "I can conveniently forget about the means of observation i.e., about conscious mind" (205). But the problem becomes that in quantum physics the entities that appear in the theory are not those of conscious experience. The crucial difference is that whereas classical physics tells us about the world as it is, quantum theory tells us only about what will happen when we observe the world. Following an expansion of this discussion, Squires comes to the point that "What is certainly true is that, for some reason, in discussions of the measurement problem of quantum theory, very similar questions are asked to those which occur in discussions of consciousness: are macroscopic systems responsible; is it something to do with complexity or is it something *new* required; can this something new be regarded as a part of physics or not; can cats do it or only humans?" (206). From this base he goes on to comment that "at the very least we can say that we have met two things, conscious mind and the 'something' that can make observations, which we do not understand and which seem not to be in present physics. It is therefore worth exploring the possibility that they are in some way related to each other" (207).

It is important to realize that Squires is not here attempting to introduce some mystical element, for he goes on later (221) to state that "conscious mind is itself made from the observed objects of the external world, either exclusively, as in materialism, or at least in the sense that it requires such objects to interact (through brains etc.) with that world."

As he moves toward a conclusion Squires poses the question, What is conscious mind? It should be noted that he had earlier written "confident answers can only be expected from those who have not thought too much about the questions" (225). When, however, he comes to give his own answer to the question, he is, as we might expect, suitably tentative and open-minded. Thus he writes (237): "Naive materialism can hardly even start [to answer the question]. A statement that everything is matter is without content since we do not know what matter is. We want to say that it is particles, quarks and leptons etc., but what are these? In most versions of quantum physics they do not really exist, without minds to observe them" (237). He sums up his own provisional conclusions when he writes, "Perhaps the boot strap idea of Geoffrey Chew, the process philosophy of Alfred North Whitehead, and a new understanding of quantum theory will one day come together to give a coherent picture of the relation between conscious mind and the physical world" (237). He notes further, "Until that time we will not let the mystery of the origin of conscious mind prevent us from recognizing its importance as an *ingredient* of reality. Nor will we forget that our experiences are not just a guide to the nature of the world; they are themselves a part of the world" (237).

Mathematician Sir Roger Penrose has also written about consciousness. He has written in depth about modern theoretical physics and the nature and excitement of mathematics. In *The Emperor's New Mind* he argues that the widely believed and strongly argued contention over many years that the human brain is a digital computer is a view that cannot be sustained in the light of a proper understanding of the nature of mathematics and the implications of theoretical physics. In marshalling his arguments he puts together a range of evidence from mathematics and physics, as well as metamathematics. He is an eloquent advocate, not only of conveying a proper view of the wonders of mathematics as practiced by leading mathematicians, but also of his belief in the uniqueness of human individuals, whom he regards as mysterious and awesome beings.

It is instructive to compare Penrose's views with those of Squires. Penrose, like Squires, raises the question, "How is it that a material object (a brain) can actually evoke consciousness?" (523). And "How is it that a consciousness, by the action of its will, can actually influence the (apparently physically determined) motion of material objects?" (523). In identifying what he refers to as the passive and active aspects of the mind–body problem he foreshadows a view we shall find later as a centerpiece of Roger Sperry's views about the active role played by consciousness in life and in brain activity. As a strong believer in and advocate of natural selection, Penrose believes it is important to consider the question, "What selective advantage does a consciousness confer on those who actually possess it?" (523). In this way, though himself a mathematician, he raises questions that are also foremost in the minds of biologists, such as "What are minds for?"

Penrose points out that those who are primarily interested in artificial intelligence (AI) are concerned first and foremost with a very important aspect of consciousness he prefers to call intelligence. However, for him, the question of intelligence remains subsidiary to that of consciousness. Thus he writes, "I do not think that I would believe that true intelligence could be actually present unless accompanied by consciousness" (526). He continues: "On the other hand, if it does turn out that the AI people *are* eventually able to simulate intelligence without consciousness being present, then it might be regarded as unsatisfactory not to define the term intelligence to include such simulated intelligence. In that case the issue of 'intelligence' would not be my real concern here. I am primarily concerned with 'consciousness'" (526). It is at this point that he enters his main contention: "When I assert my own belief that true intelligence requires consciousness, I am implicitly suggesting (since I do not believe the strong AI contention that the mere *enaction* of an algorithm would evoke consciousness) that intelligence cannot be properly simulated by algorithmic means, i.e. by a computer, in the sense that we use that term today" (526). Later he writes, "I shall argue strongly . . . that there must be an essentially non-algorithmic ingredient in the act of consciousness" (526). In passing, and noting the lack of consensus about where in the animal kingdom consciousness is to be found, he notes that there is as yet no generally accepted criterion for the manifestation of consciousness.

In developing his arguments Penrose leans heavily on his intimate knowledge of mathematical thinking, viewed both from the inside as a distinguished mathematician and from the outside through discussing mathematical thinking with other mathematicians and reading what his forebears, such as Hadamard, have written on the topic. In so doing he comes to what, on the face of them, may seem rather surprising conclusions. Like Squires, he leans heavily on Godel's theorem. He writes: "It has, indeed, been an underlying theme of the earlier chapters that there seems to be something non-algorithmic about our conscious thinking. In particular, a conclusion from the argument . . . concerning Godel's theorem, was that, at least in mathematics, conscious contemplation can sometimes enable one to ascertain the truth of a statement in a way that no algorithm could" (533). He continues: "I am putting forward the argument here that it is this ability to divine (or intuit) truth from falsity (and beauty from ugliness!) in appropriate circumstances, that is the hallmark of consciousness" (533).

Developing his argument further he asserts that "we are driven to the conclusion that the algorithm that mathematicians actually use to decide mathematical truth is so complicated or obscure that its very validity can never be known to us" (540). And "The message should be clear. Mathematical truth is *not* something that we ascertain merely by use of an algorithm." "I believe," he argues, "that our consciousness is a crucial ingredient in our comprehension of mathematical truth" (540). Penrose quotes strong support from the distinguished French mathematician Hadamard[12] who had written, "But with Poincaré, we see something else, the intervention of the sense of beauty playing its part as an indispensable means of finding. We have reached the double conclusion:

that invention is choice, that this choice is imperatively governed by the sense of scientific beauty" (544–45). He finds a further ally in Dirac's[13] claim that "it was his keen sense of beauty that enabled him to divine his equation for the electron while others had searched in vain" (545). For him this judgment-forming capacity is the hallmark of consciousness, is something that the AI people have no concept of how to program on a computer, and is a central feature of advanced mathematical thinking. Thus, he writes,[14] "With mathematics, the factual content is small" (553). Reflecting on the fact that in his own experience he finds "words almost useless for mathematical thinking" (549), he notes that some other forms of thinking such as philosophizing seem to be much better suited to verbal expression. And he goes on to wonder why "so many philosophers seem to be of the opinion that language is essential for intelligent or conscious thought!"

As he moves toward the end of his argument he reiterates (577) that "I *am* arguing for some kind of an active role for consciousness, and indeed for a powerful one, with a strong selective advantage" (577). Finally, he says, "I have presented many arguments intending to show the untenability of the viewpoint—apparently rather prevalent in current philosophizing—that our thinking is basically the same as the action of some very complicated computer" (578). He remains critical when he notes that "Science seems to have driven us to accept that we are all merely small parts of a world governed in full detail (even if perhaps ultimately just probabilistically) by very precise mathematical laws. Our brains themselves, which seem to control all our actions, are also ruled by these same precise laws. The picture has emerged that all this precise physical activity is, in effect, *nothing more* than the acting out of some vast (perhaps probabilistic) computation—and hence our brains and our minds are to be understood solely in terms of such computations" (579). For Penrose, "It is hard to avoid an uncomfortable feeling that there must always be something missing from such a picture" (579). So he says, "In my own arguments I have tried to support this view that there must indeed be something essential that is missing from any purely computational picture. Yet I hold also to the hope that it is through science and mathematics that some profound advances in the understanding of mind must eventually come to light. . . . Consciousness, for me seems to be," he says, "such an important phenomenon. . . . it is the phenomenon whereby the universe's very existence is made known" (580). Thus, "beneath all this technicality is the feeling that it is indeed 'obvious' that the conscious mind cannot work like a computer, even though much of what is actually involved in mental activity might do so" (580).

Penrose's fascinating and stimulating views above all point to the tremendous complexity of the issues involved when considering the nature of consciousness. He is anxious to avoid trivializing these issues by implying that there are simple answers to these complex questions, but as the final quote indicates, he is, at the same time, eager that they should be investigated with the full resources available to modern science and that includes the investigations of neuroscientists and biologists, to whose views we now turn.

Consciousness in Psychology

Around the middle of this century, within mainstream psychology, especially in North America, the only way to smuggle in the concept of mind seemed to be to call it something else. At that time, the study of thinking, for example, was certainly not a mainstream topic in psychology. As Jerome Bruner[15] pointed out, it was "too mentalistic, too subjective, too shifty." You could find a way of talking about aspects of mind, such as problem solving, if you came at it in an oblique way, as Kohler had done with his studies of insightful behavior in chimpanzees. Bruner reports George Miller as saying, "You're supposed to get at the mind through the eye, ear, nose and throat if you are a real psychologist." Another earlier form of camouflage used successfully was that of Edward Tolman, who had studied what he called "vicarious trial and error," which was his way of smuggling consciousness into learning theory.

Bruner graphically illustrates how the main texts in psychology around the middle of this century, what he calls the advanced "high-status" ones such as Woodworth's *Experimental Psychology* (late 1930s) and Steven's *Handbook of Experimental Psychology* (1951), devoted only very brief treatments to anything remotely like thinking. Of Woodworth's text, only 77 of the 823 pages dealt with problem solving, and that included animal studies and thinking. The contrast in Steven's book was even greater—only 27 pages were given to a chapter on cognitive processes out of its 1,362 pages. This seems hardly believable in the 1990s, when cognitive psychology is so dominant. But mind is not synonymous with consciousness. Mind is a label that we use to refer to the remarkable things that human beings, and no doubt other creatures, can do in handling the vast amounts of information bombarding them all the time, reflecting on that information, and then going beyond it in anticipating and planning. In a sense consciousness is an instrument of mind. There is a lot more to mind than consciousness and, as Bruner points out, even philosophers spent their time not so much elucidating it for us, as telling us how to talk about it! So while from the beginning of the cognitive revolution, which Bruner dates from 1952, mind entered increasingly into discussions in main-line psychology, it was several decades before consciousness began to be taken seriously. And when it was it was not primarily cognitive psychologists who took the lead but neuropsychologists.

Neuropsychology and Consciousness

Neuropsychologists did not suddenly get together and declare that the time had come to study consciousness. Rather, as often happens in science, developments in related disciplines or unexpected results on a narrow front within the discipline opened up new frontiers for investigation on a topic that had lain dormant for some time. As regards the neuropsychology of consciousness, two significant things happened over the past two decades. First were the quite remarkable developments in techniques for imaging the brain, notably and most recently the use of magnetic resonance imaging (MRI) and studies of cerebral blood flow. These developments, combined with increasing sophistication of the analysis of event-related potentials taken at the surface of the skull, led to the possibility of hitherto unimagined fine-grained patterns of analysis of brain activity taken while people were actually undertaking specific cognitive tasks. The second development is what Weiskrantz[16] described as "the virtual epidemic of dissociations discovered by neuropsychologists whereby residual processing occurs in the absence of acknowledged awareness." He was referring to the remarkable findings in a small group of patients suffering from amnesia, who nevertheless showed good retention of certain specific types of events even though their professed knowledge of these events was minimal. Weiskrantz was also referring to his own work on blind sight, a condition in which, due to lesions of the cerebral cortex, half the visual field is, to all intents and purposes "blind," but nevertheless, patients, in spite of their own expectations, are still able, under certain experimental conditions, to report at above chance level the presence or absence of visual stimuli. Studies of blind sight led to studies of blind touch, prosopagnosia (the inability to recognize faces) and various other forms of agnosia, dyslexia, unilateral neglects, and aphasia.

The capacity to undertake a task in the absence of, or independent of, explicit awareness of what is happening has been closely scrutinized also in experiments with normal subjects. Experiments on repetition priming, backward central masking, lexical decision, and subliminal perception have all contributed to knowledge in this field. The focus of studies by neuropsychologists has been to regard consciousness as conscious awareness or, when consciousness is not present, lack of awareness. How such conscious awareness emerges in the first place has been viewed differently by different scientists. Sperry, for example, regards the emergence of conscious awareness as resulting from the increasing complexity of the nervous system without finding it necessary, at this stage, to specify what it is about complexity that allows this remarkable qualitative attribute to emerge. Others such as Crick and Koch have sought to link the question of awareness to what they call the binding problem. This is a problem of how the multiplicity of specialized visual neurons that exist in the brain cohere into a single visual image that emerges into consciousness. Weiskrantz thus identifies the combination of rapidly developing imaging techniques, together with the evidence of the epidemic of dissociations between "overt" and "covert" processes both in neuropsychology and in human experimental psychology, as the bodies of knowledge that generated new and important insights into mechanisms underlying different forms of awareness. He comments that the evidence produced by experimental psychologists and neuropsychologists working in this field should provide philosophers of mind with important material which, by its nature, will to some extent relieve them from too much dependence on the armchair! A similar view, although perhaps expressed in a somewhat more forthright way, is given by Crick:[17] "The study of consciousness is a scientific problem. . . . If there is any lesson to be learned from this book it is that we can now see ways of approaching the problem experimentally. There is no justification for the view that only philosophers can deal with it. Philosophers have had such a poor record over the last 2,000 years that they would do better to show a certain modesty rather than the lofty superiority that they usually display. Our tentative ideas about the workings of the brain will almost certainly need clarification and extension. I hope that more philosophers will learn enough about the brain to suggest ideas about how it works, but they must also learn how to abandon their pet theories when the scientific evidence goes against them or they will only expose themselves to ridicule." While Crick's statement is a bit strong, it is a salutory reminder of the crucial importance of the empirical approach.

Given these two developments in neuropsychology we may ask what sort of things neuropsychologists today are saying about consciousness. The 1990 international conference at St. Andrews, organized by David Milner and Michael Rugg and referred to earlier, may be taken as typical of the state of the art as neuropsychologists address the problem of consciousness by studying awareness and lack of awareness in brain-damaged and normal people.

Michael Posner and Mary Rothbart posed the question, What is the relationship between the study of attention and the understanding of consciousness? They argued that the evidence points to the existence of three networks in the brain involved in selective attention: the posterior and anterior attention systems and the visual system. Posner[18] has no doubt that "the study of attention is fundamental to understanding conscious processing" (191). He believes that as the anatomical basis in cognitive operations of the attentional networks becomes clearer, the extent of the relationship will be further clarified. At the same time he acknowledges that his view is only one of several tenable views today. Thus others such as Bisiach would argue that "the concept of consciousness involves such a highly distributed system that the specification of its anatomical basis is not a meaningful exercise" (115). Posner, however, pointed out that "a similar view would have been tenable in the study of word reading a few years ago" (91). However, recent PET studies seem to have shown that although reading or listening involves much of the brain, the specifiable computations that compose the task of processing its major constituents are very localized (Posner et al., 1988). Posner believes that a similar resolution between distribution and localization will be possible in the study of consciousness. He has no doubt that further research aimed at deepening our understanding of the relation between the brain's attention networks and conscious experience remains one effective way of understanding more about consciousness.

Edoardo Bisiach,[19] another participant in the St. Andrews conference, while sharing many of Posner's views, nevertheless emphasizes that "we must conclude that the mechanisms by which conscious experience of a relatively complex situation is achieved are indeed widely distributed in neural space and sub-divided into several processes. None of these, so far as we know from observations of brain damaged subjects, centralizes in itself the role of a conscious homunculus" (120). He reiterated this view later when discussing how the contents of awareness achieve their apparent unity when they are presented to consciousness. As far as the awareness of the external world is concerned, this is fairly straightforward. So he writes, "When the elements of what is going to be the content of phenomenal experience swarm from the endogenous activity of the nervous system in a disorderly way they might be integrated by the intervention, as it were, of the brain's editorial staff. In the awareness of the external world, the coherence of phenomenal experience largely reflects the coherence of the environment; a slight amount of retouching is evident in phenomena such as the visual completion occuring in the blind spot, the phoneme restoration effect (Warren 1970), or intriguing illusions (reviewed by Dennett and Kinsbourne 1991) such as the color changes during illusory movement or the 'cutaneous rabbit' phenomenon" (123). These he contrasts with the case of internally generated experiences. To give the reader the "flavor" of how neuropsychologists are grappling with the problem of understanding consciousness, consider Bisiach's approach. Note how he ties it down to the empirical data already gathered from studies of both brain-damaged people and normal subjects.

Coherence is probably achieved with reference to a model set by previous exposure to the environment and through induction; this leaves much room for inventiveness but imposes constraints, vestiges of which are retained even in dreaming and schizophrenia. Conformity with such a model is likely to require a great deal of pruning and re-adjusting of pre-conscious activity, whereas it may admit non-veridical intrusions and the recollections of previous experiences. At any rate, the process of coherent cross integration of phenomenal experience *does not require a mind within the mind—let alone a mind above the mind—any* more than a resident architect is required for the shaping of a cluster of H_2O molecules into a snow crystal. The result of this process may be a more or less complete temporary relaxation achieved through a distributed counterbalance of different computing representations arising within the expanse of the neural network. The fact that in wakefulness thought processes are radically different from those occurring in dreaming suggests that there are progressive levels of cross integration. . . . However this does not imply the endorsement of an intelligent homunculus responsible for the highest level: (relative) rationality may still be conceived to result from a virtual machine distributed across a vast expanse of the cerebral cortex (123).

Particularly relevant to gaining a deeper understanding of human nature is Bisiach's main thesis: "I have argued—*against the cartesian tradition—that there is no definite brain center for conscious experience.* Clinical and experimental data collected in patients suffering from unilateral spatial neglect and related disorders, indeed, suggest that conscious experience rests entirely on a virtual mechanism distributed over brain circuits that are still very poorly understood. This distribution, however, seems to be both horizontal (across and within sensory modalities) and vertical, in so far as conscious experience appears to be shaped not only by afferent occurrences but also by the kinds of actions that happen to be undertaken on the basis of such occurrences. The spread of such mechanisms in neural space entails the possibility of local failures and the dissociability of conscious experience into contrasting states" (131). He returns to his opening question and the one we pose here: "To what extent do the data reviewed in this chapter (i.e., neuropsychological evidence) contribute to an understanding of consciousness?" (131). He believes that in seeking to tie down this question to one that can be addressed in an empirical way one must begin by narrowing objectives and selecting an operational definition of consciousness. Thus he writes, "If we select each time just one of the possible operational definitions of consciousness (e.g., the ability to report verbally the contents of our mental processes), then it is clear that such data tell us a great deal. Conflicting conclusions, however, seem to be reached if we refer to different operational definitions, since we have confronted instances in which what is verbally reported fails to be witnessed by non-verbal responses and instances in which the opposite is true. But here indeed seems to lie the main moral we can draw from the corpus of empirical data so far collected: any intuition to the contrary notwithstanding, consciousness is far from being unitary" (132).

In concluding our look at what neuropsychologists are writing about consciousness we consider the contents of a special issue of the international journal *Neuropsychologia* (1995) devoted to the topic of "The Biology and Neuropsychology of Consciousness." Its title reminds us that neuropsychological research is but one partner in the study of the biology of consciousness. We shall continue to keep in mind the question of whether there are any special issues at stake for the Christian believer. Are there any claims from within this research or implications to be taken from it that challenge or impact traditionally held Christian beliefs? We believe not. And to indicate why, we note the main points made by Jean Delacour[20] in his introduction. Delacour, widening his brief from the *neuropsychology* of consciousness to the *biology* of consciousness, believes that the scientific study of consciousness is not only possible but already well advanced. He sees emerging among scholars a consensus that rejects dualism as well as what he calls eliminative monism. He writes, "The sterility of dualism has been stressed repeatedly and it is now a classical introduction to a text on consciousness with Descartes playing the role of a 'straw man.' The insufficiency of eliminative monism is less obvious, since it can be easily masked by scientific arguments; moreover, this philosophical position fits well with reductionism, which until recently was dominant in neurosciences. However," he goes on, "consciousness as a fact of experience withstands any form of reductionism" (1061).

As regards defining consciousness he finds far less of a consensus. It helps, he believes, to focus separately on the subjective and objective aspects of consciousness, which is "a continuous succession of states having a characteristic structure." This is reminiscent of William James's idea of the stream of consciousness. Delacour recognizes the stable subject aware of itself as being identical though passing through a succession of states. And these conscious states point beyond themselves to "intentionality," expressed by sentences such as "I hope that . . ." or "I see that . . ." or "I imagine that . . ." or "I believe that . . ." The question of whether all conscious states are intentional remains controversial. The other main property that Delacour identifies in conscious representations is that they involve, more or less explicitly, what he calls "global models of the self, of the alter ego and of the world." These two properties—intentionality and global modeling—are intimately related and it is their conjunction that gives conscious representations their special and, he thinks, perhaps unique characteristic. Parting company with some of the views expressed by Penrose, Delacour believes that conscious representations *are* closely tied to language. Consciousness and language are, he believes, of primary importance for workers on artificial intelligence. At the same time he agrees with Penrose that from the AI standpoint all cognitive activity amounts to symbolic thinking and in this sense consciousness is a certain type of algorithm. Like Penrose, he acknowledges that "the symbol is not a specific marker of consciousness. Most of the contents of consciousness are *not* symbolic perceptions, images, schemas, scripts, frames" (1062).

As regards the objective aspects of consciousness, he notes that consciousness is most often but not exclusively associated with wakefulness. Drawing on recent literature, he identifies the main features of consciousness as "(1) the integrated, coherent, controlled character of behavior; (2) detection and adaptation to novelty; (3) goal directed behavior, with flexibility and the completion of a given task or plan in variable conditions; (4) use of language; (5) use of certain forms of representation as exemplified by declarative memory; (6) metacognition" (1065). These features he thinks can be considered as more or less specific objective criteria. The first three, at least, he says are fulfilled by many artificial systems. He notes that the objective description is compatible with the subjective one, so that at times precise correspondences between the two are possible. But, he warns, "subjective and objective descriptions may disagree on the unified, integrative nature of consciousness" (1065).

In answering the question of what consciousness is for, Delacour has no doubt that consciousness has "real, material functions, which exclude both epiphenomenalism and metaphysical conceptions. It is a recurring and lasting state, extending over most of wakefulness and a sizeable part of sleep; it is associated with most significant behaviors, especially with social interactions. There are two principal groups of functional concepts: one from artifical intelligence and the other from evolutionary biology" (1066). He believes that the rule and symbol models of cognition from artificial intelligence alone cannot give vital leads to explicating the biology of consciousness. He believes that is well illustrated by David Marr's thesis on the independence of the functional and implementation levels in a cognitive machine. For this reason he believes it is preferable to look for the functions of consciousness in living organisms, not in AI machines. He believes this, first, because in the present state of our knowledge consciousness seems to be an exclusive property of living organisms; second, because a description of consciousness in terms of evolutionary biology may lead more directly to its neurobiological basis. Evolutionary biologists see consciousness as having evolved as a means of optimizing the functioning of increasingly complex nervous systems. But such integration is not a merely passive process. He writes, "This synthesis is not passive, merely reflecting the anatomical organization of the visual system which is in great part parallel, consisting in numerous cortical modules (more than 20), relatively specialized in the analysis of the different features of visual objects. Visual perception sets into play anticipations, a priori categories, as shown by the perceptual illusions and constancies, the filling in of 'the blind spot,' and the 'completion' phenomena of the lesions of the visual system" (1068). He also notes the social aspects of consciousness, particularly in its relationship to language. Thus, consciousness may indeed have a social origin that would, in turn, account for its intentional modeling structure. He notes that "as primate cognitive activities seem to be mostly stimulated by social life, models of the social group may be the basis for other models: the self, alter ego and physical world." And in this regard, he adds, "If consciousness has a biological value, it should exist in some form in animals" (1068).

In a later section, reviewing the neurobiology of consciousness, he covers much the same ground that we have covered earlier in this chapter. It is interesting that he picks up a point we noted from the writings of Bruner. In discussing some of the dissociations in, for example, blind sight, he comments, "These dissociations demonstrate that a major part of cognitive activity is unconscious. Contrary to what was wrongly assumed by Descartes, mind and consciousness are not equivalent. Another lesson from neuropsychology is that there is not a unique 'center' of consciousness" (1070). His tentative conclusion is that "a complete view of the neural basis of consciousness is still impossible. However, the preceding data suggest that two opposing concepts seem inadequate. Contrary to holistic views, consciousness, due to its divisibility and its modularity, is not an emergent property of the whole brain. On the other hand, it is not the function of a unique center as assumed by Strehler. Clearly many structures playing different roles are involved. This is in agreement with the notion that consciousness is not a separate faculty but a certain activity mode of basic cognitive functions—memory, perception, action planning. Its basis is likely to be a certain type of interaction of different neural systems rather than the special product of one of them. But how is this interaction achieved? What is the origin, the basis of the unified, integrative character of consciousness?" (1070). This he recognizes is the most difficult part of the problem and it is here that he thinks that it is tempting to invoke some new, still to be discovered, mysterious property of the nervous system to provide an answer. However, he believes that "the difficulty is intractable only for pure reductionist concepts of the nervous system attempting to explain the integrative aspects of consciousness by a special cell or molecule" (1071). He has no doubt that "dogmatic reductionism is the other main philosophical obstacle to the neurobiology of consciousness. Hunting for the consciousness molecule may be sterile and its failure may strengthen the dualistic position" (1071). While acknowledging that consciousness may ultimately only be explained by a new and yet to be discovered physics, he argues that neurobiology, in its present state, based on physical techniques that allow its impressive advances, is able to reveal the material basis of consciousness. And, he concludes, "The only condition is that the neurobiology of consciousness should be integrative, essentially based on data from a living, intact brain, functioning under conditions where consciousness is possible" (1072).

Taking Stock

1. Consciousness, a topic of primary interest to psychologists a century ago, had, fifty years later, almost dropped from sight as an issue to research or to write about. By the 1950s psychologists in North America were able to foist on generations of students of human behavior the doctrinaire refusal to acknowledge human consciousness as worthy of serious study or as a potent factor in human behavior.

Today scientists, however distinguished and almost without exception, acknowledge its mysterious nature. Thus, Crick wrote, "This book is about the mystery of consciousness"; Sir Roger Penrose marvels over "how is it that a material object (a brain) can actually evoke consciousness"; Squires puzzles, "Where, within physics, does mind and consciousness appear? . . . Can physical things be conscious?"; Sir John Eccles writes of the "tremendous intellectual tasks (that face us) in our efforts to understand baffling problems that lie right at the center of my being."[21] But to acknowledge frankly the enormity of the task we face, as scientists, in seeking to understand this mysterious something that we label consciousness does not constitute an excuse (or even a reason) for going on to assert "so far science cannot explain consciousness so this is where God is to be seen at work." To follow that route would be to resurrect the God-of-the-gaps approach to portraying the relationship of scientific knowledge and truth given by revelation. Indeed, these same scientists who readily acknowledge the mysterious nature of consciousness all seem agreed that it is a timely topic for scientific study, as perhaps never before.

Just as the remarkable discoveries of the cosmologists have done nothing to explain away but rather to increase our wonder as we see more

clearly how "the heavens declare the glory of the Lord," so as we continue to unravel the mysteries of consciousness we shall increasingly
marvel as we become aware, as even Crick acknowledged, when he
quoted with approval the psalmist's statement that "We are fearfully and
wonderfully made."

2. In the past decade scientists from diverse disciplines, including
physics, theoretical physics, mathematics, biology, neuroscience, and
neuropsychology, have written about consciousness—some specula-
tively, some from an increasing base of empirical data. They differ on
many things, but on one they agree: It is a vitally important topic. So
important, in the view of Crick, that "every laboratory working on the
visual system of man and the other vertebrates will have a large sign
posted on its walls reading CONSCIOUSNESS NOW." For Squires it is
important because "everything we know, we know by means of the conscious mind." For Penrose it is important because, he writes, "I believe
that our consciousness is a crucial ingredient in our comprehension of
mathematical truth" and thus "I am arguing for some kind of an active
role for consciousness, and indeed a powerful one, with a strong selective
advantage." And he goes on: "Consciousness for me seems to be such an
important phenomenon . . . it is the phenomenon whereby the universe's
very existence is made known."[22]

3. The study of consciousness can no longer be left to philosophers—and
that includes the philosophical psychologists. Thus, Weiskrantz's comment that experimental psychologists and neuropsychologists should
provide philosophers of mind with important material which, by its
nature, will to some extent relieve them from too much dependence on
the armchair, and Crick's assertion that "the study of consciousness is a
scientific problem. . . . There is no justification for the view that only
philosophers can deal with it. . . . I hope that more philosophers will
learn enough about the brain to suggest ideas about how it works, but
they must also learn to abandon their pet theories when the scientific
evidence goes against them or they will only expose themselves to
ridicule."[23] Would it be unfair to replace reference to "philosophers," in
this quote from Crick, by "philosophical theologians" and for it still to
be a timely warning as they write about human nature?

4. There will be no quick and easy answers available from the scientific
study of consciousness. Even so there is already enough data to warn
against accepting either of two supposed solutions to the problems, dualism and eliminative monism, which have been and continue to be
widely canvassed by some.

5. Consciousness as a topic of investigation is entering ever more firmly into the scientific arena. Handwaving statements without empirical data just will no longer suffice.

Perhaps we may take encouragement from unexpected developments in more basic sciences such as physics. Maybe there is a higher coherence framework, as yet undiscovered, which will eventually help us make sense of all the data.

6. Despite Crick's attempt to set up a conflict between what he takes as the religious view of human nature, which he believes argues for a "hypothetical immortal soul" (xii), and the view that "people have souls, in the literal and not merely metaphorical sense," we believe there is no necessary conflict between the biblical view of human nature (as outlined in chapter 6) and the emerging picture from scientific research. Both point to one set of physical events that require analysis from two (at least) distinct perspectives in order to begin to do justice to what is being discovered scientifically.

Polkinghorne,[24] who prefers to talk about a new regime rather than a coherent framework, has written of the seeming irrationality (until recently) of the superconductivity state: "It was simply the case that there was a higher rationality than that known in the everyday world of Ohm. After more than fifty years of theoretical effort an understanding of current flow in metals was found which subsumed ordinary conduction and superconductivity into a single theory. The different behaviors correspond to different regimes, characterized by different organizations of the states of motion of the electrons in the metal. One regime changes into the other by a phase change (as the physicists call it) at the critical temperature" (75).

Could it be that the same material "stuff," brains, of animals as well as humans, due to changes in structural complexity, at some point undergo something analagous to "a phase change" so that new properties of mind, consciousness, and a capacity for spiritual awareness emerge in humans? Patient, hard work by dedicated psychologists and neuroscientists may yet give us fresh insights into how, indeed, "we are marvellously and wonderfully made."

CHAPTER 11

Explaining Consciousness Now

A Contemporary Issue

Everything in scientific enquiry should be exposed
to remorseless criticism. The evolutionary assumption
implies that consciousness is efficacious—that it is not an
epiphenomenon. . . . There is no more mystery in our
inability as scientists to give an explanation of an individual
consciousness than there is in our inability to explain why
there is something rather than nothing. There is a mystery,
perhaps, but it is not a scientific one.
—Gerald Edelman, *Bright Air, Brilliant Fire,* 1992

NEUROBIOLOGICAL ASSESSMENTS OF CONSCIOUSNESS

SCIENTIFIC DATA do not come with a label attached giving their interpretation. This is graphically illustrated by the data gathered by scientists seeking to understand consciousness. The views of four biologists,
who over the past forty years have received the Nobel Prize in Medicine
or Physiology and have written about consciousness, well illustrate this
diversity of explanations. In chronological order of the award of their
prizes they are Francis Crick, Sir John Eccles, Gerald Edelman, and Roger
Sperry. We shall look briefly at how each views consciousness and its
biological substrate. In so doing, we may begin to appreciate something
of the complexity of the issues involved (if the previous chapter had not
already demonstrated that) and, at the same time, be warned against any
simplistic solutions to the problems we face.

Francis Crick

Francis Crick is arguably the most influential biologist of the twentieth century as joint discoverer with James Watson of the structure of DNA. As we indicated in the previous chapter, recently Crick has given his views on the mind, the brain, and consciousness in his *The Astonishing Hypothesis.*[1] The opening pages set the stage. He writes, "This book is about the mystery of consciousness—how to explain it in scientific terms. I do not suggest a crisp solution to the problem. I wish I could, but at the present time this seems far too difficult" (xi). Continuing with this modest approach, his preface ends, "I am still groping with these difficult problems, but I hope the reader will find this introduction to them of some interest." He has no doubt that "now is the time to think scientifically about consciousness (and its relationship, if any, to the hypothetical immortal soul) and . . . the time to start the *experimental* study of consciousness in a serious and deliberate way" (xii).

Crick's astonishing hypothesis is "that you, your joys and your sorrows, your memories and your ambitions, your sense of personal identity and free will, are in fact no more than the behavior of a vast assembly of nerve cells and their associated molecules" (3). In this opening sentence he discloses his presuppositions, which pervade the book. His philosophy and metaphysical position are those of a materialist reductionist. He gives the reader a clearly written, ingeniously illustrated, and lucid account of the tightening of the links between mind and brain, generously spiced throughout with his personal speculations of what it might all mean. He is continually self-critical and often, having convinced his reader of the plausibility of one interpretation of the data he presents, he then immediately exposes all the flaws in his own arguments. He even seems sensitive to the possible misinterpretations of his constant reiteration that "you are *no more than* the behavior of a vast assembly of nerve nets and their associated molecules" or "that you are *nothing but* a pack of neurones," when toward the end (261), he writes, "The words *nothing but* in our hypothesis can be misleading if understood in too naive a way."

Crick found the views of David Marr, the young English scientist who first trained in mathematics before going on to study the brain, as one of the most insightful approaches to the beginnings of understanding how the brain works. In his book *Vision*, Marr had argued that the main job of vision was to derive some form of representation of shape; other features, such as brightness, color, and texture, were, in his view, of secondary importance to shape. He took the view that the brain builds within itself a symbolic representation of the visual world, making explicit those aspects that are only implicit on the retinal image.

Marr thought that the total job could not be done in one simple step, but there was a sequence of representations, which he called the "primal sketch," the "two and a half D sketch," and the 3-D model. Sadly Marr died at age thirty-five. Crick, lamenting the great loss to theoretical biology, remained convinced that had Marr lived he would not have remained fixed in his ideas but would have developed further approaches to brain theory as a subject to study.

From this Crick goes on to ask the question, "What style of explanation shall we need to understand the brain?" He does not believe, as he puts it, that, for example, visual perception requires the solving of elaborate equations, as he believes is often implied by artificial intelligence researchers. Rather, he shares the views of his colleague Ramachendran that perception "uses rules of thumb, short cuts, and clever sleight of hand tricks that are acquired by trial and error through millions of years of natural selection. This is a familiar strategy in biology but for some reason it seems to have escaped the notice of psychologists who seem to forget that the brain is a biological organ" (77). And, therefore, Crick underlines, and agrees with the view of Ramachendran, that "the best way to resolve some of these issues may be actually to open the black box [the brain] in order to study the responses of nerve cells, but psychologists and computer scientists are often very suspicious of this approach" (77–78). It is, I believe, interesting that toward the end of his book, Crick, anxious, it seems, to maintain a balance, says that "to say that our behavior is based on a vast, interacting assembly of neurones does not diminish our view of ourselves but enlarges it tremendously" (260). Indeed, earlier in the same paragraph, referring to the vast increase in our knowledge about biology and the world in general, he comments that "this new knowledge has not diminished our sense of awe but increased it immeasurably. The same is true of our detailed biological knowledge of the structure of plants and animals, and of our own bodies in particular. The psalmist said, 'I am fearfully and wonderfully made,' but he had only a very indirect glimpse of the delicate and sophisticated nature of our molecular constitution" (260). But soon he returns to the main thrust of his book, which is that "if the scientific facts are sufficiently striking and well established, and if they support the Astonishing Hypothesis, then it will be possible to argue that the idea that man has a disembodied soul is as unnecessary as the old idea that there was a Life Force. This is in head-on contradiction to the religious beliefs of billions of human beings alive today. How will such a radical challenge be received?" (261). We, however, saw in chapter 7 that the whole idea of disembodied souls is not a biblical idea and hence the thrust of Crick's criticism is removed at a stroke.

Sir John Eccles

Our next Nobel Laureate is the distinguished physiologist Sir John Eccles.[2] His views contrast strongly with those of Crick. Whereas the thrust of Crick's book is to deny any substantive case for dualism (a view consistent with his presupposition as a materialist reductionist), Eccles, a Roman Catholic, believes in some form of dualism of mind and body. On this view a conscious, nonphysical entity labeled *mind is* separate and independent from the brain and is able to exert its influence on the processes within the brain. Eccles seeks to work out how this mind–brain interaction may plausibly take place. He views the brain as possessing circuits of neurons, at times so delicately poised that the minutest of influences produced by the mind can tip the activity of the brain one way or the other. The influence he proposes is clearly nonphysical. In some of his writings he develops this model further and sees the conscious self, which he believes is a separate entity, as communicating directly with the dominant left half of the brain in most right-handed individuals. On this view freedom of will and freedom of action are safeguarded by means of the consciously willed influence of the conscious self over the brain. Other biologists, such as J. Z. Young,[3] would not share this view. Thus Young writes, "The clinical evidence does not support the idea that there is some entity or spirit that can exist apart from the brain. Nor is it necessary to postulate, as Eccles and some other dualists seem to wish, that our 'minds' constitute some special force acting to control the cells of the brain. It is indisputable that we have consciousness, but must we say we have 'a mind' in the sense of an entity acting upon the world?" Young goes on to argue that, on his view, "proper consideration of the nature of persons and their brains and of living systems in general will show that a common terminology can help in the study of all aspects of man. We can profitably use such terms as information, action, choice, aim and even value in connection with physical as well as mental events." Thus, he argues, "Consciousness is an aspect of the functioning of the brain, not something that can exist apart from it. My brain and my body are inseparable from myself" (12).

Returning now to Eccles's views, we need to recognize that while there is certainly no knock-down, unambiguous scientific evidence to repudiate the position that he takes, nevertheless, the accumulating evidence over the past few decades of the intimate and ever-tightening link between mind and brain makes his hypothesis increasingly dubious. Eccles has invoked the indeterminancy of physical events noted in the Heisenberg principle applying to physical systems as giving support to the likelihood of a possible locus for the influence of mind over brain. We shall return to a further consideration of Eccles's views later in this chapter when we examine how different interpretations of the same set of scientific data are offered by Crick and Eccles.

Gerald Edelman

Gerald Edelman[4] received the Nobel Prize in 1972 for his work in immunology. Recognizing the possibility that there were close similarities between neural and immunological memory, he has subsequently written at length about the mind–brain and consciousness problem. In natural organisms learning that occurs in the nervous system is by means of the selection of specific responses in light of environmental events and internal experience and in this way, so the argument goes, the survival of organisms is ensured. Certainly muscles, bones, and glands all manifest alterations with use. Survival then depends on systems that are variable, not rigidly fixed and deterministic, and this flexibility is the secret of a successful life. J. Z. Young had long argued that some of the difficulty in understanding memory disappears if we follow through on this idea and assume that the remarkable accuracy of nervous connections that we observe is achieved by selection and elimination as a result of experience. On this view, the detailed fits between organisms and their environments have been achieved by the process of natural selection. And a similar process, he argues, is seen in the production of antibodies by the immune system of the body and hence the analogies of natural selection and immunology seem a promising way of attacking this problem.

The central plank of Edelman's views is his exposition of what he calls neural Darwinism. From his deep knowledge of the importance of the process of recognition in immunology, Edelman asks the question, What justification is there for considering brain science also as a science of recognition? The detailed answers that he gives to this question are beyond the scope of this brief review, but basically he believes that brain science and the study of behavior are concerned with the adaptive matching of animals to their environments. And thus he says, "In considering brain science as a science of recognition I am implying that recognition is not an instructive process. No direct information transfer occurs, just as none occurs in evolutionary or immune processes. Instead, recognition is selective" (81). Linked with this view is a theme that recurs throughout his writings: "The brain is not a computer" (81). Thus, (82) "the individuality and structural diversity of brains even within one species is confounding to models that consider the brain to be a computer. Evidence from developmental studies suggests that the extraordinary anatomical diversity at the finest ramifications of neural networks is an unavoidable consequence of the embryological process.

That degree of individual diversity cannot be tolerated in a computer system following instructions. But it is just what is needed in a selective system." Instead, he proposes his own theory, which he calls the theory of neuronal group selection (TNGS).

This theory, he says, is based on three essential tenets. First, developmental selection, the dynamic primary processes of development, leads to the formation of the neuroanatomical characteristic of any given species. Thus the genetic code does not provide a specific wiring diagram for this "primary repertoire," as he calls it, but rather imposes a set of constraints on the selectional process. He believes that "even within such constraints, genetically identical individuals are unlikely to have identical wiring, for selection is epigenetic." His second tenet provides another mechanism of selection at work but this does not involve an alteration of the anatomical pattern in general. Rather, it assumes that during behavior synaptic connections in the anatomy are selectively strengthened or weakened by specific biochemical processes. It is this mechanism, he believes, that underlies memory and a number of other functions by effectively laying down a variety of circuits within the anatomical network by a process of selection. It is this set of variant functional units that he calls the "secondary repertoire." His third tenet is concerned with how the selectional events described in his first two tenets connect psychology to physiology. He believes that it suggests how brain maps interact by a process called reentry. This, he says, is "perhaps the most important of all the proposals of the theory, for it underlies how the brain areas that emerge in evolution coordinate with each other to yield new functions" (85).

Edelman's theory, like any provocative new theory, has not been without its critics. Two concepts of his theory that have come under the most intense attack are those of neuronal groups and of selection itself. Neurophysiologists such as Horace Barlow, as well as Francis Crick, have, he notes, attacked the notion of the existence of such groups. Edelman believes, however, that contrary to these initial criticisms, "experimental findings have emerged since the TNGS was first proposed that directly demonstrate the existence of neuronal groups and the functions of reentry." Further details are beyond our consideration here but we note these to indicate that there is lively debate within the community of experts on this particular aspect of Edelman's theory. This does not concern him. Indeed, he notes shortly afterwards (97) that "everything in scientific enquiry should be exposed to remorseless criticism." With these comments in mind, we move on now to our primary consideration here: Edelman's views on consciousness.

Edelman believes it is necessary to make what he calls a fundamental distinction between what he labels primary consciousness and higher-order consciousness. Primary consciousness is "the state of being mentally aware of things in the world—of having mental images in the present. But it is not accompanied by any sense of a person with past and future. It is what one may presume to be possessed by some non-linguistic and non-semantic animals. . . . In contrast," he goes on, "higher-order consciousness involves the recognition by a thinking subject of his or her own acts or affections. It embodies a model of the personal, and of the past and the future as well as the present. It exhibits direct awareness—the non-inferential or immediate awareness of mental episodes without the involvement of sense organs or receptors. It is what we as humans have in addition to primary consciousness. We are conscious of being conscious."

In developing his views of consciousness, Edelman spells out three assumptions he says are part of the underpinnings of his theory. He labels these the physics assumption, the evolutionary assumption, and the qualia assumption. Briefly stated, these assumptions, in Edelman's own words, are as follows.

"The physics assumption is that the laws of physics are not violated, that spirits and ghosts are out; I assumed that the description of the world by modern physics is an adequate but not completely sufficient basis for a theory of consciousness. Modern quantum field theory provides a description of a set of formal properties of matter and energy at all scales. It does not, however, include a theory of intentionality, of a theory of names for macroscopic objects, nor does it need them. What I mean by physics being just adequate is that I allow no spooks—no quantum gravity, no action at a distance, no super physics—to enter into this theory of consciousness" (113).

"The evolutionary assumption is also reasonably straightforward. It is that consciousness arose as a phenotypic property at some point in the evolution of species. Before then it did not exist. This assumption implies that the acquisition of consciousness either conferred evolutionary fitness directly on the individuals having it, or provided a basis for other traits that enhance fitness. The evolutionary assumption implies that consciousness is efficacious—that it is not an epiphenomenon (merely the redness of the melting metal, when pouring is what counts)" (113).

He notes that when he gets to his third assumption he comes to something much more subtle. He begins by defining what he calls qualia. These, he says, constitute "the collection of personal or subjective experiences, feelings, and sensations that accompany awareness. They are phenomenal states—how things seem to us 'as human beings.'" He then goes on to note that since qualia, according to his definition, are experienced directly only by individuals, the methodological difficulty that he faces at once becomes obvious. Thus, he says, "We cannot construct a phenomenal psychology that can be shared in the same way as a physics can be shared. . . . What is directly experienced as qualia cannot be fully shared by another individual as an observer" (114). And thus he notes the paradox. In order to do physics we must employ our conscious life, our perceptions, and our qualia. But, he goes on, "in my intersubjective communication, I leave them out of my description, assured that fellow observers with their own individual conscious lives can carry out the prescribed manipulations and achieve comparable experimental results. When for some reason qualia do affect interpretations, the experimental design is modified to exclude such effects; the mind is removed from nature" (114). However, he points out that "in investigating consciousness, we cannot ignore qualia. The dilemma is that phenomenal experience is a first person matter, and this seems, at first glance, to prevent the formation of the completely objective or causal account." He then asks the question, Is this a completely hopeless situation? He thinks not.

Edelman's third assumption, as a basis for his theory of consciousness, is that "it is sensible to *assume* that, just as in our selves, qualia exist in other conscious human beings, whether they are considered as scientific observers or as subjects" (115). Hence he wants to build a theory of consciousness based on the assumption that qualia do indeed exist in other human beings. And so he continues: "This *qualia assumption* distinguishes between higher order consciousness and primary consciousness. Higher order consciousness is based on the occurrence of direct awareness in a human being who has language and a reportable subjective life. Primary consciousness may be composed of phenomenal experiences such as mental images, but it is bound to a time around the measurable present, lacks concepts of self, past, and future, and lies beyond direct descriptive individual report from its own standpoint" (115).

In developing his theory of consciousness based on these three assumptions, Edelman faces and brings out into the open certain basic problems about trying to study consciousness as a scientific subject. Thus, he writes, "There is something peculiar about consciousness as a subject of science, for consciousness itself is the individual, personal process each of us must possess in working order to proceed with *any* scientific explanation. Even though I may be unaware of what I have forgotten or repressed or of unconscious factors that drive my behavior, I feel as if the process of consciousness is all of a piece, at least in my healthy state. And so it is natural that I demand an explanation of my own consciousness in terms satisfactory to myself. But I must realize that it is not a scientific act to do so, nor would I expect it to be. After all, no one says to a physicist, 'You have explained energy and matter in terms of symmetry relations, and you have approached the beginnings of the universe in your theories. But you have not *really* explained *why* there is something rather than nothing.' To attempt such an explanation would be fruitless; under these circumstances no science based on experiment could recommend itself as better than any other. A scientific explanation cannot be given" (138). He then goes on to ask, why "are we tempted to demand a scientific explanation of how it feels personally to be conscious? It is the certainty of consciousness to ourselves and its relation to the idea of self that makes us want to demand more of a psychologist than of a physicist or a cosmologist. But the demand is not a scientifically reasonable one."

Hence, his reply to the question he posed would be, as he says, in exactly the same form as one given by a physicist, who would say, "I have offered you a theory in terms of known structures and relationships, one based on experimental facts. The theory says that, if you perform an operation on structure said to be important for properties of consciousness, those properties will be predictably altered or may even disappear. . . . So it is with other tests; the theory of consciousness *can* have operational components. But it must, if it is a good theory, also unify all kinds of pertinent facts and deepen our understanding" (139).

Roger Sperry

We now arrive at the fourth of our Nobel Laureates, Roger Sperry. His interests, both in terms of research and of the problems he studied, are much more centrally placed in the contemporary landscape of late-twentieth-century psychology than that of the other biologists whom we have considered.

Sperry on several occasions reflected on the fact that the 1950s were dominated by what he describes as a materialistic philosophy that maintained the so-called psychophysical or mind–brain identity theory. This view was made explicit by, among others, D. M. Armstrong, a philosopher from Sydney, Australia, who stated that "we can give a complete account of man in purely physico-chemical terms" and that in a "purely electro-chemical account of the workings of the brain," the mind is nothing but the brain. Sperry also quotes Armstrong, writing in 1968, that "man is nothing but a material object having none but physical properties."

Commenting on the neural substrate of any brain processes that mediate conscious awareness, Sperry noted that it is composed of elements and forces within forces. These he saw as ranging from subnuclear and subatomic particles, at the lower levels, upwards through molecular, cellular, and simple to complex neural systems. Thus, he comments, "At each level of the hierarchy, elements are bound and controlled by the enveloping organizational properties of the larger systems in which they are embedded. Wholistic systems' properties at each level of organization have their own causal regulatory roles, interacting at their own level and also exerting downward control over their components, as well as determining the properties of the system in which they are embedded. It is postulated that at higher levels of the brain these emergent system properties include the phenomena of inner experience as higher order categories in the brain's hierarchy of controls."[5] And he continues in the same vein when he writes, "As is the rule for part–whole relations, a mutual interaction between the neural and mental events is recognized: the brain physiology determines the mental effects, as generally agreed; but also the neuro-physiology, at the same time, is reciprocally governed by the higher subjective properties of the enveloping mental events." It is this last statement that is the crux of Sperry's new emphasis in his theory of consciousness. In seeking to set his theory alongside those of earlier theories, he writes, "The resultant mind–brain model, in which mind acts on brain and brain acts on mind, is classified as being 'interactionist' in contrast to mind–brain 'parallelism' or mind–brain 'identity.' The term 'interaction,' however, is not the best for the kind of relationship envisaged, in which mental phenomena are described as primarily supervening rather than intervening in the physiological processes" (165). Thus, for Sperry, "in the revised mind–brain model consciousness becomes an integral working component in brain function, an autonomous phenomenon in its own right, not reducible to electrochemical mechanisms." And he goes on: "Because it is neither traditionally dualistic nor physicalistic, the new mentalist paradigm is taken to represent a distinct third philosphical position. It is emergentist, functionalist, interactionist, and monistic." Thus, he argues, "The mind has been restored to the brain of experimental science. The qualitative, colorful and value rich world of inner experience, long excluded from the domain of science by behaviorist materialist doctrine, has been reinstated."

RECAPITULATION: ONE SET OF DATA, FOUR INTERPRETATIONS

It is instructive now to compare and contrast the views on consciousness of these four Nobel Laureates. On his own admission a self-confessed materialist reductionist, Francis Crick happily asserts, "You are *nothing but* a pack of neurones"; "You . . . are *no more than* the behavior of a vast assembly of nerve cells and their associated molecules." After 250 pages of brilliant exposition of relevant scientific evidence, he states: "To repeat: consciousness depends crucially on thalamic connections with the cortex. It exists only if certain cortical areas have reverberatory circuits (involving cortical layers 4 and 6) that project strongly enough to produce significant reverberations . . ."[6] However, he immediately goes on to say, "I hope nobody will call it the Crick Theory of Consciousness" (252). Indeed, he inserts an immediate apologia by saying, "While writing it down, my mind was constantly assailed by reservations and qualifications. If anyone else produced it, I would unhesitatingly condemn it as a house of cards. Touch it, and it collapses. This," he says, "is because it has been carpentered together, with not enough crucial experimental evidence to support its various parts. Its only virtue is that it may prod scientists and philosophers to think about these problems in neural terms, and so accelerate the experimental attack on consciousness" (252).

By contrast, Sir John Eccles, from his earliest writings to his most recent publications, advocates a strong emphasis on what may be called the dualism of substance. Consciousness "is dependent on the existence of a sufficient number of such critically poised neurones, and, consequently, only in such conditions are willing and perceiving possible. However, it is not necessary for the whole cortex to be in this special dynamic state." And, he goes on, "on the basis of this concept [of activity of the cortex] we can face up anew to the extraordinary problems inherent *in a strong dualism. Interaction of brain and conscious mind, brain receiving from conscious mind in a willed action and in turn transmitting to mind in a conscious experience.*" But, he goes on, "let us be quite clear that for each of us the primary reality is our consciousness—everything else is derivative and has a second order reality. We have tremendous intellectual tasks in our efforts to understand baffling problems that lie right at the center of our being."[7]

What Gerald Edelman finds so daunting about consciousness "is that it does not seem to be a matter of behavior. It just is—winking on with the light, multiple and simultaneous in its modes and objects, ineluctably ours. It is a process and one that is hard to score. We know what it is for ourselves but can only judge its existence in others by inductive inference. As James[8] put it, it is something the meaning of which 'we know as long as no-one asks us to define it'" (111). And, then, later, having introduced his concept of qualia he comments, "We cannot expect any theory of consciousness to render obvious to a hypothetical qualia-free animal what qualia are by any linguistic description. To maintain intersubjective communication and carry out scientific correlation, which is a human activity, we *must* assume qualia. Qualia cannot be derived as experiences from any theory." Having made a comparison with some of the problems faced by modern physicists in understanding aspects of cosmology, he writes, "Our cosmological comparison is not so far afield; we may ask modern physics to explain certain aspects of cosmology beginning at the earliest moment, consistent with the understanding given to us by modern physical theory. But we cannot ask a theory of physics to give a satisfactory answer to Gottfried Leibniz's question of why there is something rather than nothing." He picks up this theme later on (on p. 139) when he raises the question, "Why is there a mystique about consciousness?" And, he comments, "A reasonable answer seems to be that each consciousness depends on its unique history and embodiment. And given that a human conscious self is constructed, somewhat paradoxically, by social interactions, yet has been selected for during evolution to realize mainly the aims and satisfactions of each biological individual, it is perhaps no surprise that as individuals we want an explanation that science cannot give." He goes on: "But there is no more mystery in our inability as scientists to give an explanation of an individual consciousness than there is in our inability to explain why there is something rather than nothing. There is a mystery perhaps, but it is not a scientific one."

From Roger Sperry[9] we have a series of succinct statements that encapsulate his view. First, "consciousness is conceived to be a dynamic emergent property of brain activity, neither identical with nor reducible to, the neural events of which it is mainly composed" (312); "consciousness exerts potent causal effects in the interplay of cerebral operations"; "in the position of top command at the highest levels in the hierarchy of brain organization, the subjective properties were seen to exert control over the biophysical and chemical activities at subordinate levels." He emphasizes (384) "that consciousness phenomena *are not conceived as nothing but neural events.*" At the same time, he admits that the term that he uses, namely, interaction, a psychophysical relation, is perhaps not the best descriptor.

Bringing together these four views we note that several have emphasized the mysterious nature of consciousness. They unashamedly argue that it just won't do to pretend that consciousness is something secondary to our other activities as human beings and as scientists. All our endeavors and achievements in whatever walk of life, including the scientific enterprise, are dependent ultimately on this remarkable phenomenon of individual consciousness. If ever the ontological priority of mind needed to be emphasized, it is surely forcefully achieved in the varied approaches of these four scientists writing on this common issue. At the same time they all believe that consciousness is a proper topic for scientific investigation.

Gerald Edelman emphasized that we must understand and accept the limitations of what a scientific theory about consciousness can offer and not demand more than is demanded of, for example, a theory in physics. If anything stands out from these attempts of leading scientists this century in grappling with this problem of consciousness, it is that it is totally to misunderstand the topic if one thinks that it is possible to come up with some simplistic explanation of so mysterious a phenomenon. It is here that we return to a point made earlier when we emphasized that no scientific data come with a little label giving an interpretation. Interpretations have to be created and different interpretations are possible of the same set of data. This we believe is well illustrated by the data on the neural substrate of consciousness. The presuppositions of the investigating scientist exclude certain explanations and give primacy to others. A specific example of this is found in the results of a series of experiments by Libet and his co-workers, which all four scientists agree are relevant to the problem of understanding consciousness.

THE TIMING OF CONSCIOUS AWARENESS— SAME DATA, DIFFERENT INTERPRETATIONS

Libet[10] and his colleagues, over a period of several decades, reported experiments studying the timing of events in the brain in relation to mental phenomena. They devised ways of comparing the times at which events occur in the human brain with those at which mental intentions are reported. Some time ago it was shown that electrodes attached to the head can record a slow negative potential shift a second or more before someone receives a signal that he is expecting and to which he will respond by making a movement. This was labeled the *contingent negative variation* (CNV). A related, but considerably more interesting, discovery was that a similar kind of readiness potential (RP) occurs before a person makes a voluntary action. What Libet and his collaborators have shown is that this readiness potential change in the brain takes place as much as a half second before a subject mentally decides that he intends to make a movement. One way in which they showed this was to ask their volunteers to sit and watch a television screen on which a spot was going around in circles in a clockwise direction at a rate of one revolution every 2 1/2 seconds. Subjects were asked simply to decide, of their own free will, to bend a finger and then to note the position of the spot on the tube at the moment they made their freely chosen decision. Through an electrode attached to the subject's head it was possible to record the readiness potential changes in her brain. These changes began on average 350 milliseconds before the time she reported that she "wanted" or "intended" to act. This was long before the time of actual movement of the finger, which was also detected by electrodes attached to it. It seems that this readiness potential arises from the activities of neurons in what is known as the premotor area of the cortex. There are probably activities occurring in other parts of the brain at still earlier times before such an intended action. The importance of the work by Libet and his collaborators was that they showed us that the brain seems to be at work before a subject's conscious intention to act. Libet stated it in one of his publications as follows: "The brain evidently 'decides' to initiate, or, at least, prepare to initiate the act at a time before there was any reportable subjective awareness that such a decision has taken place. It is concluded that cerebral initiation even of a spontaneous voluntary act, of the kind studied here, can and usually does begin *unconsciously.*"

In a more recent series of studies, Libet has reported on the effects of stimulating part of the thalamus concerned with sensations such as touch and pain.[11] This work was done on people who had volunteered to collaborate since they had already had electrodes implanted in their brains for the relief of intractable pain. The details of the experimental technique are complicated and will not be given here. The results, however, showed that even when the train of pulses into this part of the brain was too brief to elicit conscious awareness, nevertheless the subjects could perform above chance in indicating, guessing if necessary, whether a particular light had been put on for a second or more. In order to become aware of the stimulus the subjects seemed to require significantly longer trains of impulses. Libet's interpretation of his data was that a certain duration of the pulse train was required for conscious awareness to occur. These studies, although not on vision, nevertheless may help explain some aspects of blind sight, which we described earlier. Thus, as Francis Crick has pointed out, the pathway from the lateral geniculate nucleus to visual areas such as V4 may be too weak to produce visual awareness yet still be strong enough to have some influence on the person's behavior. As an aside, we may note that although the experiments just mentioned are not in any sense conclusive, they do, however, indicate ways in which an experimental approach to at least one aspect of consciousness is possible within neural science and experimental psychology. Our brain's information processing occurs apart from (and sometimes before) our conscious awareness.

Some of Libet's[12] earlier experiments have been viewed as evidence to support a dualist view of mind and brain. Sir John Eccles,[13] for example, has inferred from these and similar data that "there can be a temporal discrepancy between neural events and the experiences of the self-conscious mind," and that "this antedating procedure does not seem to be explicable by any neuro-physiological process." This is certainly a plausible view on the evidence currently available. What we don't know in this situation is whether the cortical activity that was elicited and measured was in fact the *immediate* correlate of the conscious experience.

Delacour has pointed out[14] there may be two separate systems, one dedicated to consciousness and one to unconsciousness. However, such a dichotomy is, he believes, unlikely in view of the fact that "conscious and unconscious states are gradual and not all or nothing realities and that most cerebral activity that occurs in conscious states, even during reflective cognitive operations, is unconscious." Moreover, he writes, "No center for consciousness has been found." He notes that, contrary to one view that has been expressed, the brain is not equally potential with respect to consciousness. Here he refers, as did Francis Crick, to the system that is closely involved in cortical arousal and to which he attaches special importance. As Delacour notes, "Thanks to the pattern of its projections, it [the thalamo-cortical projection] may be the basis of the main functional feature of conscious experience, its unified, integrated character." However, Delacour is eager to point out, "this does not mean that it is *the* 'system of consciousness'; a better formulation would be that the induction and maintenance of conscious state depends mainly on a certain activation mode of this system, characterized, among other things by a higher level of excitability of thalamo-cortical neurones and a discharge mode in which interspike intervals are stochastically independent."

What is clear is that as a result of certain lesions in the brain, consciousness may be fragmented. That would raise the question of whether the blind sight phenomenon mentioned earlier involves the existence of two subsystems within the visual system, only one of which gives access to conscious experience. Following through on this idea, Delacour speculates that a particular representation is conscious under two conditions: "One a global one which is the 'state' of consciousness. This state would allow the assembly corresponding to the representation to interact with other assemblies; two, a local condition, that is a property of the assembly itself. Its access to consciousness may depend, for example, on its reaching a critical size." It is at this point that Delacour refers to Libet's results that we are presently considering. He interprets some of Libet's data as showing that this size criterion may indeed be an economical explanation of the fact that consciousness is crucially dependent on time. Thus the transition from an unconscious mental event to a conscious one may depend on an increase in duration of appropriate neural activities. A critical duration for access to consciousness would be (following Libet's work) several hundred milliseconds, which is perhaps the time required for an assembly to reach the critical size and coherence.

Like Crick, Delacour concludes that what these data indicate is that, in principle, the neurobiology of consciousness is not only possible but already in progress. And, he continues in an optimistic mood, "our thesis is that neurobiology, in its present state, based on physical techniques which allowed its impressive advances, is able to reveal the material basis of consciousness. The only condition is that the neurobiology of consciousness should be integrative, essentially based on data from the living, intact brain, functioning under conditions where consciousness is possible." It is noteworthy that at this point, in commenting on threats to the scientific study of consciousness, he adds, "*dogmatic reductionism is the other main philosophical obstacle to the neurobiology of consciousness. Hunting for the consciousness molecule may be sterile and its failure may strengthen the dualistic position.*"

We would agree with Donald and Valerie Mackay[15] who, commenting on Libet's results, wrote: "If we take as the correlate of conscious perception the supervisory matching response to cortical disturbance, a more parsimonious explanation [than Eccles] seems possible. The data could equally be interpreted as showing that the direct neural correlates of the elicited sensation were in some different region of the brain, and a simple conditional coding operation allows the time label to be computed by a backward extrapolation from the output of the integrative process to the putative start of the stimulus. (This may not be the right explanation, but until it and others like it have been ruled out, Libet's data have not been shown to be neurophysiologically inexplicable.)" Thus the dualism of Eccles, while tenable, is neither necessary nor the most parsimonious explanation.

TAKING STOCK

1. One thing emerges clearly from this brief review of the range of current opinions about the status of the scientific study of consciousness. It is that conscious experience is no longer regarded, as often in the past, as being, from a scientific viewpoint, too subjective, too private, and therefore too far removed from the relative certainties of physics, chemistry, and cell biology to warrant serious study. Conscious experiences are certainly private and they are frequently subjectively tinted, *but they are the bedrock of all experience* and it is the only place from which any of us can start. Privately and subjectively, we either do or do not observe something happening in our laboratories, we do or do not measure the position of the pointer on the scale. We shall certainly want to ask our colleagues to repeat our observations and see whether they confirm our findings while remembering that *their* reports are about *their* very private experiences. The same happens whether you look down a micro-

scope, observe the color of a visual stimulus, or take a reading from a scientific instrument. It is here and here only that science can begin.

2. The second theme we have noted is that there is, currently, intensive scientific activity by those dedicated to developing a greater understanding of consciousness, what it is and what its neural substrate is. However, we have also noted that the data do not come nicely labeled with interpretation. Equally competent, equally distinguished scientists from different disciplines and with different presuppositions look at the same set of data and arrive at different conclusions. For our part, we have, on balance, taken the view that it is unnecessary, and would be unwise from the scientific studies of consciousness (as well as unbiblical), to feel obliged to adopt a dualist view of the relation of mind and brain. A more parsimonious view, and we believe one more probable on the basis of the evidence currently available, is that to do justice to the complexity of the one set of neurochemical brain events occurring during conscious experience we must give ontological priority to mental life. As Christians, we believe that we can be peaceably open-minded about questions such as whether consciousness is a property of other animals beside ourselves. In this regard the work of primatologists certainly points to the presence of mind-like, conscious, reflective, and deceptive behavior in the highest nonhuman primates.[16] Again, as we have noted elsewhere in this book, there are no issues at stake here for the biblically informed Christian who recognizes that we share some properties with animals.

The upshot of all this is that the scientist who is a Christian can be enthusiastically committed to, and involved in, work at the cutting edge of neuroscience and neuropsychology aimed at elucidating the mysterious nature of our ubiquitous experience of consciousness. In so doing we shall, as Francis Crick reminded us (perhaps surprisingly), be filling out a little more of just how "fearfully and wonderfully made" we really are.

As scientists we shall continue to be, as Edelman[17] reminded us, concerned that "everything in scientific enquiry should be exposed to remorseless criticism." At the same time we also agree with Edelman that "the evolutionary assumption implies that consciousness is efficacious—that it is not an epiphenomenon."

While each of the scientists noted the mysterious nature of some aspects of consciousness, none of them concluded that we must not study it or that we shall never understand it. Rather, as Edelman put it, "there is no more mystery in our inability as scientists to give an explanation of an individual consciousness than there is in our inability to explain why there is something rather than nothing. There is a mystery perhaps, but it is not a scientific one" (139).

CHAPTER 12

DETERMINISM, FREEDOM, AND RESPONSIBILITY

The future of the universe is not completely determined
by the laws of science as Laplace thought. God still has
a few tricks up his sleeve.
—Stephen Hawking, Waterstone Lecture, 1995

IF YOU SIMPLY REFLECT back on what happened in the past twenty-four hours, recall what you did and what you said, you will find that most of it was based on an unquestioning assumption that, in the main, human behavior is predictable. In this sense, at least, psychological determinism is not some kind of special demonic prejudice held by atheist materialist psychologists, but is an implicit working assumption that most of us hold most of the time. Why would we go to such lengths to devise and apply certain methods to facilitate the learning of physics, French, or mathematics if we did not believe that the effectiveness of some methods was greater than that of others? The same applies in a church situation. Why would we bother with a Sunday school if we didn't think that in some sense it is effective in influencing the children taking part? As a general working orientation, therefore, determinism amounts to little more than taking an attitude that says that human behavior seems to exhibit regularities (laws), that these regularities seem to be susceptible to rational causal explanations (theories), and that for this reason it is sensible to set up our research programs in order to push our understanding of these laws and theories to the limits? We all tend to operate, provisionally at least, on the working assumption that any domain of behavior, whether it be learning French, learning to ski, undergoing psychotherapy, composing music, translating Latin, or whatever else, is in some sense orderly and predictable, that is to say, lawful in the scientific sense of the word. Thus, if a particular behavior seems to be capricious, our natural reaction is not to accept it as such but rather to subject it to more careful study, hoping to find the hidden laws we expect *really* to apply. This kind of determinism, which applies not only within psychology but also in other domains, is often labeled *methodological determinism* and as a procedure is shared by psychologists and biologists as well as by schoolteachers and preachers.

Some who criticize contemporary secular psychology do so on the grounds that it makes the metaphysical assumption of determinism. There is no doubt that there is some truth in this statement as it applies to psychologists in general, but it remains misleading and inaccurate stated this way. There is an important difference between what may be called a working orientation toward the world, what we have just called methodological determinism, and an inflexible and absolute ontological presupposition about the way the world is. Almost all scientific psychologists are determinists or near determinists in the sense of adopting methodological determinism. If they did not hope, and indeed expect, to identify regularities in human behavior that would enable them to explain, predict, and control it, there would be little point in the whole enterprise in which they are engaged. What point would there be in undertaking an experiment on how schoolchildren learn mathematics or on the effects of particular drugs on the efficiency of the behavior of industrial workers or on comparing the efficacy of two competing types of psychotherapy, if the experimenter studying each of these at root believed that they were intrinsically capricious? If that were so, then the "laws" being looked for in each experiment wouldn't really be laws at all. The results of any experiment would not be applicable to further instances of the same kind of situations as those being studied.

If the tentative application of a methodological determinism turns out to be reasonably successful, then the next step is to move on and to say, "Well, it seems likely that in all areas of the study of behavior, if only we could understand it sufficiently, we shall find that it follows exceptionless regularities. Where there are exceptions is probably due to our lacking complete information and, therefore, from a procedural point of view we will assume that determinism does apply." This next stage has sometimes been called empirical determinism.

If we were now to go beyond methodological determinism and empirical determinism and adopt a position that was popular fifty years ago, we would say that all human acts are instantiations of the laws of physics and chemistry. This is an extrapolation from our limited ability to explain and predict behavior. Certainly no psychologist can prove any such universal proposition. In practice the predictability we are normally able to obtain, even in the experimental laboratory, is largely of a probabilistic type. That is to say, by suitable detailed knowledge and/or manipulations of the organism's history, together with the knowledge of its momentary state and current external situation, we can render its subsequent responses highly probable. To go beyond this we would have to move to metaphysical determinism and if we did this we would then want to say that all human psychological events instantiate universal laws and that we hold this view as an absolute ontological presupposition that no empirical evidence could be allowed to gain say. Most psychologists hold with methodological determinism, and empirical determinism, and it used to be the case that quite a number held metaphysical determinism, though with the demise of logical positivism this is less common today than it was fifty years ago.

The outcome of four decades of study of the neural substrate of mental life has, as we have indicated, pointed to an ever-tightening link between mind and brain. In this sense, some have argued that the human person and all his functions are complexes of events that can, at least in principle, be formulated in physical and chemical terms. That is not to deny that distinctly psychological events take place or that they are less "real" than their physical component events. The thesis being put forward is that descriptive and causal statements made in familiar psychological language can be translated without residue, at least in principle, into statements in physiological language. More sophisticated holders of these views readily acknowledge that a "psychological" statement such as "Smith laughed when he noticed the logical fallacy" cannot be completely translated into physiological language simply because the term *fallacy* designates a logical (normative) concept rather than a physiological state. But the reason for that is that the original statement you are trying to translate was not, in itself, purely causal or descriptive. It is the evidence for this tightening of the link between mind and brain that has led Christian psychologists to reexamine with a fresh urgency the question of the determinism of human behavior and the question of whether we do in fact enjoy any real freedom of choice. To give the reader the general flavor of the debate on these issues at the present time we shall briefly describe the views of some of the leading thinkers in this field in recent years. Their views differ because their presuppositions differ, while they share many basic Christian beliefs.

A Preliminary Cautionary Tale

In a moment, we consider the views of different scientists, expressed in some cases a few years ago. It is salutary to record how, at the cutting edge of contemporary research, some of their at that time legitimate assumptions are now being called into question. Most recently (November 1995) the well-known physicist Stephen Hawking of A *Brief History of Time* fame has publicly proclaimed that predicting the future is not just difficult; it is impossible.[1] Starting from the views of the French philosopher Laplace, who asserted that if at any one time we knew the positions and speeds of every particle in the universe, we could predict its future as well as tracing its past, Hawking claimed that such a philosophy, which had become the unwritten creed of scientists, turns out to be an illusion. So said Hawking, "These scientists have not learned the lesson of history. It is just a pious hope that the universe is deterministic in the way that Laplace thought. The universe does not behave according to our preconceived ideas; it continues to surprise us." The reasons for these changed views had, according to Hawking, all emerged from twentieth-century science—quantum theory, the uncertainty principle, and more recent ideas about black holes. "The situation changed," said Hawking, "when I discovered that black holes aren't completely black. Quantum mechanics causes them to send out particles and radiation at a steady rate. The result came as a total surprise to me." What all this means, he said, was that information will be lost when black holes are formed and that will mean we can predict even less than we thought on the basis of quantum theory. But what has this got to do with everyday life? Hawking believes a lot. He argues that the uncertainty principle implies that space is full of tiny black holes, a hundred billion billion times smaller than the nucleus of the atom. And because they are so small, the rate at which information is lost is very low, which is why the laws of science appear to be deterministic to a very good approximation. Following the implications of all this, Hawking concludes that it means that the universe is constructed in a way that is intrinsically indeterminate. He concluded his lecture: "One can calculate probabilities, but one cannot make any definite predictions. . . . Thus the future of the universe is not completely determined by the laws of science and its present state as Laplace thought. God still has a few tricks up his sleeve."

The scientific jury is still out on many of these issues. The purpose of noting Hawking's most recent views is to warn us against endowing any of the views to be reviewed now with a finality that they do not deserve. The need for an open, but not an empty, mind never changes.

Proposed Solutions to the Problem

Several solutions have been proposed. One approach comes from those who, while conceding that the body is a physically determinate stuff, maintain that mind is not bound to the body but enjoys a certain autonomy. Such views are often, though not exclusively, held by those with interests in subjects such as parapsychology, extrasensory perception, psychical research, and so on. It is a defensible view. In 1950 Peter Laslett[2] edited a book entitled *The Physical Basis of Mind,* in which a number of distinguished biologists reached something approaching a consensus to the effect that the neural activity of the brain somehow interacts with the private world of the mind. The question remains, however: Is it necessary to hold a dualist view in order to safeguard man's freedom?

Another form of dualism that has been canvassed has been labeled *dualism of descriptive categories.* On this view, freedom and determinism are concepts belonging to two different language systems. Its advocates argue that both are necessary to do justice to our present scientific knowledge and to the experience of human freedom. Thus, for example, theoretical physicist Nils Bohr speaks of freedom and determinism as complementary descriptions, drawing attention to the analogy of wave-particle models in physics. Certainly this view avoids some of the difficulties of the dualism of stuff approach. Yet others simply point out that, while determinism is a useful postulate within science, that does not mean that it is a universal rule throughout the world. It is one thing, they argue, to employ it as a useful rule of procedure for scientific enquiry, yet another to go on to assert that such a rule expresses an intrinsic property of the created order. Among psychologists, Carl Rogers took a similar view. He wrote that "responsible personal choice, which is the core experience of psychotherapy, and which exists prior to any scientific endeavor, is an equally prominent fact in our lives. To deny the experience of responsible choice is as restricted a view as to deny the possibility of behavioral science."

Yet another form has been advocated by some, who, having accepted the force of the scientific evidence, see a clue to the solution to the problem within science itself. Their appeal is to a particular scientific principle—the Heisenberg principle of indeterminacy in physics. The best-known champion of such a view has been physiologist Sir John Eccles.[3] On his view the main features of the situation are as follows. First, some form of mind–brain liaison occurs in the cerebral cortex. The will can influence neural activity without violating physical laws because the energy involved in such influence is within the limits of the Heisenberg uncertainty principle.

In the simplest possible terms the Heisenberg principle states that, where there are certain pairs of variables that specify what is happening at the level of interactions of the then smallest known particles, such as electrons, peculiar relationships are operative; the more accurately one of the quantities is known, the less accurately can the other quantity be predicted. For example, the more accurately the position of an electron is measured in an experimental setup, the greater is the uncertainty in any prediction about its velocity. The errors of measurement, therefore, that come in under these circumstances are not the ordinary type of error that can be reduced by improving the sensitivity of the apparatus; they are, so it is asserted, inherent in the structure of matter.

When this is applied to our present problem, the picture that emerges is one of neural activity influenced by nonphysical factors. Thus Eccles believes that mind, being a nonphysical factor, either may influence individual quantum events, these effects then being amplified throughout the cortex, or, more probably, there could be a coordinated shifting of probabilities in many such events simultaneously.

We may make a number of comments on Eccles's view. First, the indeterminacy allowed by the Heisenberg principle becomes more and more negligible the bigger the objects that we are studying. While for the study of electrons it is far from negligible, nevertheless, by the time we get to the size of the neuron, which is a million million times heavier than an electron, it is already becoming negligible. Second, the brain, as far as we can see at the moment, seems to be organized on a teamwork basis so that one brain cell behaving unpredictably would make no significant difference to the overall functioning of the brain. Third, the random fluctuations in the brain attributable to Heisenberg's principle are extremely small compared with other fluctuations known to us, such as those due to thermodynamic changes, random fluctuations in the blood supply, and so on. In fact, what we must conclude here is that such unpredictable disturbances could as easily be used to excuse me from responsibility as to credit me with responsibility for my choices.

There is one aspect of this latter view we might label as *modified dualism*, which is extremely vulnerable to further scientific advances if we are to take seriously the opinions of other distinguished scientists such as Einstein and Bohm. They have contended that the Heisenberg indeterminacy principle is simply an expression of our present ignorance in this field of science. Thus, while Nils Bohr was convinced that uncertainty is not a product of our ignorance but a fundamental limitation on our human knowledge permanently preventing us from knowing whether certain events are determinate or not, his view was not shared by Einstein and Bohm. In such circumstances the reader may well feel (as does the writer), Who, then, are we to decide? But perhaps we can push the question one stage farther back, and ask, Do we need to pin our defense of freedom on the Heisenberg uncertainty principle? That, as we shall see later, is one of the questions that Donald Mackay[4] kept in mind in his discussions of freedom and determinism.

Former professor of mathematical physics at Cambridge University,

Dr. John Polkinghorne[5] refers to "the perpetual puzzle of the connection of mind and brain." He points out that if you are a thoroughgoing reductionist the answer to this puzzle is easy: "Mind is the epiphenomenon of brain, a mere symptom of its physical activity." But, as he points out, "the reductionist program in the end subverts itself. Ultimately it is suicidal." It destroys rationality, and replaces thought with electrochemical neural events. Such events cannot confront one another in rational discourse; they are neither right nor wrong, but just happen. Thus, writes Polkinghorne, "If our mental life is nothing but the humming activity of an immensely complexly connected computer-like brain, who is to say whether the program running on the intricate machine is correct or not?" And later he goes on: "The very assertions of the reductionist himself are nothing but blips in the neural network of his brain. The world of rational thought discourse dissolves into the absurd chatter of firing synapses. Quite frankly, that cannot be right and none of us believes it to be so" (209). In arguing in this way, Polkinghorne is echoing Professor J. B. S. Haldane,[6] who many years ago wrote, "If my mental processes are determined wholly by the motions of the atoms in my brain, I have no reason to suppose that my beliefs are true . . . and hence I have no reason for supposing my brain to be composed of atoms."

There are several ways of thinking about this problem and it will remain a puzzle for those of us involved to work at for many years to come. But until we know better how to integrate the activities of mind and brain, let us at least hold fast to our basic personal experience of choice and responsibility without denying the neurological insight that our mental activity is incarnated in our brains. These are complementary aspects of the whole person, just as wave and particle are complementary aspects of light.[7]

DOES CHAOS THEORY HELP?

Recently there has been much discussion, in both the popular and the scientific press, of the science of chaos. This word is used to describe the irregular, unpredictable behavior of deterministic nonlinear dynamic systems. This is not new and doesn't contain new fundamental physics. What is new is the realization that many real-world physical problems contain chaotic elements. The capability provided by modern high-speed computers to simulate chaotic behavior has provided fresh stimulation to the study of chaos, with wide-ranging applications in physics, chemistry, and biology.

Chaos theory is most often talked about in the field of meteorology. Some claim that if chaology is taken to its logical extremes then all of our predictions about such things as global warming will, whether the best or the worst, ultimately be rendered meaningless, since its central tenet is that there is no such thing as a reliable prediction. Best known of all is the so-called butterfly effect, which says that an insect batting its wings and disturbing the air in China today can next month affect storm systems in New York or the temperature of London in August.

As popular writers have pointed out, chaos is to a certain extent what we make of it. Some see chaos theory as nothing less than that third great revolution in the physical sciences, and, like the two that went before, it refutes Newtonian principles. Such advocates would assert that the simplest systems are now seen to create extraordinarily difficult problems when it comes to predictability. They suggest that only a new kind of science could begin to cross the great gulf between knowledge of what one thing does, whether it be one water molecule or one neuron of the brain, and what billions of them will do. The relevance of this to our present discussion is that there are some who believe that ideas from chaos theory may assist in grappling with the puzzles about processes in the brain. A *Scientific American*[8] article on chaos published in 1986 closed with these words:

> Even the process of intellectual progress relies on the injection of new ideas and on new ways of connecting old ideas. Innate creativity may have an underlying chaotic process that selectively amplifies small fluctuations and molds them into macroscopic coherent mental states that are experienced as thoughts. In some cases the thoughts may be decisions, or what are perceived to be the exercise of will. *In this light, chaos provides a mechanism that allows for free will within a world governed by deterministic laws* (my italics).

Concerning the possible relevance of chaos theory to problems of personal freedom, John Houghton,[9] former professor of physics at Oxford, has commented that

> we have no doubt about our freedom to make choices; we are making them all the time. The choices are, of course, restricted by the structure of space and time in which we exist. They are also constrained by our environment or our circumstances, and our behavior is undoubtedly in some ways preconditioned by our upbringing and our past experience. But not entirely so; our freedom to choose is real. In particular, we are constantly faced with choices between good and evil and are only too well aware of a propensity to choose the evil rather than the good.

Clearly there is nothing remotely "scientific" about ignoring or minimizing our primary experience that we make choices all the time. To try to pretend on any ideological reductionist grounds that the common human experience of freedom to choose is an illusion is blatantly unscientific special pleading. It amounts to sweeping universally shared and agreed empirical data under the carpet.

What Constitutes Freedom to Choose?

The topic of free will and choice has a very long history in the writings of philosophers. A reference to such writings alerts us to the fact that it is a problem to know how we should define freedom of choice. Relevant to our present discussion is the philosophers' reminder that there have been two distinct definitions of freedom, often referred to as the liberty of spontaneity and the liberty of indifference.[10] To understand the difference between the two, consider a situation where a person is faced with a choice of selecting porridge or stewed fruit for breakfast. She chooses porridge. Now if we were able to set up the exact same circumstances in force at the moment the choice was made, and that would include a specification of the state of the whole universe including the person's brain, then, so it is said, two possibilities exist:

1. The liberty of spontaneity, according to which the person would always choose porridge, since choosing porridge is what the person wanted to do.

2. The liberty of indifference, according to which the person would have the ability to take either porridge or stewed fruit.

The liberty of spontaneity is often referred to as a compatibilist view of freedom. This is because it is compatible with determinism. The liberty of indifference is referred to as a libertarian view of freedom.

The Liberty of Indifference

The writings of Christian scientists such as John Polkinghorne[11] and Arthur Peacocke[12] construe freedom in terms of the liberty of indifference. Polkinghorne believes that anything less than this would relegate us to being automata. If, as Polkinghorne seems to assume elsewhere, we accept a nondualist view of mind, then the independence from all physical circumstance he invokes seems to imply an independence from the previous state of the mind. The problem then becomes in what sense the choice that does take place can be said to be caused by the mind. In effect, it looks as if this definition of freedom gives us too great an independence in that it produces an independence from our own selves; we are not the source but only the scene of the choice.

Polkinghorne has argued that the liberty of indifference is necessary if we are to understand our rationality. He asks, "If the brain is a machine, what validates the program running on it?" He argues that in order to discern truth we require that human rational judgment shall enjoy an autonomous validity and that this would be negated if it were the byproduct of mere physical necessity. In this context we need to remember that "mere physical necessity" is the unbelievably complex system of the brain. It looks as though the autonomy of objectivity Polkinghorne wishes to defend is more than the autonomy from past circumstance that the liberty of indifference provides. What, we must ask, would validate the truth-discerning capacities of this freedom? It looks as though the explanation of our rationality is difficult whatever view of freedom we take. It is indeed as Polkinghorne has pointed out hard to conceive how evolutionary necessity would ensure the "subtlety and fruitfulness of human reason."

THE LIBERTY OF SPONTANEITY AND LOGICAL INDETERMINACY

Donald Mackay[13] gave the whole debate on free will a new twist by defining freedom in a new way consistent with the other definition of liberty, the liberty of spontaneity.

In presenting his views Mackay asks us to imagine the following scenario. We consider a person (call him A), whose behavior we are studying and whose next choice we seek to predict. We can think of a superscientist who is able to look into A's brain, to see its complete state and on the basis of this, so it is claimed, the scientist would be able to predict the future brain state of A. But, asks Mackay, would A himself be correct to believe the prediction being made by the superscientist if it were offered to him? His answer is no. Mackay argues that if the superscientist's predictions were presented to A, then it would in fact alter A's brain state, and so the prediction would immediately be invalidated. Since, therefore, by definition no change can take place in what A believes without a correlated change in his brain state, it follows that no completely detailed specification of the present or immediately future state of his brain would be equally correct whether or not A believed it. If it were correct before A believed it, then it must be incorrect in some detail after A comes to believe it; conversely, if the specification were adjusted so that it would become correct if and when the brain state were changed by A's believing it, then it would not be correct unless A believed it.

Thus, Mackay envisages the further situation that supposes that our superscientist could, in fact, formulate a new prediction that would take into account the effect of offering it to A and would only be correct if A believed it. The question, then, is, Would such a prediction command A's unconditional assent? Mackay answers no. A would obviously be entitled to believe it. However, A would be equally entitled to disbelieve it, as a prediction is true if and only if A believes it. Putting this in a more formal way, we can say there does not exist a complete description of A's future, which would have an unconditional claim to A's assent, in the sense that A would be correct to believe and mistaken to disbelieve it, if only A knew it. Mackay argues that in this sense A's future is *logically indeterminate* and that from A's point of view the future is open and up to A to determine. For Mackay this is the essence of freedom, as he asserts that it is not brains but persons who choose. It is at the level of our conscious experience that there is an indeterminacy, irrespective of any indeterminacy at the level of the brain. Mackay remained uneasy with other definitions of freedom that do not explicitly distinguish between these two levels and he suggested that it is a mistake to try to secure our freedom by trying to exploit physically indeterminate processes in the brain, along the lines of Eccles's arguments.

In presenting his argument Mackay quite openly assumed what he called a worst-case scenario. As he[14] put it in his Gifford lectures, "We are going to set ourselves the toughest case: We are going to be asking, what if—and it is a strongly underlined *if*—the whole of this system as summarized here were a determinate system in the physical sense? That is to say, if every physical event had its adequate determinants in other and earlier physical events, would it follow that we have no choice, everything is inevitable, and we couldn't have done otherwise?" Mackay is here arguing that if we can demonstrate freedom in such a restricted world then, a fortiori, it can certainly be established in the real world. He makes it clear elsewhere that, in fact, he believes it is highly unlikely that the world is totally physically determinate. The second point, which is not always understood, is that the argument is not concerned with what A would actually do when he was offered the prediction but it is rather making a logical point about what it would be correct for A to believe. Mackay is also emphasizing that his logical indeterminacy argument applies to statements that involve what he calls the cognitive mechanism—the part of the brain embodying a person's beliefs. Indeed, he suggests that we should only be held responsible for those actions that are physically dependent on our cognitive mechanism. And Mackay also believes that the way he defines freedom is fully compatible with theological determinism, that is, in a universe where God determines all that is and, therefore, on this view, divine sovereignty and human freedom are reconciled.

Mackay's argument has been discussed and critiqued widely by many logicians and philosophers, as well as scientists; there is no doubt that the logical point he wishes to make is firmly established. For some of Mackay's critics the problem centers on whether it is proper to equate logical indeterminacy with the notion of freedom in the way that he does.

Thus we see that Mackay has no desire to appeal to unpredictability to retain the kind of freedom that he believes is required. Indeed, he[15] comments, "In so far as quantum events disrupted the normal cause and effect relationships between the physical correlates of my rational deliberation, such events might be held to diminish rather than enhance my responsibility for the outcome." To attempt to retain the idea of freedom by an appeal to physically indeterminate processes produces the further question of how, in that case, the choice that is made can be attributable to a personal agent. Polkinghorne tackles this problem by referring to the inherent openness of complex dynamical systems. For him the future would be contained within an envelope of possibilities so that the actual pathway followed could be selected by input of information by the mind. This sounds like the introduction of a new form of dualism by the back door. It is this kind of top-down operating causation that for Polkinghorne could be the locus of human freedom. He has elsewhere argued strongly for the kind of dual-aspect monism we adopted elsewhere in this book. On the face of it, then, there seems to be some conflict between his acceptance of a dual-aspect monism and his attempt to exploit the openness of complex dynamic systems in the way he does.

A group of Cambridge research scientists[16] have recently compared the different views of Mackay, Polkinghorne, and Peacocke, and have written regarding Polkinghorne's view that "the difficulty is that to attribute the information input to an act of the mind, it needs to be preceded by a mental decision on the desired outcome. But if the mind is embodied, this decision would already have a physical correlate and so the information input cannot be the point of choice. Freedom must lie elsewhere. Alternatively, if the information input is not seen to be the result of a previous state of the mind, then we get back to the original problem of the liberty of indifference—what causes this information input, chance? Also its attempts to explain the freedom of a non-dualistic mind through the openness of physical processes are likely to meet this problem" (127). Jonathan Doye and his colleagues aptly summarize the position in which we remain when they write, "Both views held by our authors [Mackay, Polkinghorne, and Peacocke] have difficulties which need to be addressed.

Put starkly, the following questions remain: Is the liberty of spontaneity really free, and is the liberty of indifference really a result of our willing? Neither view appears to be philosophically or empirically necessitated and consequently, it needs to be opened to review in the light of its implications in other areas, particularly theology. However, we note the general point that the liberty of spontaneity can be more easily reconciled with God's sovereignty, than the liberty of indifference" (128).

SUMMING UP

We can note a number of aspects of this so-called problem of determinism and free will. First—and this is a point that is often overlooked—if there is a problem, it is one of our own making. From an empirical point of view the common experience of almost all of us is that in our "normal" condition we spend our time making free choices and engaging in deliberately chosen actions. As the philosophers say, the experience of freedom of choice has an ontological priority over anything that we may subsequently say about the basis of this in our brains. It is our assumption that because we have had so much success in the physical sciences and because we are convinced of the physical determinism (at least, according to Stephen Hawking, to a very good approximation) of the world in which we live (within the bounds and under the conditions appropriate and bearing in mind Heisenberg indeterminacy, chaos theory, and information loss in black holes) that we go on to assume that, as a physical system, the brain also is physically determinate. Given that assumption, the problem then faces us, In what sense can our choices be seen as being free? We have reviewed a number of approaches to this problem, none of which is entirely satisfactory, but all of which help us better to understand the issues involved and to give some assurance of our freedom of choice and behavior. Each of them in their different ways enables us to affirm that if we are prepared to maintain an open mind we can still affirm our personal responsibility. It could be argued that the greater the knowledge we have of the biological foundations of our behavior and of how what we do to ourselves affects the workings of the neural substrate of our minds, the more responsible we become for our actions. The appropriate attitude to adopt toward ourselves is to give primacy to the exercise of our personal freedom. Yet we seldom do that. Unfortunately, we readily blame the environment for our failures while being all too ready to take credit for our successes. When thinking of attitudes toward others, there is surely wisdom in taking seriously some of the research that shows how people are significantly shaped by their social, environmental, and cultural contexts. On this view, we should regard ourselves as agents responsible for our actions but always be ready to entertain the possibility that others have been unduly influenced by their social and physical environment and to make allowances accordingly. Philip Johnson-Laird[17] writes, "Any scientific theory of the mind has to treat it as an automaton." But, he went on, "this is in no way demeaning or dehumanizing, but a direct consequence of the computability of scientific theories. *Above all, it is entirely consistent with the view that people are responsible* agents."

It would be fair to say that for many Christian psychologists the kind of problems we have been talking about so far in this chapter are not really the most pressing ones. They are more concerned that, given all that we now know about the biological substrate of mental life and of behavior, of its variability as with any other biological system, we must assume that we are consequently confronted with varying degrees of responsibility. We have indicated some of these problems earlier in the domains of sexual orientation, aggression, and alcoholism. There seems little doubt that because of their genetic endowment, the biochemistry of the brain, or undetected abnormalities in the structures of the brain, some people may find it easier to make some decisions than others and some may find it more difficult to follow a particular course of action than others. That being so, the problem then becomes responsibility for making moral choices, for which, according to Scripture, we are accountable.

Clearly our present behavior is dependent on our genetic endowment and our early upbringing—the social, cultural, and physical environment in which we have grown up. These factors could certainly make it more difficult for some people than others to become and to be Christians. There is nothing in Christianity, however, to deny that people differ and certainly nothing to suggest that persons will be judged for failing to make decisions which, by their very constitution, they could not make.

That having been said, it is well to remember that the crux of being a Christian is not having a full intellectual grasp of a set of theological doctrines, nor is it a matter of coming to God with an attitude of gratitude, nor is it being able to analyze all the factors that make us feel a need to come to terms with him, if he does exist. Rather, in essence, it is exercising, however feebly, however haltingly, however vaguely at first, a capacity that we all have grown up with, however much of a battering it may have taken due to the circumstances of our lives: the capacity to respond as one person to another. The Christian assertion is that the other person is not an abstract God defined in terms of absolutes, but rather a loving, compassionate, and caring friend, Jesus Christ himself, aptly described in the Gospels as "the friend of sinners." It is at this point that one is thankful for the experience of millions who can testify that, in making the smallest move in response to the glimmer of an understanding of such love, they were led on to the awareness that

God himself had already moved toward them and that a loving welcome awaited them. It is in these terms that Christ's invitation "Come unto me" is as meaningful today as it ever was.

TAKING STOCK

1. Determinism is not a new problem thought up or generated by psychologists and neuroscientists. Failure to distinguish among methodological determinism, empirical determinism, and metaphysical determinism has generated unnecessary confusion and conflicts.

2. If there is a problem of determinism it is of our own making, since our shared common experience is that we do have freedom to choose within the limits of our physical makeup. We may choose to jump over a twenty-foot wall but fail lamentably in the attempt due to our anatomical and physiological limitations!

3. In recent years we have been made more acutely aware of the possible problems of psychological determinism by the accumulating evidence of the tightening of the link between mind and brain, and behavior and brain.

4. Various solutions have been proposed to the problem of determinism. The dualism of Eccles, the top-down emergent properties of mind of Sperry, appeal to the nature of open dynamic systems by Polkinghorne, demonstration of the logical indeterminacy of a choice by Mackay. All have features in their favor. However, if we pay attention to Stephen Hawking's recent pronouncement that "the future of the universe is not completely determined by the laws of science as Laplace thought. God still has a few tricks up his sleeve," we may find that such pronouncements may, to a degree, relieve the pressure on us to resolve these problems of determinism.

5. On balance we lean toward Mackay's suggested portrayal and solution of the problem since it seems to do most justice to the theological teaching about God's general providential care of all things at all times.

6. We conclude that nothing in contemporary neuroscience or psychology can be appealed to in order to excuse us from serious considerations of the claims of Christ. There are Christian evidences available for all to study and the challenge is for us to examine them with an open mind and a willingness to be convinced. "If any man is willing . . . then he shall know."

CHAPTER 13

THE FUTURE OF SCIENCE AND FAITH

Beyond Perspectivalism?

It seems to me that perspectivalism leaves too many
unanswered questions to be the final word on the relationship
between Christianity and psychology.
—Mary Van Leeuwen, *The Person in Psychology*, 1985

Christian philosopher Steven Evans[1] has described six ways Christians
relate religious beliefs to psychological knowledge. "Perspectivalists"
are, he says, jealous to maintain the integrity of the scientific enterprise
and are anxious to keep it unsullied by personal philosophies which, at
times, are smuggled in unawares and undeclared. They are vigilant to
avoid the intrusion of what is sometimes called scientism, the extension
of the scientific method into a metaphysical position. He believes that
perspectivalism implies the incompleteness of science and this, he says,
may be envisaged in two different ways. There are those who see the
boundaries of science as territorial in nature. According to this view, he
says, certain areas of reality are strictly off limits to the scientific investigator; he labels such thinkers the territorialist kind. The other kind he
portrays as those who see the scientific approach as only one of several
possible ways of perceiving reality, hence the term "perspectivalist."

Another group of thinkers he labels the "reinterpreters" of the Christian view. These are those who wholeheartedly accept the truth of the so-
called scientific view of man and then go on to reinterpret the image of
the personal to make it consistent with what they believe is the current

scientific view. He again further subdivides these into those who basically believe that when the scientific data, on the one hand, and a personal understanding, on the other, are rightly interpreted, then the image of the personal will turn out to be compatible with the mechanistic, which he takes to be the scientific view. His other subgroup in this category are those who, he says, believe that nothing essential is lost by modifying the image of the personal so as to make it compatible with the mechanistic view.

The third group, seeking to resolve these issues, tend, he says, to focus their analysis on the nature of the scientific enterprise and the extent to which it is properly applicable to current psychological research. Some of these directly attack the unity of science; he labels them the humanizers of science. Within this camp he identifies two groups. Some are opposed in principle to the positivist view of science as a whole and are keen to emphasize the need to, what they call, humanize science in general; these are the generalists. The other group are those who object to the view that there is only one acceptable scientific method, and while recognizing that a positivist view of science may be applicable in some sciences, believe it is not in others; these he refers to as the particularists. Their principal concern is with humanizing those sciences that primarily deal with humankind. Such writers aim to contrast the methods used in studying humankind with what they regard as a methodological imperialism that those who see all sciences as natural sciences want to impose on all scientific research.

Evans himself seems to come down in favor of the perspectivalist version of a limits of science position. He writes (145) that "such a view allows for a unified view of the person which is congenial to the Bible's emphasis on the unity of the person and the resurrection of the body." With Evans we would agree that taking up this position need not mean that other models for integration have nothing to offer. It is likely that a thorough discussion of just which parts of the vast territory currently covered by psychology are properly seen as similar to the natural sciences would help resolve some of the issues presently raised by the so-called humanizers of science. The point is that what is important is not the particular label that is attached to the enterprise but whether or not, at the end of the day, it is seeking to submit its claims to the nature of reality as we are able to study it. It is certainly true that those like the present writer who have been portrayed by Evans as perspectivalists work primarily in the cognitive/biological/neuroscience part of the current psychological landscape (as outlined in chapter 1), whereas those who emphasize the humanizer approach tend to work in the personology territory of psychology dealing with theories of personality and sundry clinical aspects of the discipline.

As we indicated in chapter 6, when offering a brief biblical cameo of the nature of humankind, there are dangers to be alert to in relating the biblical and the scientific accounts of human nature. These were well expressed by Mary Van Leeuwen[2] when she wrote, "We return to the knotty question as to what these core human characteristics comprise from a biblical perspective. Let it be pointed out," she went on, "that although scripture does contain material which, when systematized, helps us to answer this question, it does not do so in a way that renders psychological and other social scientific theorizing redundant." We would agree. We would say that they give accounts from different perspectives and that for the Christian, each enriches the other. Thus we would fully endorse Mary Van Leeuwen's statement when she continues: "What the bible rather gives us, in its journey through salvation history, are some broad categories in terms of which we should think about humanness and in light of which we can judge the adequacy of more systematic personality theories, especially as regards their core statement." In the same book Van Leeuwen perceptively foreshadowed the need for us to reexamine, and possibly modify and amplify, the brand of perceptivalism she believed characterized our views at that time. Thus, she wrote (68), "despite these encouraging qualities, it seems to me that perspectivalism leaves too many unanswered questions to be the final word on the relationship between Christianity and Psychology"—a view picked up recently by Colin Russell[3] and John Brooke[4] as regards the more general relationship of science and faith.

Help from the Historians of Science

As we indicated in chapter 2, some historians of science, such as Colin Russell and John Brooke, have recently suggested that the notion of science and faith representing complementary perspectives on the same set of reality could, in order to more accurately depict what *actually* has happened, be amplified and modified. We agree. As a step in that direction we now offer one way of doing this. Since the primary readership of this book is likely to be psychologists or students studying psychology, it seems appropriate to suggest how a widely held theory of the visual system, familiar to psychologists, physiologists, and neuroscientists generally, may provide a useful model of how a constructive relationship between science and faith may be thought about.

Relating Psychological Science and Christian Belief: A Model from the Neuropsychology of Vision

The perspectivalist model has served us well and will, in many respects, continue to do so. It has often been portrayed as the plan and the elevation drawings of a three-dimensional structure. Both contain important information, but any attempt improperly to intermix them will lead to confusion. These are not to be seen as competitors; both are necessary to provide a full picture of the reality they portray. This is essentially a static model of perspectivalism. Others have used the idea of perspectives somewhat more loosely, or figuratively. Thus they have seen the two accounts as complementary, much as wave and particle accounts of light tell us different things about light as we study it under different experimental conditions.

Bearing in mind the points made by Brooke and Russell about the ongoing reciprocal interactions between science and faith it could be argued that we need a more dynamic model that would help us capture aspects of the relation between science and faith accounts missed or underplayed in the rather static perspectives model. With this in mind let us consider a model of how the visual system works and see if it provides a more adequate account of how knowledge from the domains of science and faith come together in practice.

For the nonspecialist reader, a brief introduction may help. As we view the world around us we pick up information through our senses of sight, smell, touch, and taste. It is generally agreed that the visual system has to be able to accommodate two somewhat distinct functions—one concerned with acting on the world and the other with representing it. How the brain achieves these ends is intensively studied by neuropsychologists, neurophysiologists, neuroscientists, and, in recent years, computer scientists. The retina of the eye, which on embryological grounds can be considered part of the central nervous system, transduces the electromagnetic radiation hitting the photoreceptors into physiological signals that can be understood by the brain while at the same time performing several computations on those signals. From the retina there are numerous projections (pathways) carrying different sorts of information to the so-called primary visual cortex and the higher visual areas of the cortex.

In the late 1960s a number of different functional dichotomies of the visual system were proposed, for example, by Trevarthen,[5] who referred to "ambient" versus "focal" vision. Schneider[6] identified two visual systems, one that localized the stimulus in space and another that identified the stimulus. Then in 1982, Ungerleider and Mishkin[7] argued that "appreciation of an object's qualities and of its spatial features depends on the processing of different kinds of visual information in the inferior temporal and posterior parietal cortex respectively." Most recently, and of special relevance to our present discussion, is the theory put forward by David Milner and Mel Goodale. They see "the output requirements for a visual coding system serving the visual control of action as quite different from the requirements for a system sub-serving visual perception" (42). They also note that "while it is true that different channels in the mammalian visual system are specialized for different kinds of visual analysis (broad band versus color opponent; magno versus parvo) at some point these separate inputs are combined and transformed in different ways for different purposes" (65). They continue: "In other words, both cortical streams process information about the intrinsic properties of objects and their spatial location, but the transformations they carry out reflect the different purposes for which the two streams have evolved" (66, 67).

While there is then what Milner and Goodale[8] call "a quasi-independence of the two visual streams" (201), nevertheless, "there will be reciprocal cross-connections between areas in the two streams" (202). For the organism to operate at optimum capacity in its world there is a need for cooperative action of the two streams. Is there a useful analogy between the way the visual system processes its inputs, analyzes them, uses them, and ultimately applies them for effective action, and how we seek out, analyze, process, and integrate the knowledge of ourselves and our world given, on the one hand, by the scientific enterprise, and on the other, in what God has chosen to reveal to us? We may note several things.

First, the data that are gathered are not all of a kind, and to benefit fully, we must subject these data to *appropriate* forms of analysis. Both are important, both are relevant, but they are different. Second, after appropriate analysis in the relevant channel, the information is brought together to enrich the total picture of the world that is available. Third, along the way there are opportunities for reciprocal cross-connections between the two streams that positively supplement and guide each other. Fourth, while the analysis from one stream is able to provide a detailed analysis of the world as it is, the analysis from the other stream is primarily given to make possible effective action in the world as it is. Does this perhaps not remind us that, while through the scientific enterprise we gain a remarkable understanding of the way the world is, in addition, through what God reveals to us and teaches us in Scripture we discover how, the more effectively, to act within the world as we find it. The two streams are not conflicting or competing; rather, they are complementary and enriching one another to the benefit of both. Is this not the way we should think about how positively and productively to integrate the knowledge given in the distinct domains of science and faith?

Expressing it thus brings to mind the quotation from Colin Russell that we included in chapter 2, where, commenting on the network of relationships between science and theology, he wrote, of the view he was putting forward, "It merely recognizes that in the interpretation of such data, theological and scientific ideas are often intermingled in one brain, as they are indeed in society. Hence one might expect some degree of mutual influence; and such turns out to be the case."[9]

More specifically, we believe it suggests a way of thinking about the evidence concerning our human nature, all gathered by our common conscious experience, as being capable of being analyzed in two distinct ways that ultimately flow together to provide an enriched composite picture at the highest level. We have outlined in detail in earlier chapters the way that is adopted by those who work within the scientific enterprise. That approach enables us to build up a substantial composite picture of the mechanisms that may be at work, in the moment-by-moment, ongoing activity of human beings, as they take in information from their environment, process it, store it, and, as appropriate, act on it. We have also noted that there is an altogether different stream of knowledge about human nature that comes to us from the writings of wise men down through the centuries, such as the remarkable insights of great writers such as Shakespeare, and these also provide enduring insights into our human nature, as do the insights of philosophers, poets, artists, and others. This stream of information, for the Christian, is subordinate to a source of knowledge and information about human nature that takes primacy over all else; this is the knowledge given to us by God through revelation in Scripture and above all in the person of Jesus Christ. The Bible, as we saw in chapter 6, is full of profound insights into human nature and teaching as to how God would have us live our lives day by day, individually, in social interactions with others, and, above all, in relationship with him.

In the theory of two cortical visual systems, we have a picture of how all of the information in the visual world that hits the retina of the eye proceeds upstream via two largely separate pathways, each having their independent and distinctive processing functions, from time to time interacting through feedback loops, until eventually the outputs of their processing are brought together at what we might describe as a superordinate level. So, in like manner, we may think of the knowledge given to us about human nature, on the one hand, through the endeavors of scientists and, on the other hand, through the insights of wise men, and for us as Christians primarily by God through revelation, as coming together for each of us to enrich our overall understanding of the mystery of human nature. The purpose and function of what is happening in the two streams is distinct. The knowledge gained through the scientific enterprise enables us, as we have seen, to build models of the cognitive and neural mechanisms that analyze our experience through the sensory modalities as well as that stored in memory. But that is only part of the total story. The other part given through revelation also gives us profound insights into human nature and primarily how we should act day by day and moment by moment. As we have noted repeatedly, the Hebrew knew nothing of a purely intellectual attitude toward creation and life in general; the Old Testament seems to know nothing of a purely intellectual reaction to life. The Word of God speaks to and is written on the heart; it is never given simply as academic information. God reveals his purposes so that we may act in a manner that acknowledges his lordship and is shown in the day-to-day outworking in all activities—our relationships to one another, our relationship of stewardship with the created order, and above all our relationship of thankful, loving obedience to a compassionate, loving Father God. Finally, perhaps we could extend the analogy and note how the occasional feedback loops between the two streams in the cortical visual system model also have their counterparts in the occasional interactions between the scientific enterprise and Christian beliefs noted and documented by Russell, Brooke, and Hooykaas (chapter 2). These kinds of reciprocal interactions may be mutually beneficial and enhance the ultimate composite picture that is built up only finally within the individual. It is this aspect of the relationship Russell has sought to capture in his term "symbiosis." Thus the data, theological and scientific, while distinctive in themselves, are ultimately intermingled in one brain, as they are also in society. In this sense, one expects a continuing degree of mutual influence and enrichment, as turns out to be the case.

TAKING STOCK

That psychology has developed relatively recently as a scientific discipline affords its Christian practitioners the opportunity, in seeking to relate psychological knowledge to Christian belief, to learn from the experiences of scientists of better established disciplines of earlier generations. The experiences of cosmologists, astronomers, geologists, and biologists, as indicated in chapter 2, provide invaluable lessons, as well as giving timely warning of pitfalls to be avoided, as we seek to relate knowledge derived from research in psychology to truths revealed in the Scriptures. It is worth asking whether there are any guidelines that we can propose to help us in the ongoing task of relating psychology to Christian belief. Such guidelines should help us avoid overreacting to each new discovery reported by psychologists which, at first sight, may seem to challenge some long-held Christian beliefs, in the way some did (as indicated in chapter 6) in response to the feature article "In Search of the Mind" that appeared in *Time* magazine in July 1995.

1. Since man, according to Scripture (Gen. 1–2), is part of the created, natural order, we have a positive Christian mandate to study our nature as well as other parts of creation. There is no biblical warrant for a "hands off" policy when it comes to the study of human nature. The positive mandate that Christians have to seek to understand the created order and to exercise responsible stewardship over it applies equally to humankind proper. There is nothing new in this; witness the long history of medical research. There will in addition be the special motivation for the Christian to seek at all times and in all places wherever possible to increase our knowledge so as to relieve the suffering of fellow human beings and ensure that we may live peaceably with all men. To that extent psychological knowledge potentially has great benefits for humankind.

2. It is difficult to overemphasize the point that the Bible does not give us a complete psychology in the late-twentieth-century scientific sense. The Scriptures embody truth not just for today and for our generation but for all people, past, present, and future. As C. S. Lewis put it so eloquently when discussing the ever-present temptation to abuse Scripture by claiming that buried within it, if only we could find it, are specific political theories, social theories, and scientific theories, "that is not how Christianity works. When it tells you to feed the hungry it does not give you lessons in cookery. When it tells you to read the scriptures it does not give you lessons in Hebrew and Greek, or even in English grammar. It was never intended to replace or supersede the ordinary human arts and sciences: it is rather a director which will set them all to the right jobs, and a source of energy which will give them all new life, if only they would put themselves at its disposal."

In the context of the present discussion we may note the views of John S. Reist Jr.[10]: "Whatever truths or information most secular introductory psychology textbooks contain, the biblical view declares that such information can never comprehensively describe a human being without references to God, the image of God and their implications" (160). And he continues, "The bible is not a psychology text, nor does it theorize about human nature or action" (162).

3. We need to learn from past episodes of encounters between science and faith. This is especially true of those sciences which, as we have said, were root disciplines of different specializations of contemporary psychology. These include physics, biology, and medicine. We learn how, in the past, particular interpretations of passages of Scripture, long accepted

as *the* only acceptable interpretation, have, in the light of new truth given through science, needed to be rethought. If the cosmologists had to learn that when they read in Psalm 96:10 that "the earth is fixed that it cannot be moved" was not denying the possibility that the earth is rotating in space, and if the geologists had to learn that the early chapters of Genesis were not making claims about the age of the universe, and if the biologists had to learn that Genesis was not making claims about the scientific process giving rise to the origin of species, so psychologists have to learn that the references to human nature found throughout Scripture are not given as a basis for building up a scientific theory of how the human organism functions, but rather convey eternal truths that remain unchanged whatever the current personality theories say or what neuroscience suggests about the mind–brain link. Hard lessons have already had to be learned in psychological medicine, especially in regard to its views of mental illness. Mercifully, gone are the days when anyone manifesting abnormal behavior was assumed to be possessed by an evil spirit and burned as a witch. Instead, today, they are recognized as people suffering from an illness and in need of help, and the very best care that contemporary psychological and medical knowledge can afford. The temptation to abuse Scripture by misusing it and imposing personal interpretations on it is ever present.

4. Psychology's claims to be a science are justified today by its solid achievements in both pure and applied research. Claiming the status of a science implies also acknowledging the limits of science. These limits are not imposed by Christian belief but are shared by humanists and others and are an intrinsic part of the effective methods devised by scientists as part of the scientific enterprise. Scientists who are Christians have, for many years, criticized the views of some social scientists and philosophers who argue that all truth, including scientific knowledge, is subjective. Recent continuing concerns over this issue have been highlighted by some leading scientists today. Thus, Max Perutz, Nobel Prize winner in molecular biology, has criticized some social scientists for teaching students that scientific results are subjective. Some Christians, mistakenly believing that by weakening the objectivity of scientific knowledge they might strengthen the claims of religious knowledge, have succumbed to the temptation to join such views. As Max Perutz[11] said, "This is a caricature of modern science, yet it represents what future teachers, civil servants, journalists and politicians are taught." And he continued: "The bulk of scientific knowledge is final. If it were not, jet planes could not fly, computers would not work, and atom bombs would fail to explode." Perutz also criticized those scientists attacking religion, writing, "My view of religion and ethics is simple: even if we do not

believe in God, we should try to live as though we did." We have a duty, I believe, to join in counteracting the widely held belief that all scientific knowledge is subjective. It may not make us popular with some of our social science colleagues, but so be it.

5. As in other sciences, all claims must in principle be testable and in practice be defended by relevant evidence. As in other sciences, appropriate training in specialist skills and techniques are necessary in order, properly and fairly, to evaluate any claims. This point is especially pertinent to the claims of psychology. Since we are our own psychologists and use our own everyday "folk psychology" as we, of necessity, make immediate snap judgments day to day as we go through life, it is a perfectly understandable reaction for us to think that we can all immediately evaluate any claims made by psychologists. It is difficult at times to recognize that properly to evaluate the claims of psychologists requires extensive training. While this is readily recognized in, say, the fields of nuclear physics or molecular biology, it seems much more difficult for the man in the street to accept as regards the claims made by psychologists since we are all up to a point our own ready-made experts. When psychologists make claims that are extrapolations from their ongoing research, but which have not, as yet, been tested, their predictions should be taken seriously, should be critically evaluated, and should be held in the "not proven" category.

6. We must constantly be alert to the confusion that arises when everyday words are taken over by a specialist area in psychology and given technical operational meanings. Failure to recognize this subtle, and at times not so subtle, change in the meanings of words is a source of much unnecessary confusion and apparent conflict. For example, most of the discussions of guilt found in psychological literature arise in a clinical context. When the psychotherapist is using it, he or she almost always is using it as a shorthand for "guilt feelings." The psychotherapist is not concerned with indicating an objective forensic state, but a psychological event or state. The person may feel guilty, but not be guilty of the offense from which his or her experience of guilt is said to be derived. There is no reason why two distinguishable states, "feeling guilty" and "being guilty," should exist in any direct proportion. In fact, in the pathological state they certainly do not. Contrast this with theologians' use of the word "guilt," in which they refer to an objective ethical or forensic relation between a man and God. Christians believe that a man's objective sinful and alienated relation to God, with the attendant effects upon relations to fellow men, normally give rise to a psychological state of guilt. In examining the ways in which psychologists and theologians describe basic human needs

we noted how each may enrich the other but that any attempt to incorporate the one into the other is likely to lead to confusion.

7. Since each of us is a complex system, simultaneously part of a larger social system and composed of smaller systems which in turn are composed of ever smaller subsystems, any aspect of human behavior and cognition chosen for investigation may be analyzed at different levels. Each level entails its own questions and appropriate methods for answering them. While the account given at each level may be complete *within* itself that does not mean that *by* itself it constitutes a full account of the phenomenon under investigation. Each level complements the others. So, for example, consider memory. While neuropsychologists study cerebral localization of the different kinds of memory, such as short-term memory, working memory, episodic memory, and procedural memory, as well as the chemical codes and neural networks in which information is stored, cognitive psychologists investigate memory in nonphysical terms, as a partly automatic and partly effortful process of encoding, storing, and retrieving information. Social psychologists study how our moods and social experiences affect our recall of past events. This recognition by psychologists of the importance of levels of explanation reminds us that the decision to adopt a reductionist position is not part of science but may be linked with materialist presuppositions held for other reasons.

8. We need to recognize and be alert to the way in which psychologists, however distinguished scientifically, each have their own personal cherished beliefs that are not part of their science per se but may all too easily intrude into their attempts to generalize their findings and to explore their wider implications. This point has been well documented by psychologists such as Paul Vitz with his criticism of the "selfism" built in to the theories of four prominent humanistic psychologists, Eric Fromm, Carl Rogers, Abraham Maslow, and Rollo May. Another example of psychological research that has received widespread publicity is that of Lawrence Kohlberg. His influential theory of moral development is today incorporated into many modern school curricula for moral and values education. Kohlberg argued that children develop morally as their thinking proceeds through a sequence of stages, from a preconventional morality of pure self-interest, to a conventional morality concerned with gaining others' approval or doing one's duty, to (in some mature people) a postconventional morality of self-chosen principles. Critics have questioned Kohlberg's assumption that morality is more a matter of thinking rather than acting, and they even more strongly question the humanistic individualism of his assumption that the highest and most mature moral

stage is exhibited by those who make moral judgments in accord with their self-chosen convictions. As one critic has argued, Kohlberg's moral ideal is little more than an articulate liberal secular humanist view masquerading as psychological truth. This illustrates how, at times, hidden values and assumptions can penetrate seemingly scientific and academic psychology. In such a way their assumptions may influence how psychologists construct, confirm, and label their concepts so that they seem to support their own presuppositions.

The task of the psychologist who is a Christian, as Donald Mackay once put it, is "to tell the story like it is," knowing that the Author is at all times at our elbow, a silent Judge of the accuracy with which we claim to describe the world he has created. Our human failings may, for a time and in some domains, limit our attaining objective value-free knowledge. That is not something to be gloried in but rather to be acknowledged in a spirit of repentance and to be accompanied by a fresh resolve to press on ever more firmly toward the goal of such knowledge. To believe, as some have implied, that the inability to achieve this goal could justify a dismissal of the whole idea of value-free knowledge as a "myth" would in fact be as irrational and as irreligious as for the Christian to dismiss the idea of righteousness as a "myth" on the grounds that we can never perfectly attain it. The Christian psychologist's responsibility is to be as faithful as he or she possibly can to reality. Since the Christian believes that God has written the book of nature and we are part of that nature, it remains our calling to read it as clearly and accurately as we can, remembering that we are humble stewards of the creation, answerable to the Giver for all the data we gather and for their accuracy. In this regard we share our commitment to be answerable to reality, at all times, with our fellow scientists, as is well exemplified by Paul Gross and Norman Levitt's recent comment: "Reality is the overseer at one's shoulder, ready to rap one's knuckles or to spring the trap into which one has been led by overconfidence, or by a too-complacent reliance on mere surmise. Science succeeds precisely because it has accepted a bargain in which even the boldest imagination stands hostage to reality. Reality is the unrelenting angel with whom scientists have agreed to wrestle."[12]

9. Our presuppositions not only influence the interpretation of our scientific data; they also, at times powerfully, influence the interpretations we impose on the "data of Scripture." In that sense *all* our ideas are vulnerable to error and bias. For that reason we must always be wary of absolutizing either our theological or our scientific ideas. As the Reformation motto "ever reforming" suggests, so our religious and scientific ideas must always be subject to test, challenge, and revision when required. It

is as important to sit down humbly before the data of Scripture, as the data of creation gleaned through our scientific enterprise. It is as easy to unthinkingly bring along our prior conceptions and to seek to impose them upon the one as upon the other. Believing that the data from nature and the biblical data both reveal God's truth, we can peaceably allow the scientific and theological perspectives to challenge and inform each other. But, as we have noted above, we shall do this ever conscious that science and theology operate at different levels of explanation and mindful of the distinctive natures of scientific theory and theological doctrine.

NOTES

Preface to 2006 Templeton Foundation Press Edition

1. D. Rees and S. Rose, eds., *The New Brain Sciences: Perils and Prospects* (Cambridge: Cambridge University Press, 2004), 298.
2. D. Buss, ed., *The Handbook of Evolutionary Psychology* (West Sussex: John Wiley & Sons, 2005).

Chapter 1: Approaching Modern Psychology

1. H. Feinstein, *Becoming William James* (Ithaca: Cornell University Press, 1984), 313.
2. H. Gardner, "Scientific Psychology: Should We Bury It or Praise It?" *New Ideas in Psychology* 10, no. 2 (1992): 179–90.
3. J. Ziman, *Reliable Knowledge* (Cambridge: Cambridge University Press, 1978).
4. H. Vande Kemp, "Sorcerer as a Straw Man—Apologetics Gone Awry: A Reaction to Foster and Ledbetter," *Journal of Psychology and Theology* 15, no. 1 (1978): 19–26.
5. B. F. Skinner, "A Case History in Scientific Method," in S. Koch, ed., *Psychology: A Study of a Science*, vol. 12, *General Systematic Formulations, Learning, and Special Processes* (New York: McGraw Hill, 1959), 359–79.
6. F. H. Crick, *The Astonishing Hypothesis: The Scientific Search for a Soul* (London: Simon & Schuster, 1994).
7. F. Watts, "Talking through His Neurones," review of Crick's *The Astonishing Hypothesis, Church Times*, May 27, 1994.
8. N. L. Munn, *Psychology* (Boston: Houghton Mifflin, 1946).
9. D. G. Myers, *Psychology*, 2nd ed. (New York: Worth, 1988).
10. Z. J. Lipowski, "Psychiatry: Mindless or Brainless, Both or Neither," *Canadian Journal of Psychiatry* 34, no. 3 (1989): 24–54.
11. A. Damasio, *Descartes' Error: Emotion, Reason and the Human Brain* (New York: Grosset/Putnam, 1994), 118.

Chapter 2: Science and Faith: Learning from the Past

1. C. A. Russell, *Cross Currents: Interactions between Science and Faith* (Leicester: InterVarsity, 1985).

2. R. Hooykaas, *Religion and the Rise of Modern Science* (Edinburgh: Scottish Academic Press, 1971).

3. W. K. C. Guthrie, *Greek Philosophy* (Cambridge: Cambridge University Press, 1957), 190.

4. Russell, *Cross Currents*, 29.

5. Ibid., 55.

6. N. Carpenter, *Philosophia Libera* (Oxoniae, 1622).

7. Russell, *Cross Currents*, 4.

8. J. W. Draper, *History of the Conflict between Religion and Science*, International Scientific series (London, 1874).

9. A. D. White, *History of the Warfare of Science with Theology in Christendom* (London: Macmillan, 1896).

10. Russell, *Cross Currents*, 6.

11. G. M. Marsden, *Understanding Fundamentalism and Evangelicalism* (Grand Rapids: Eerdmans, 1991).

12. S. B. Ferguson and D. F. Wright, eds., *New Dictionary of Theology* (Leicester: InterVarsity, 1988).

13. J. H. Brooke, *Science and Religion—Some Historical Perspectives* (Cambridge: Cambridge University Press, 1991).

14. R. K. Merton, *Science, Technology and Society in Seventeenth Century England* (San Francisco: Harper & Row, 1970).

15. Brooke, *Science and Religion*, 5.

16. S. B. Ferguson and D. F. Wright, *New Dictionary of Theology*, (Downer's Grove: Intervarsity Press) 625–26.

17. L. Hearnshaw, *A Short History of British Psychology* (London: Methuen, 1964).

18. E. G. Starbuck, *The Psychology of Religion* (London: W. Scott, 1899).

19. G. S. Spinks, *Psychology and Religion* (London: Methuen, 1963).

20. R. H. Thouless, *Introduction to the Psychology of Religion* (Cambridge: Cambridge University Press, 1923).

21. B. F. Skinner, *Beyond Freedom and Dignity* (New York: Bantam, 1972), 116.

22. R. W. Sperry, "Psychology's Mentalistic Paradigm and the Religion/Science Tensions," *American Psychologist* 43, no. 8 (1988): 607–13.

22. G. W. Allport, *The Individual and His Religion* (London: Constable, 1951), viii.

24. F. C. Bartlett, *Religion as Experience, Belief, Action* (Oxford: Oxford University Press, 1950), 3–4.

25. H. Vande Kemp, "The Sorcerer as a Straw Man—Apologetics Gone Awry: A Reaction to Foster and Ledbetter," *Journal of Psychology and Theology* 15, no. 1 (1987): 19–26.

26. M. S. Van Leeuwen, *The Person in Psychology* (Grand Rapids: Eerdmans, 1985), 73–74.

27. J. D. Foster and M. F. Ledbetter, "Wheat and Tares: Responding to Vande Kemp and Other Revisionists," *Journal of Psychology and Theology* 15, no. 1 (1987): 19–26.

28. M. Shepherd, "Psychiatry and Philosophy," *British Journal of Psychiatry* 167 (1955): 287–88.

29. A. Lewis, "Dilemmas in Psychiatry," *Psychological Medicine* 21 (1991): 581–85.

Chapter 3: Neuropsychology: Linking Mind and Brain

1. Editor's Preface, in A. Kertesz, ed., *Localization and Neuroimaging in Neuropsychology* (San Diego: Academic, 1994).
2. A. Damasio, *Descartes' Error: Emotion, Reason and the Human Brain* (New York: Grosset/Putnam, 1994), 19.
3. Ibid., 10.
4. Ibid., 40.
5. P. Erdi, Review of K. Pribam's *Rethinking Neural Networks: Quantum Fields and Biological Data, Neuropsychologia* 32 (1994).
6. Preface, in H. B. Barlow, J. P. Frisby, A. Horridge, and M. A. Jeeves, eds., *Natural and Artificial Low-Level Seeing Systems* (Oxford: Oxford Science, 1993).
7. Z. J. Lipowski, "Psychiatry: Mindless or Brainless, Both or Neither," *Canadian Journal of Psychiatry* 34, no. 3 (1989): 249–54.
8. M. Dolan, "Psychopathy—A Neurobiological Perspective," *British Journal of Psychiatry* 165 (1994): 151–59.
9. Damasio, *Descartes' Error*, 125–26.
10. R. W. Sperry, "American Psychological Association," *Psychological Science Agenda* (September–October 1994): 10–13.
11. R. W. Sperry, "Psychology's Mentalist Paradigm and the Religion/Science Tension," *American Psychologist* (1988): 607–13, 609.
12. J. Z. Young, *Philosophy and the Brain* (Oxford: Oxford University Press, 1987), 19.
13. Damasio, *Descartes' Error*, 260.
14. Z. J. Lipowski, "Psychiatry: Mindless or Brainless, Both or Neither," *Canadian Journal of Psychiatry* 34, no. 3 (1989): 249–54.

Chapter 4: Neuropsychology and Spiritual Experience

1. See *Nature* 378 (1995): 176–79.
2. G. D. Weaver, "Senile Dementia and a Resurrection Theology," *Theology Today,* (1986) 444–56.
3. W. Sargant, "The Physiology of Faith," *British Journal of Psychiatry* 115 (1969): 505–18.
4. W. Sargant, *The Mind Possessed* (London: Heinemann, 1973), 13.
5. J. E. D. Esquirol, *Des Maladies Mentales* (Paris: Bailliere, 1838).
6. B. A. Morel, *Traité des Maladies Mentales* (Paris: Masson, 1860).
7. W. Penfield and H. Jaspers, *Epilepsy and the Functional Anatomy of the Human Brain* (London: Churchill, 1954).
8. H. Dewhurst and A. W. Beard, "Sudden Religious Conversions in Temporal Lobe Epilepsy," *British Journal of Psychiatry* 117 (1970): 497–507.
9. R. H. Thouless, *An Introduction to the Psychology of Religion* (Cambridge: Cambridge University Press, 1923).
10. F. Dostoeyevski, *The Idiot*, trans. Henry and Olga Carlisle (New York: Signal–Classics, 1969).
11. Ibid.
12. D. M. Bear and P. Feddio, "Quantitative Analysis of Interictal Behaviour in Temporal Lobe Epilepsy," *Arch. Neurol.* 34 (1977): 454–67.

13. D. M. Bear, "The Temporal Lobes: An Approach to the Study of Organic Behavioural Changes," in M. D. Gazzaniga, ed., *Handbook of Behavioural Neurobiology*, vol. 2, *Neuropsychology* (New York: Plenum, 1979).

14. D. M. Tucker, R. A. Novelly, and P. J. Walker, "Hyperreligiosity in Temporal Lobe Epilepsy: Redefining the Relationship," *Journal of Nervous and Mental Disease* 175, no. 3 (1987): 181–84.

15. M. A. Persinger, "Religious and Mystical Experiences as Artifacts of Temporal Lobe Function: A General Hypothesis," *Perceptual and Motor Skills* 557 (1983): 1225–62; idem, "People Who Report Religious Experiences May also Display Enhanced Temporal Lobe Signs," *Perceptual and Motor Skills* 58 (1984): 163–97; idem, "Propensity to Report Paranormal Experiences Is Correlated with Temporal Lobe Signs," *Perceptual and Motor Skills* 59 (1984): 583–86; idem, "Striking EEG Profiles from Single Episodes of Glossalalia and Transcendental Meditation," *Perceptual and Motor Skills* 58 (1984): 127–33.

16. K. Makarec and M. A. Persinger, "Temporal Lobe Signs: Electroencephalographic Validity and Enhanced Scores in Special Populations," *Perceptual and Motor Skills* 60 (1985): 831–42.

17. M. A. Persinger and K. Makarec, "Temporal Lobe Epileptic Signs and Correlative Behaviours Displayed by Normal Populations," *Journal of General Psychology* 114, no. 2 (1987): 179–95.

18. W. S. Brown and C. Caetano, "Conversion, Cognition and Neuropsychology," in H. N. Malony and S. Southard, eds., *Handbook of Conversion* (Birmingham: Religious Education Press, 1992), 147–58.

19. G. Davies, *Genius and Grace: Sketches from a Psychiatrist's Notebook* (London: Hodder & Stoughton, 1992).

20. S. Judge, "Brains and Persons," (paper presented to the Christianity in Science annual conference, London, 1995).

21. A. Sims, "Psyche—Spirit as well as Mind," *British Journal of Psychiatry* 165 (1994): 441–46.

Chapter 5: Linking the Brain and Behavior

1. R. Dawes, *House of Cards: Psychology and Psychotherapy Built on Myth* (New York: Free Press, 1994).

2. J. Money, "Sin, Sickness or Status? Homosexual Gender Identity and Psychoneuroendocrinology," *American Psychologist* 42 (1987): 384–99.

3. J. Bancroft, *Human Sexuality and Its Problems*, 2nd ed. (Edinburgh: Churchill Livingstone, 1989).

4. J. Bancroft, "Homosexual Orientation," *British Journal of Psychiatry* 164 (1994): 437–60.

5. D. Myers, *Exploring Psychology*, 3rd ed. (New York: Worth, 1996).

6. D. F. Swaab and E. Fliers, "A Sexually Dimorphic Nucleus in the Human Brain," *Science* 228 (1985): 1112–15.

7. S. LeVay, "A Difference in Hypothalamic Structure between Heterosexual and Homosexual Men," *Science* 153 (1991): 1034–37.

8. M. Lassonde and M. A. Jeeves, eds., *Callosal Agenesis: A Natural Split Brain?* (New York: Plenum, 1994).

9. F. J. Kallman, "Comparative Twin Study of the Genetic Aspects of Male Homosexuality," *Journal of Nervous and Mental Disease* 115 (1982): 288–98.

10. J. M. Bailey and R. C. Pillard, "A Genetic Study of Male Sexual Orientation," *Archives of General Psychiatry* 48 (1991): 1089–96,

11. J. M. Bailey, R. C. Pillard, M. C. Neale, et al., "Heritable Factors Influence Sexual Orientation in Women," *Archives of General Psychiatry* 50 (1993): 217–23.

12. D. H. Hamer, S. Hu, V. L. Magnuson, et al., "A Linkage between DNA Markers on the X Chromosome and Male Sexual Orientation," *Science* 261 (1993): 321–27.

13. Bancroft, "Homosexual Orientation."

14. W. Byrne and B. Parsons, "Human Sexual Orientation: The Biologic Theories Reappraised," *Archives of General Psychiatry* 50 (1993): 228–39.

15. S. Rose, lecture presented at the Edinburgh Science Festival, 1992.

16. A. Damasio, *Descartes' Error: Emotion, Reason and the Human Brain* (New York: Grosset/Putnam, 1994), 77–78.

17. Rose, lecture.

18. J. R. W. Stott, *The Message of Romans* (Leicester: InterVarsity, 1994).

Chapter 6: Human Nature: Biblical and Psychological Portraits

1. J. R. W. Stott, *The Message of Romans* (Leicester: InterVarsity, 1994), 189.

2. G. W. Allport, *The Individual and His Religion—A Psychological Interpretation* (London: Constable, 1951).

3. Stott, *Message of Romans*, 108.

4. F. C. Bartlett, *Remembering* (Cambridge: Cambridge University Press, 1932).

5. D. Myers, *Psychology*, 2nd ed. (New York: Worth, 1992).

6. F. H. Crick, *The Astonishing Hypothesis: The Scientific Search for the Soul* (London: Simon & Schuster, 1994).

7. *New Bible Dictionary*, 2nd ed. (Leicester: InterVarsity, 1982).

8. J. E. Colwell, "Anthropology," in *New Dictionary of Theology* (Leicester: InterVarsity, 1988), 28–30.

9. J. D. G. Dunn, "Holy Spirit," in *New Bible Dictionary*, 2nd ed. (Leicester: InterVarsity, 1982).

10. B. Reichenbach, *Is Man the Phoenix? A Study of Immortality* (Grand Rapids: Eerdmans, 1978).

11. J. W. Cooper, *Body, Soul and Life Everlasting* (Grand Rapids: Eerdmans, 1989).

12. M. Scharlemann, *What Then Is Man?* (St. Louis: Concordia, 1958).

13. D. Willard, *The Spirit of the Disciplines* (San Francisco: Harper & Row, 1988).

Chapter 7: Human Nature and Animal Nature: Are They Different?

1. W. H. Thorpe, *Animal Nature and Human Nature* (London: Cambridge University Press, 1974).

2. B. A. Hinde, "Animal-Human Comparisons," in R. L. Gregory, ed., *The Oxford Companion to the Mind* (Oxford: Oxford University Press, 1987), 25–27.

3. G. Ettlinger, "Humans, Apes and Monkeys: The Changing Neuropsychological Viewpoint," *Neuropsychologia* 22, no. 8 (1984): 685–96.

4. R. Passingham, *The Human Primate* (Oxford: Oxford University Press, 1982).

5. R. Byrne, *The Thinking Ape* (Oxford: Oxford University Press, 1982).

6. R. W. Byrne and A. Whiten, eds., *Machiavellian Intelligence: Social Expertise and the Evolution of Intellect in Monkeys, Apes and Humans* (Oxford: Oxford University Press, 1988).

7. A. M. Fairbairn, *The Philosophy of the Christian Religion* (London: Hodder & Stoughton, 1902).

8. S. Rose, lecture presented at the Edinburgh Science Festival, 1992.

9. Ibid.

10. C. J. Labuschagne, "Creation and the Status of Humanity in the Bible," in V. Brummer, ed., *Interpreting the Universe as Creation* (Kampen: Pharos, 1991).

11. F. Andersen, lecture manuscript.

12. K. Ward, "Is God a Person?" in E. Vanden Brink et al., eds., *Christian Faith and Philosophical Theology* (Kampen: Pharos, 1992).

Chapter 8: Personology and Psychotherapy: Confronting the Challenges

1. S. Evans, *Preserving the Person* (Leicester: InterVarsity, 1977).

2. M. Van Leeuwen, *The Person in Psychology* (Grand Rapids: Eerdmans, 1985).

3. A. E. Bergin, "Psychotherapy and Religious Values," *Journal of Consulting and Counseling Psychology* 48 (1980): 95–105.

4. R. Dawes, *House of Cards: Psychology and Psychotherapy Built on Myth* (New York: Free Press, 1994).

5. G. Miller, review of R. Dawes's *House of Cards, Psychological Science* 6, no. 3 (1995): 129–32.

6. D. Myers, *Psychology*, 2nd ed. (New York: Worth, 1992).

7. P. C. Vitz, *Psychology as Religion: The Cult of Self-Worship* (Grand Rapids: Eerdmans, 1977).

8. Bergin, "Psychotherapy and Religious Values."

9. Van Leeuwen, *Person in Psychology.*

10. Dawes, *House of Cards.*

11. P. E. Meehl, *Clinical versus Statistical Prediction: Analysis and Review of the Literature* (Minneapolis: University of Minnesota Press, 1954).

12. M. J. Lambert, D. A. Shapiro, and A. E. Bergin, "The Effectiveness of Psychotherapy," in S. L. Garfield and A. E. Bergin, eds., *Handbook of Psychotherapy and Behavior Change*, 3rd ed. (New York: Wiley, 1986).

13. Dawes, *House of Cards.*

14. S. L. Jones, "A Constructive Relationship for Religion with the Science and Profession of Psychology: Perhaps the Boldest Model Yet," *American Psychologist* 49 (1994): 184–99.

15. Van Leeuwen, *Person in Psychology*.

16. B. McKeown, "Myth and Its Denial in a Secular Age: The Case of Behaviorist Psychology," *Journal of Psychology and Theology* 9 (1981): 19.

17. Jones, "Constructive Relationship for Religion."

18. H. J. Van Till, R. E. Snow, J. H. Stek, and D. A. Young, *Portraits of Creation* (Grand Rapids: Eerdmans, 1990).

19. H. Aguinis and M. Aguinis, "Integrating Psychological Science and Religion" (response to S. L. Jones), *American Psychologist* 50 (1995): 541–42.

Chapter 9: Human Needs: Psychological and Theological Perspectives

1. M. Van Leeuwen, *The Person in Psychology* (Grand Rapids: Eerdmans, 1985).

2. K. Boa, "Theological and Psychological Accounts of Human Needs: A Comparative Study" (D. Phil. thesis, Oxford University, 1994). I am pleased to acknowledge my indebtedness to him, though my treatment and conclusions at times differ from his.

3. S. Freud, *The Future of an Illusion* (London: Hogarth, 1927), 239.

4. S. Freud, *An Outline of Psycho-analysis* (London: Hogarth, 1949), 5.

5. E. H. Erikson, *Identity and the Life Cycle* (New York: Norton, 1959), 165; idem, *Child and Society*, 2nd ed. (New York: Norton, 1963), 80.

6. A. H. Maslow, *Toward a Psychology of Being*, 2nd ed. (New York: Van Nostrand Reinhold, 1968), 21–23; idem, *Motivation and Personality*, 3rd ed. (San Francisco: Harper & Row, 1987), 30.

7. Maslow, *Psychology of Being*, iii.

8. Ibid., 206.

9. C. R. Rogers, *A Way of Being* (Boston: Houghton Mifflin, 1980), 49.

10. C. R. Rogers, *On Becoming a Person* (Boston: Houghton Mifflin, 1961), 123.

11. E. Fromm, *The Heart of Man* (London: Routledge & Kegan Paul, 1964), 116–17.

12. E. Fromm, *The Sane Society* (London: Routledge & Kegan Paul, 1956), 25.

13. J. E. Sullivan, *The Image of God* (Dubuque: Priory Press, 1963).

14. See O. O'Donovan, *The Problem of Self-Love in St. Augustine* (New Hare: York University Press, 1980), 99; J. Burnaby, *Amor Dei* (London: Hodder & Stoughton, 1938), 70–71.

15. E. Gilson, *The Christian Philosophy of St. Thomas Aquinas*, trans. L. K. Shook (London: Victor Gollanz, 1957), 375.

16. K. E. Kirk, *The Vision of God* (London: Longmans, 1932), 380, 384.

17. J. Edwards, *A Treatise on Religious Affections* (1746; Grand Rapids: Baker, 1982), 131, 138, 140, 162.

18. K. Rahner, *Spirit in the World*, trans. J. B. Metz (London: Sheed & Ward, 1968).

19. K. Rahner, *Faith in a Wintry Season*, trans. P. Imhof, H. Biallowons, and H. D. Egan (New York: Crossroad, 1990).

20. J. R. W. Stott, *The Message of Romans* (Leicester: InterVarsity, 1994), 88.

21. P. Vitz, *Psychology as Religion: The Cult of Self-Worship* (Grand Rapids: Eerdmans, 1977).

22. A. Farrer, *Saving Belief* (London: Hodder & Stoughton, 1964), 12.

Chapter 10: Consciousness Now: A Contemporary Issue

1. F. H. Crick, *The Astonishing Hypothesis: The Scientific Search for the Soul* (London: Simon & Schuster, 1994).
2. W. James, *The Principles of Psychology* (Cambridge: Harvard University Press, 1890).
3. A. D. Milner and M. Rugg, eds., *The Neuropsychology of Consciousness* (New York: Academic, 1992).
4. J. Delacour, "The Biology and Neuropsychology of Consciousness," *Neuropsychologia* 33, no. 9 (1995): 1061–1192.
5. E. Squires, *Conscious Mind in the Physical World* (Bristol: Adam Hilger, 1990).
6. K. R. Popper and J. C. Eccles, *The Self and Its Brain* (Berlin: Springer-Verlag, 1990), 23.
7. Squires, *Conscious Mind*, 17.
8. P. C. W. Davies, *God and the New Physics* (London: Dent, 1983).
9. Squires, *Conscious Mind*.
10. R. Penrose, *The Emperor's New Mind* (Oxford: Oxford University Press, 1989).
11. Squires, *Conscious Mind*.
12. J. Hadamard, *The Psychology of Invention in the Mathematical Field* (Princeton: Princeton University Press, 1945), 31.
13. P. A. M. Dirac, "Pretty Mathematics," *International Journal of Theoretical Physics* 21 (1982): 603–5.
14. Penrose, *Emperor's New Mind*.
15. J. Bruner, *In Search of Mind* (New York: Harper & Row, 1983), 105.
16. L. Weiskrantz, "Introduction and Dissociated Issues," in A. D. Milner and M. Rugg, eds., The Neuropsychology of Consciousness (New York: Academic, 1992), 2.
17. Crick, *Astonishing Hypothesis*, 258.
18. M. Posner, in Milner and M. Rugg, eds., *Neuropsychology of Consciousness*.
19. E. Bisiach, in ibid.
20. J. Delacour, "Biology and Neuropsychology of Consciousness."
21. J. C. Eccles, ed., *Brain and Conscious Experience* (Berlin: Springer-Verlag, 1966), 327.
22. Crick, *Astonishing Hypothesis*, 253; Squires, *Conscious Mind*; Penrose, *Emperor's New Mind*, 577.
23. Crick, *Astonishing Hypothesis*, 258.
24. J. C. Polkinghorne, *One World* (London: SPCK, 1986), 75.

Chapter 11: Explaining Consciousness Now: A Contemporary Issue

1. F. H. Crick, *The Astonishing Hypothesis: The Scientific Search for the Soul* (London: Simon & Schuster, 1994).
2. J. C. Eccles, *Evolution of the Brain: Creation of the Self* (London: Routledge, 1989).
3. J. Z. Young, *Philosophy and the Brain* (Oxford: Oxford University Press, 1987).

4. G. Edelman, *Bright Air, Brilliant Fire: On the Matter of the Mind* (London: Penguin, 1992).

5. R. W. Sperry, in R. L. Gregory, ed., *The Oxford Companion to the Mind* (Oxford: Oxford University Press, 1987), 164–65.

6. Crick, *Astonishing Hypothesis*, 252.

7. Eccles, *Evolution of the Brain*, 327.

8. W. James, *The Principles of Psychology* (Cambridge: Harvard University Press, 1890).

9. C. Trevarthen, ed., *Essays in Honor of Roger W. Sperry* (Cambridge: Cambridge University Press, 1990), 382–85.

10. B. Libet, A. G. Curtis, E. W. Wright, and D. K. Pearl, "Time of Conscious Intention to Act in Relation to Onset of Cerebral Activity (Readiness-Potential): The Unconscious Initiation of a Freely Voluntary Act," *Brain* 106 (1983): 640ff.

11. B. Libet, "Electrical Stimulation of Cortex in Human Subjects, and Conscious Memory Aspects," in A. Iggo, ed., *Handbook of Sensory Physiology* (Berlin: Springer-Verlag, 1973), 2:743–90.

12. Ibid.

13. Eccles, *Evolution of the Brain*.

14. J. Delacour, "The Biology and Neuropsychology of Consciousness," *Neuropsychologia* 33, no. 9 (1995): 1061–1192.

15. D. M. Mackay and V. Mackay, "From Cell Biology to Behavior and Conscious Experience," in *Fundamentals of Medical Cell Biology*, vol. 6: *Neurobiology, Thermobiology and Cytobiology* (JAI, 1992), 6:247–62.

16. R. W. Byrne, *The Thinking Ape* (Oxford: Oxford University Press, 1994).

17. Edelman, *Bright Air, Brilliant Fire*, 97.

Chapter 12: Determinism, Freedom, and Responsibility

1. S. Hawking, *The Waterstone Lecture* (London, 1995).

2. P. Laslett, ed., *The Physical Basis of Mind* (London: Macmillan, 1950).

3. J. C. Eccles, ed., *Brain and Conscious Experience* (Berlin: Springer-Verlag, 1966).

4. D. M. Mackay, *The Clockwork Image* (London: InterVarsity, 1974).

5. J. C. Polkinghorne, *One World* (London: SPCK, 1986).

6. J. B. S. Haldane, *Possible Worlds* (London: Chatto & Windus, 1945), 209.

7. Polkinghorne, *One World*.

8. J. P. Cruchfield, J. D. Farmer, N. H. Parkhard North, and R. W. Shaw, "Chaos," *Scientific American* 225 (1986): 38–49.

9. J. Houghton, *Does God Play Dice?* (Leicester: InterVarsity, 1988), 123.

10. A. Kenny, *The God of the Philosophers* (Oxford: Clarendon, 1979).

11. J. C. Polkinghorne, *Science and Christian Belief* (London: SPCK, 1990).

12. A. R. Peacocke, *Theology for a Scientific Age: Being and Becoming—Natural, Divine, Human* (London: SCM, 1993).

13. D. M. Mackay, *The Open Mind and Other Essays: A Scientist in God's World* (Leicester: InterVarsity, 1988).

14. D. M. Mackay, *Behind the Eye* (Oxford: Blackwell, 1991), 193.

15. Mackay, *Open Mind*, 61.

16. J. Doye, I. Goldby, C. Line, S. Lloyd, P. Shellard, and D. Tricker, "Contemporary Perspectives on Chance, Providence and Free Will: A Critique of Some Modern Authors," *Science and Christian Belief* 7 (1995): 117–39.
17. P. Johnson-Laird, *Mental Models* (Cambridge: Cambridge University Press, 1983), 477.

Chapter 13: The Future of Science and Faith: Beyond Perspectivalism?

1. C. S. Evans, *Preserving the Person: A Look at the Human Sciences* (Madison: IVCP, 1979).
2. M. Van Leeuwen, *The Person in Psychology* (Grand Rapids: Eerdmans, 1985), 191.
3. C. A. Russell, *Cross Currents: Interactions between Science and Faith* (Leicester: InterVarsity, 1985).
4. J. H. Brooke, *Science and Religion—Some Historical Perspectives* (Cambridge: Cambridge University Press, 1991).
5. C. B. Trevarthen, "Two Mechanisms of Vision in Primates," *Psychol. Forschung.* 31 (1968): 299–337.
6. G. E. Schneider, "Two Visual Systems: Brain Mechanisms for Localisation and Discrimination Are Dissociated by Tectal and Cortical Lesions," *Science* 103 (1969): 895–902.
7. L. G. Ungerleider and M. Mishkin, "Two Cortical Systems," in D. J. Ingle, M. A. Goodale, and R. J. W. Mansfield, eds., *Analysis of Visual Behavior* (Cambridge: MIT, 1982), 578.
8. A. D. Miller and M. A. Goodale, *The Visual Brain in Action* (Oxford: Oxford University Press, 1995).
9. C. A. Russell, *Dictionary of Theology* (Leicester: InterVarsity, 1988).
10. J. S. Reist, *Man and Mind: A Christian Theory of Personality* (Hillsdale: Hillsdale College Press, 1987).
11. M. Perutz, *Times Higher Educational Supplement*, November 25, 1994.
12. P. R. Gross and N. Levitt, *Higher Superstition* (Baltimore: Johns Hopkins University Press, 1994), 234.

Index